Fair Play

Fair Play

Sports, Values, and Society

Robert L. Simon

Hamilton College

Westview Press

BOULDER • SAN FRANCISCO • OXFORD

Published in 1991 in the United States of America by Westview Press, Inc., 5500 Central Avenue, Boulder, Colorado 80301-2847, and in the United Kingdom by Westview Press, 36 Lonsdale Road, Summertown, Oxford OX2 7EW

Library of Congress Cataloging-in-Publication Data
Simon, Robert L., 1941–
　Fair play : sports, values, and society / Robert L. Simon.
　　p.　cm.
　Rev. ed. of: Sports and social values. 1985.
　Includes bibliographical references and index.
　ISBN 0-8133-7973-3 – ISBN 0-8133-7974-1 (pbk.)
　1. Sports—Social aspects.　2. Sports—Social aspects—United
States.　I. Simon, Robert L., 1941–　　Sports and social values.
II. Title.
GV706.5.S56　1991
306.4'83'0973–dc20
　　　　　　　　　　　　　　　　　　　　　　　　　　91-31293
　　　　　　　　　　　　　　　　　　　　　　　　　　CIP

Printed and bound in the United States of America

The paper used in this publication meets the requirements
of the American National Standard for Permanence of Paper
for Printed Library Materials Z39.48-1984.

10　　9　　8　　7　　6　　5　　4　　3　　2　　1

*To my parents, who perhaps now
will finally believe that the many hours I spent
playing ball instead of doing homework really
were "field research" after all*

Contents

Preface

Sports play a significant role in the lives of millions of people throughout the world. Many men and women participate actively in sports, and still more are spectators, fans, and critics of sports. Even those who are uninvolved in sports, bored by them, or critical of athletic competition often will be significantly affected by them, either because of their relationships with enthusiasts or, more important, because of the impact of sports on our language, thought, and culture.

Because sports are a significant form of social activity, which affect the educational system, the economy, and perhaps the values of citizens, they raise a wide range of issues, some of which are factual or empirical in character. Social scientists, historians, physicians, and writers have raised many such issues that concern sports. For example, sociologists may be concerned with whether or not participation in sports affects the values of the participants, and psychologists might try to determine what personality features contribute to success or failure in competitive athletics.

However, in addition to factual and explanatory questions, sports also raise philosophical issues that are conceptual and ethical in character. Conceptual questions concern how we are to understand the concepts and ideas that apply in the world of sports. What are sports anyway? How are sports related to rules? Do those who intentionally break the rules of a game even play it or are they doing something else? Are there different forms of competition in sports? Is it possible to compete against oneself?

Ethical questions raise the moral concerns many of us have about sports. Should sports be accorded the importance they are given in our society? Is there too much emphasis on winning and competition? Are college sports getting out of hand? Why shouldn't we cheat in a game if it will bring us a championship? What, if anything, makes the use of steroids to enhance performance in sports unethical? How should men and women be treated in sports if they are to be treated equitably and fairly? Should we be aiming more for excellence in competition among highly skilled athletes or should we place greater value on more participation? *Fair Play* examines such questions and evaluates the principles to which thoughtful people might appeal in trying to formulate answers.

Not only are questions in the philosophy of sports important in their own right, they can also serve as a useful introduction to broader philosophical issues. Most students come to philosophy courses with knowledge of sports, and many have a deep interest in ethical issues raised by sports. This initial interest can serve as a launching pad to introduce students to the nature and value of philosophical inquiry.

Perhaps most important, issues in the philosophy of sports are of great intrinsic interest and are well worth our attention. Philosophical questions force us to stretch our analytical powers to the fullest and to question basic presuppositions. Those that arise in the philosophical examination of sports, like any others, require us to test and evaluate fundamental justificatory principles and engage in rigorous critical inquiry.

Fair Play never would have been written had it not been for the challenges to my own views of sports put forth by friends, colleagues in the philosophy department at Hamilton College, and students. I cannot acknowledge and sort out all my intellectual debts here, but I would like to thank the original editors of the first edition of this book, Ray O'Connell and Doris Michaels of Prentice-Hall, for their initial encouragement, and particularly Spencer Carr of Westview Press for his insights as to how the original edition could be expanded and improved upon. I also thank David Fairchild for his helpful comments on an earlier draft of this edition.

I also express my special appreciation to my wife, Joy, not only for her critical help with the manuscript but also for putting up with an abnormal number of fits of abstraction ("Earth calling Bob" became one of the phrases used most often at our dinner table) during the writing of both editions of the book. Sports have been one of the major activities my family and I have shared, so I hope they enjoy reading the finished product as much as I did writing it.

Although portions of all chapters of the first edition have been rewritten, the major changes readers of *Sports and Social Values* will find in *Fair Play* include, appropriately, a new discussion of fair play, cheating, and sportsmanship in Chapter 3; a new concluding chapter on sports and moral education; and some revisions in the often justly criticized discussion of the ethics of using performance-enhancing drugs in sports (revisions that will probably not go far enough to satisfy some critics).

Finally, without the participants in sports who demonstrate the kind of quest for excellence discussed in Chapter 2, much of the subject matter of philosophy of sports would be empty abstraction. I thank past and present staff and players in both the Hamilton College men's and women's basketball programs and the Clinton Central School's boys' and girls' basketball teams, not only for getting me away from my typewriter (in view of my attendance at basketball games, many colleagues will find it miraculous that I completed this book) but also for making the harsh upstate New York winter one of the most exciting and pleasurable times of year. And far from least, I would like to close by thanking my players on the Hamilton men's golf team for letting me try out some theories in practice and for keeping their swings grooved anyway.

Robert L. Simon

1

Introduction:
Philosophy of Sports

I would like to think that this book began on an unfortunately not atypical cold and rainy late October day in upstate New York. I had been discussing some of my generally unsuccessful competitive efforts in local golf tournaments with colleagues in the philosophy department and let drop what I thought was an innocuous remark to the effect that although winning isn't everything, it sure beats losing. Much to my surprise, my colleagues objected vehemently, asserting that winning means nothing. In their view, all that should matter are such factors as having fun and trying to improve, not defeating an opponent. I soon found myself backed into a corner by this hitherto unthreatening but now fully aroused assortment of philosophers. Fortunately for me, another colleague entered the office just at the right moment. Struck by the vehemence of the argument, although he had no idea what it was about, he looked at my opponents and remarked, "You folks sure are trying to win this argument."

This incident illustrates two important aspects of a philosophical examination of sports. First, issues arise in sports that are not simply empirical ones of psychology, sociology, or some other scientific discipline. Empirical surveys, for example, can tell us whether people do think winning is important but they cannot tell us if that is what people ought to think or whether winning really ought to be regarded as a primary goal of athletics. Second, the incident illustrated that logic could be applied to issues in the philosophy of sports. Thus, at least on the surface, it appeared that my colleagues were in the logically embarrassing position of trying hard to win an argument to the effect that winning is unimportant.

We will return to the issue of whether winning is important in

Chapter 2. For now, however, let us consider further what philosophical inquiry might contribute to our understanding of sports.

Sports, Philosophy, and Moral Values

Sports and Values

Sports play a major, if sometimes unappreciated, role in the lives of Americans. Most of us are exposed to them as children. Often as a result of our childhood experiences, many of us become participants or fans for life. Others are appalled by the character of their early exposure to sports and avoid them like the plague later in life. They may have been embarrassed by failures in front of peers or parents or have been humiliated by an insensitive physical-education instructor. Girls may have received less encouragement than boys to participate. Others may just find sports boring.

Most of us, however, retain some affiliation with sports for life, even if only as spectators. According to the recent Miller Lite Report on American Attitudes towards sports, one of the most extensive studies done in this area, 96.3 percent of the American population plays or watches or reads articles about sports with some frequency or identifies with particular teams or players. Moreover, nearly 70 percent follow sports every day and 42 percent participate daily.[1] Although intensity of involvement cannot be measured as easily as extent, the time and effort that athletes and fans devote to sports at all levels suggests that they find involvement in sports one of their most valuable and significant activities.

The situation is not unique to the United States. Intense interest in sports is virtually a global phenomenon. Whether it is ice hockey in the USSR or soccer in Europe, South America, and Africa, sports play a major role in different societies around the globe. Sports were valued by the ancient Greeks, by the Romans, and by Native Americans. Indeed, participation in sports, and the related activity of play, are characteristic of human society.

Although there is a tendency among some people to regard sports as trivial, it is not clear that such a view is justified. At the very least, it is worth reflecting what it is about sports that calls forth a favorable response among so many people from so many different cultures. Reflection upon sports raises issues that are not only intrinsically interesting but which also go beyond the bounds of sport itself. For example, reflection on the value of competition in athletics and the emphasis on winning in much of organized sports sheds light on the ethics of competition in other spheres of life, such as the marketplace. Inquiry into the nature of fair play in sports likewise will help increase our understanding of fairness in a wider social setting. Indeed, because many of our basic values, such as playing fairly, often are absorbed through involvement in athletic competition, inquiry into values in sports is likely to not only prove interesting in its own right but also to have implications of more general concern as well.

What does philosophy have to contribute to reflection about sports? It is evident even to a casual observer of our society that sports in America are undergoing intense moral scrutiny. Intercollegiate athletics, for example, are afflicted by major recruiting scandals, under-the-table payments to athletes, and charges that the whole system exploits athletes at the major intercollegiate athletic institutions who, it is alleged, fail to learn and graduate at the same rate as other students. The use of anabolic steroids to enhance performance by some athletes is widely regarded as cheating. Runner Ben Johnson was stripped of his gold medals in the 1988 Olympics after tests revealed his use of such performance-enhancing drugs. But does the use of steroids differ ethically from such other enhancements as special diets or equipment? Is the emphasis on winning and competition too great in our society? Does involvement in sports teach a success-at-all-costs attitude that cannot be defended morally?

These and similar questions raise basic issues about the kind of moral values involved in sports. These questions are not only about what people think about sports or about what values they actually hold. Rather, they are about what people ought to think. They require the identification of defensible ethical standards and their application to sports. The formulation, criticism and testing of such standards as well as their application to concrete issues are a major part of the business of philosophy of sports.

Philosophy of Sports

Misconceptions about the nature of philosophy are widespread. According to one story, a philosopher on a domestic flight was asked by his seatmate what he did for a living. He replied, perhaps foolishly, "I'm a philosopher," which is perhaps one of the greatest conversation stoppers known to the human race. His companion, apparently stupefied by the reply, was silent for several minutes. Finally, he turned to the philosopher and remarked, "Oh, and what are some of your sayings?"[2]

The image of the philosopher as the author of wise sayings can perhaps be forgiven, for the word "philosophy" has its roots in the Greek expression meaning "love of wisdom." However, wisdom is not necessarily encapsuled in brief sayings that we might memorize before breakfast. The ancient Greek philosopher Socrates provides a different model of philosophic inquiry.

Socrates, who lived in the fifth century B.C., did not leave a body of written works behind him, but we know a great deal about his life and thought through the works of his most influential pupil, Plato, and other sources. As a young man, Socrates, who was seeking a mentor from whom to learn, set out to find the wisest man in Greece. According to story, he decided to ask a religious figure, the Oracle at Delphi, the identity of the man whom he was seeking. Much to Socrates' surprise, the Oracle informed him that he, Socrates, was the wisest man in Greece. "How can that be?" Socrates must have wondered, as it was precisely because he was ignorant that he was searching for a wise teacher to begin with.

However, looking at the Oracle's answer in light of the picture of Plato's presentation of Socrates, we can discern what the Oracle might have meant. In such early Platonic dialogues as the *Euthyphro*, Socrates was portrayed as questioning various important figures of the day on such topics as the nature of piety or the essence of knowledge. Those questioned purported to be experts in the subject under investigation, but their claim to expertise was discredited by Socrates' logical analysis. These experts not only failed to know what they claimed to know but also seemed to have accepted views which they had never exposed to critical examination.

Perhaps what the Oracle had in mind in calling Socrates the wisest man in Greece was to suggest that Socrates alone was willing to expose beliefs and principles to critical examination. He did not claim to know what in fact he did not know but was willing to learn. He also was not willing to take popular opinion for granted but was prepared to question it.

This Socratic model suggests that the role of philosophy is to examine our beliefs, clarify the principles on which they rest, and subject them to critical examination. For example, in the area of science, the role of philosophy is not to compete with science in formulating and testing empirical hypotheses in biology, chemistry, and physics. Rather, philosophers might try to understand in what sense, if any, science provides objective knowledge and to examine claims about whether all knowledge of the world must be scientific in nature.[3]

If we adopt such a view of philosophy, the task of philosophy of sports would be to clarify, systematize, and evaluate the principles we believe should govern the world of sports. This task might involve conceptual analysis of such terms as "sport" and "game," inquiry into the nature of excellence in sports, ethical evaluation of such principles as "winning should be the only concern of the serious athlete," and application of ethical analysis to concrete issues, such as disagreement over whether athletes should be permitted to take such performance-enhancing drugs as anabolic steroids.

This book will be concerned primarily with the ethical evaluation of principles that many people apply to sports and the application of the analysis to specific issues. Its major focus will be on the nature of principles and values that *should* apply in sports. Thus, its concern is predominantly normative rather than descriptive. Many individuals never think of sports in moral terms. They see sports as mere instruments for gaining fame and fortune or as play, an activity we engage in for fun and recreation, but not as an activity that raises serious moral issues. However, as the headlines of our daily newspapers bring out all too frequently, moral issues of serious import do arise in sports.

But can moral issues be critically examined? Is rational argument even possible in ethics? Aren't moral views just matters of opinion? After all, who is to say what is and what is not morally incorrect? Can moral principles be rationally evaluated and defended or are they mere expressions of personal feelings that are not even the sorts of things that can be rationally evaluated or examined?

Ethics and Moral Reasoning

If reasoned ethical discourse is impossible, rational inquiry into ethical issues in sports is impossible. Although we cannot consider all possible reasons for scepticism about whether rationally justifiable moral positions can be developed, one widely cited reason for doubting the objectivity of ethics is *relativism*. Because relativism is so widely suggested as a basis for scepticism about the role of reason in ethics, a brief discussion of it will prove helpful. The remainder of this book attempts to consider moral issues in sports rationally. Clearly, if this attempt succeeds, it itself counts as an example of reasoned inquiry in ethics.

Relativism

Perhaps the most widely cited position that rejects the rationality and objectivity of ethical discourse is relativism. In his best selling book *The Closing of the American Mind*, Allen Bloom blames relativism for much of what he sees as the moral and educational decay infecting American universities. According to Bloom, "There is one thing a professor can be absolutely certain of: almost every student entering the university believes, or says he believes, that truth is relative."[4] Relativism is so widely supported, according to Bloom, because its opposite is (incorrectly, as we will see) identified with a kind of intolerant and dogmatic absolutism. The price we pay for this misidentification, however, is our inability to formulate, articulate, and defend standards we think are correct.[5] Such relativism, of course, is often applied to ethics as well as to truth. What is relativism in ethics?

According to *descriptive relativism*, the moral judgments people make and the values they hold arise from or are relative to their culture, socioeconomic state, or ethnic and religious background. For example, secular culture in the West tends to cast a permissive eye towards sexual contact between consenting adults, but such contacts have been much more strictly regulated at other times or in other places. In the world of sports, some cultures may place more value than others on winning in sports and less on, say, the aesthetic appeal of play.

What does descriptive relativism have to do with the rationality of ethical discourse? It sometimes is argued that if descriptive relativism is true, there cannot be any objectivity or rationality in ethics. No one's ethical judgments would be any more justifiable or correct than anyone else's. Rather, people's ethical judgments would be mere subjective claims based on their distinct and different backgrounds. In this view, our moral values are just the prejudices we absorbed as children. Perhaps they were presented to us as self-evident truths. In reality, they are only the blinders of our particular culture or group.

Accordingly, it sometimes is claimed that scepticism about the rationality and objectivity of ethics follows from descriptive relativism. Others, however, believe that descriptive relativism implies not scepticism but *ethical relativism*. Ethical relativism is the view that each culture's moral code is right for that culture. For example, according to ethical relativism, repressive sexual practices are morally right for those cultures that have such practices embedded in their moral codes but not for more liberal cultures or groups. Ethical relativism differs from scepticism in that scepticism denies that any ethical perspective is more justifiable or reasonable than any other. Ethical relativism, on the other hand, endorses an ethical view—namely, what is right is what your culture says is right.

What is the significance of these views for the ethical analysis of sports? If scepticism can be justified by appeal to descriptive relativism, it follows that we cannot justify any position on questions of ethics arising in sports. For example, we could not justify either the claim that the use of anabolic steroids to enhance performance is warranted or the claim that it is unwarranted. On the other hand, if ethical relativism is correct, what is morally justifiable depends on the group to which one belongs. Perhaps the use of performance-enhancing drugs is permissible for those cultures that find it permissible but not for those that find it impermissible.

Does descriptive relativism really have the sceptical implications examined above? Is relativism, in the forms discussed above, acceptable?

A Critique of Relativism

First, consider the argument that because the thesis of descriptive relativism—that moral codes of different cultures and groups conflict—is true, therefore moral scepticism is true. In order to evaluate this argument, we need to consider what general conditions an argument must meet to be acceptable. If the premises of an argument are to justify a conclusion, two fundamental requirements must be satisfied. (1) The premises must be true. *False* statements cannot be acceptable evidence for the truth of a conclusion. (2) The premises must be logically relevant to the conclusion. Otherwise, the conclusion could not follow from the premises since they would be irrelevant to it. For example, we would not accept the conclusion that "The major goal of competitive sports is winning" on the basis of the claim that "Washington, D.C., is the capital of the United States." Even though the latter claim is true, it has nothing to do with the former claim and so cannot support it.

Consider again the argument that because the moral codes of different cultures and groups conflict, no set of moral judgments or principles can be correct, reasonable, or justified. First, the argument assumes that descriptive relativism is true, but is it? If descriptive relativism claims no more than that the moral codes, principles, and judgments accepted in different societies *sometimes* conflict, it surely is true. But that leaves open the possibility that behind the apparent disagreement, there is deeper agreement on some morally fundamental values. The area of agreement might constitute the basis of cross-cultural universal values that some social scientists and sociobiologists have claimed to detect. For example, people from a wide variety of cultural, ethnic, socioeconomic, and religious backgrounds condemn incest, torture, and the random killing of members of one's community. Protests in China and Eastern Europe at least constitute evidence for the broad appeal of freedom as well.

This point can be taken further. Even surface disagreement can reflect deeper agreement in values. For instance, consider a dispute between a basketball coach and her assistant before a big game. The head coach wants to use a pressure defense to take advantage of her team's quickness and the opponent's lack of speed. The assistant argues against this strategy because it may result in overanxious defensive players committing too many fouls. In this case, there is disagreement over what tactics to follow. But behind the disagreement is a common value or principle shared by both coaches. Each is trying to select the strategy that will lead to victory.

A parallel situation is possible in ethics. Suppose culture A believes old people should be separated from the group and left to die when they no longer can contribute to the general welfare, but culture B disagrees. Clearly, there is a disagreement here, but both cultures might share deeper fundamental values as well. For one thing, the circumstances of each culture might differ. Culture A may be barely surviving at the subsistence level while culture B may be affluent and therefore can afford to care for its older members. Perhaps culture A consists of nomadic bands that must move fast to keep up with game. Arguably, each culture may accept the same basic principle of promoting the greater good for the greater number, but the principle might apply differently in the different circumstances in which each group finds itself. Accordingly, although the descriptive relativist undoubtedly is correct in pointing to moral disagreement among groups, it remains controversial whether there is fundamental disagreement about all values or whether underneath the surface disagreement cited by the relativist there is a deeper acceptance of fundamental core values by all or virtually all societies.

Suppose, however, we concede for the sake of argument that there are no universally accepted values or moral principles. The greatest weakness of the relativist argument is that even if this point is conceded, which it needn't be, moral scepticism does not follow. The premise of descriptive relativism is *logically irrelevant* to supporting moral scepticism. The mere fact that cultures or groups disagree about moral problems does not show there are no correct or justifiable resolutions to the dispute. Similarly, the mere fact that some cultures believe the world is flat and others believe it is round does not by itself establish that there is no correct answer to the question of the shape of the earth.[6] Whether or not a justifiable resolution of a dispute is possible depends in great part on whether there are justifiable modes of ethical (or scientific) inquiry that can be applied to it. Because disagreement can arise just as much from ignorance of such modes of inquiry, misapplication of them, or factual disagreement (as when one group of athletes denies and one asserts that steroids have harmful side effects), disagreement alone is not sufficient to show that no rational modes of inquiry exist, let alone that they are insufficient to resolve the issue at hand.

Of course, the failure of descriptive relativism to establish moral scepticism doesn't show there is a correct resolution to moral controversies, only that the presence of cultural or group diversity does not rule out such a resolution in advance of inquiry.

Does descriptive relativism do any better in establishing ethical relativism—the thesis that what your group or culture *says* is right or wrong for you *is* right or wrong for you. For example, is it morally right to take anabolic steroids to enhance your performance in sports just because your peer group or even your entire culture says it is right?

Once again, no such implication follows. For reasons similar to those outlined above, the mere fact that groups may disagree on ethical issues does not show that each group's moral views are right for its members. One might just as well argue that if your culture believes the earth is flat, you ought to believe the earth is flat as well. If such an absurd view were correct, we would never be justified in trying to *correct* or *change* the view of our culture or peer group even if we had strong reasons for thinking their views were unfounded. Ethical relativism has the unacceptable implication that the views of our culture or of other groups to which we belong are acceptable just as they are. But surely, even if our peer group does advocate, for example, the use of performance-enhancing drugs in sports, they are not automatically correct to do so. We need to engage in ethical inquiry and argument to see if the best reasons support their view rather than to accept it merely because it is the view of the group to which we belong.[7]

Therefore, moral disagreement among cultures, or other kinds of groups, should not deter us from engaging in moral inquiry designed to subject moral claims in sports or elsewhere to rational criticism and evaluation. Moreover, such a view does not commit us to being dogmatic or intolerant of the views of others. Indeed, tolerance and openmindedness are themselves values, which many think have objective support. If moral scepticism were true, there would be no rational basis for tolerance itself if cultures disagreed about its value. Accordingly, commitment to rational inquiry in ethics does not commit us to being arrogant dogmatists who forcibly impose our views on others. If anything, it commits us to be open to new insights of others who may be different from us, so long as we are willing to subject their views as well as our own to the test of reasoned inquiry in ethics. Thus, commitment to moral inquiry can help free us from insular prejudices and allow us to test our views by seeing if they can stand up to the reasoned criticism of others.

Moral Reasoning

How are we to distinguish good from bad moral reasoning? Philosophers and ethicists have not agreed that any one theory of moral reasoning is the correct one or even whether theories of moral reasoning are morally neutral or are themselves part of a substantive code of ethics.

At a minimum, it is doubtful if one can evaluate moral arguments with the kind of precision and rigor that would be appropriate in mathematics. This does not mean, however, that there are no acceptable standards that can be used to distinguish well-supported from poorly supported positions. Not all reasoning is of the form of mathematical proof. As Aristotle suggested, we should "look for precision in each class of things just so far as the nature of the subject admits; it is evidently equally foolish to accept probable reasoning from a mathematician and to demand from a rhetorician scientific proofs."[8] This does not mean that ethical reasoning must be imprecise or sloppy, but rather that it may be more like the making of a sound case by a skilled judicial scholar than a strict mathematical proof.

Although it is unlikely that an exhaustive or totally uncontroversial account of good moral reasoning can be provided, the following three criteria of good moral reasoning will prove especially helpful in what follows. First, moral reasoning must be *impartial*. In evaluating a moral issue, we are not asking "what's in it for me?" Rather, our goal is to see what position is supported by the best reasons, impartially considered. Moral deliberation is deliberation from a broader perspective than that of self-interest. Thus, we cannot justify the claim that "the use of steroids by Olympic athletes to enhance their performance is morally legitimate" simply by claiming "the use of steroids will help me gain a gold medal in the Olympics." The latter claim may show that the use of steroids is in the speaker's interest. It does nothing to show that personal interest is the only relevant moral factor.

R. M. Hare, distinguished professor of philosophy at Oxford University, has suggested that impartial moral reasoning requires that we imagine ourselves in the place of all those affected by the action or policy being evaluated, giving no special weight to any one perspective.[9] John Rawls of Harvard, author of the important book *A Theory of Justice*, has suggested that in thinking of social justice we must reason as if we were behind a veil of ignorance that hides from us knowledge of our individual characteristics or social circumstances.[10] Regardless of the similarities and differences between these two accounts of impartiality, each prohibits us from arbitrarily assigning special weight to our own position or interests. For example, it prohibits us from arbitrarily assigning special privileges to our own race or ethnic group because it would be irrational to do so if we had to consider such a policy impartially from the perspective of all affected, as Hare requires, or in ignorance of our own group membership, as Rawls suggests.

Second, the positions we take on various positions must be systematically *consistent*. That is, we cannot take a position on one issue that contradicts a position we have taken on another without making a change somewhere in our moral perspective so as to bring the two positions into harmony. For example, if one holds both that it is wrong to assault another person but that it is permissible for a professional hockey player to assault another player during a game, one's position appears inconsistent. Unless one can show that the two cases are relevantly dissimilar, one or the other position must be given up for both cannot be correct. If the two cases are similar in the relevant moral respects, assault in one case cannot be permissible and assault in the other impermissible, for there would be no difference between the cases to justify the difference in judgment made about them.

Third, the principles one uses in making moral decisions must be not only impartial and consistent but also must account for reflective judgments about clear moral examples. Thus, if one held a principle implying it was permissible to intentionally turn in a wrong score in a golf tournament merely to benefit oneself, and thus essentially win by lying, that would normally be grounds for rejecting, or at least questioning, that principle in the first place. Of course, and this is what makes our third criterion controversial, we must be sure that our reaction to cases is critical and reflective, rather than merely an unanalyzed, culturally conditioned response. It is all too easy to be influenced by cultural, social, or even biologically based presuppositions that cloud our appreciation of what is at stake. For example, our initial reaction that it is permissible for hometown fans to boo and wave while an opposing basketball player shoots a crucial foul shot may simply be a prejudice we share with other hometown fans. However, some of our judgments about particular cases may be reflective and unbiased and hence provide an intuitive base against which we can check our principles.

Thus, our reflective reaction to actual and hypothetical cases may be a useful guide for moral inquiry. Without consideration of cases, our principles would be empty abstractions. We would have no appreciation of their significance for action.

The more an ethical theory survives counterexample and criticism, the more confidence we would seem to be entitled to place in it. Just as we should want to expose our scientific theories to test, so we should also want to test our moral perspectives by exposing them to the criticism of others. It may make us feel good to cling to our entrenched moral views by never exposing them to opposing views. The price we pay for such a policy, however, is that we close ourselves off from discovering any errors we might make, which might be pointed out by others. We also lose opportunities for confirming our views through refutation of the objections of our critics. Just as a scientific theory gains credibility by surviving tests, so may a moral view gain credibility by continually surviving criticism in the crucible of moral debate.

From a critical perspective, a moral view can be undermined by at least three kinds of strategies. We can argue that such a view would not be held if impartially considered, that its various parts are inconsistent or inharmonious, or that the view has unacceptable implications for action. Nothing said so far, however, implies that only one moral perspective, code of ethics, or set of principles will survive moral criticism. It is possible that all who go through an extended process of moral inquiry will tend to hold the same moral view but it is equally possible that a kind of moral pluralism will flourish as well. What is unlikely, however, is that serious and extended moral inquiry will rate *all* moral perspectives as equally justified. Some will be rejected as inconsistent, biased, vulnerable to counterexample, or deficient on some other appropriate ground. Thus, while there is no guarantee that our criteria of moral reasoning are the only defensible ones or that they will yield strictly determinate results for all investigators, they at least provide guidance in the rational evaluation of moral issues. By applying them, we employ reason in ethics.

Let us turn to the discussion of moral issues in sports. We will begin with the examination of a fundamental issue: the degree of importance that should be assigned to competition and winning in sports.

2

The Ethics of Competition

"Winning is not the most important thing; it's the only thing." This widely cited claim, often attributed (perhaps falsely) to the late Vince Lombardi, famous former coach of the Green Bay Packers, raises a host of issues that are central to the moral evaluation of sports.[1] What importance should be assigned to winning in athletic competition? Consider sportswriter Grantland Rice's declaration, "When the one Great Scorer comes to mark against your name, He writes not that you won or lost but how you played the Game," as well as the rejoinder by coach Forest Evashevski that one might as well say of a surgeon that it matters not whether his patient lives or dies but only how he makes the cut.[2]

Questions about the importance of winning are closely tied to but not identical with questions about the value of competition. Should we be concerned primarily with winning or with competing well? We will begin our inquiry by considering the nature and value of competition in sports and athletics. The results will then be applied to an investigation of the importance of winning.

Competition in Sports

At first glance, competition seems built into the very nature of sports. We speak of sporting events as competitions or contests, evaluate athletes as good or bad competitors, and refer to other teams as opponents. However, the connection between sports and competition is far looser than such an initial reaction might suggest. Fishing and skiing are sports but neither necessarily involves competition. Moreover, virtually any sport can be played noncompetitively. Men and women may participate to get exercise, to forget about work, to enjoy the company of friends, or to enjoy the outdoors rather than out of any desire to compete. Another goal of participation might be improvement. Such players, often described as competing with themselves, aim not at defeating opponents but at improving their own personal performance. Still other players may have the aesthetic goal of making the movements of their sport with skill and grace. For example, playground basketball players may value outstanding moves more than defeat of opponents. A leading amateur golfer, after years of hard practice, describes her aim as "to make a swing that you know is as close to perfection as you can get. And you say, 'Boy, look at what I did.' That's all it is."[3]

However, just because a player does not have the goal of competitive success or is not motivated by it, it doesn't follow that competition isn't part of the sport. A group of people may play baseball recreationally, just to interact with friends, but the game they are playing has as its point, defined by the rules, the scoring of more runs than the opponent. Thus, if we distinguish between the goals and motives of the players and the internal point of the sport as defined by the rules, we can say that all sports are competitive insofar as they are games or contests, but even games and contests need not be played or valued because of their competitive aspect.[4]

Our concern is with how competitive sports should be *evaluated* from the moral point of view. If we are to evaluate competitive sports, however, we must be able to distinguish just what it is we are evaluating. Although any game of baseball may have as its internal goal, as defined by the rules, the scoring of more runs than the opponent, players can play baseball noncompetitively. What critics of competition in sports object to is not so much the playing of games such as baseball that have an internal competitive element. Rather, as we will see, what they object to is the competitive attitude of having the defeat of an opponent as a main desire or goal. Critics also object to this attitude being institutionalized and to competition in sports being made into a social practice.

Competition in sports can be thought of as participation in sports contests with the intent or major goal of defeating an opponent. In such clear cases, competition seems to be a zero-sum game. The aim of defeating an opponent cannot be secured by all competitors, and its attainment by one precludes its like attainment by the other in the same contest.

A further point requires some attention. The clearest cases of athletic competition involve structured games such as baseball, football, basketball, and tennis, all of which are governed by a set of rules defining permissible moves within the activity in question. For example, the rules of basketball that stipulate what it is to score, foul, or travel are such *constitutive rules*. If players were unaware of such rules or made no attempt to follow them they logically could not be playing basketball (although minimal modifications might be acceptable in informal play or other special contexts). Constitutive rules should be distinguished sharply from rules of strategy such as "dribble only if there is no faster way of advancing the ball up court." Rules of strategy are general suggestions as to how to play the game well; constitutive rules determine what counts as a permissible move within the game itself.

Fair competition is at least competition within the constitutive rules of the game. Arguably, what counts as winning is defined by the constitutive rules so successful cheaters do not really win, although successful cheats may get others to believe they have won. In this view, which will be examined in Chapter 3, because cheaters make moves not recognized by the constitutive rules of the sport, not only do they fail to prove themselves better players than fellow competitors but they have not even succeeded in playing the game in the first place.[5]

Accordingly, the paradigm of competition in sports is to be understood as the attempt to secure victory within the framework set by the constitutive rules. Participants may take part in a sport or game, even one that is competitive in the sense of having winning and losing defined internally by the constitutive rules, without playing competitively if they assign little weight to the results compared to such factors as the aesthetics of play, the social interaction between players, or the exercise and recreation involved in playing. However, the concern focused on here is the ethical evaluation of playing to win. Our goal will be to see if a morally acceptable defense of competitive sports can be developed. If such an ideal of competitive sports can be defended, it will contain guidelines enabling us to distinguish those instances of competition in sports that are ethically defensible from those that are not.

The Morality of Competition in Sports

Why is it even necessary to morally evaluate competition in sports? Isn't it enough to say simply that participants and spectators alike enjoy such competition? To critics of competition in sports, that is not enough. They argue that such competition is either inherently immoral or that it has the effect of reinforcing other social values that are undesirable. Many persons, including some professional athletes, have criticized competition and the overemphasis on winning that they claim it breeds and have proposed a more relaxed attitude toward sports, at least at most levels of amateur play, than sanctioned by the competitive creed.

On the other hand, proponents of competition in sports have argued for its moral value. General Douglas MacArthur, an American hero of

World War II, may have overstated the case when he maintained that participation in competitive sports "is a vital character builder" that "molds the youth of our country for their roles as custodians of the republic."[6] Overstated or not, the view he expresses is widely shared.

A moral evaluation of the role of competition in sports is necessary if we are to rationally assess such conflicting views. It is not enough to assume uncritically that competition in athletics must be morally permissible simply because one enjoys it. After all, a racist majority may enjoy terrorizing members of the minority racial group, but that doesn't make it right. Perhaps competition in sports is harmful or unjust in ways not acknowledged by many of its proponents. Hence, the views of the critics need to be rationally examined.

It will be useful to divide the arguments about the morality of competition in sports into two kinds. The first is concerned with the good or bad consequences of competitive practices, either on the competitors themselves or society at large. The second is concerned not with the effects of competition but with its intrinsic character.

The Consequences of Competition

One way of evaluating competition in sports is to assess its consequences. Surely, whether a practice has good or bad effects on other people is relevant to moral evaluation. However, although the strategy of evaluating consequences is sound, implementing it raises more difficulties than one might initially expect.

First, are we to look only at the effects upon the participants or are we to look more broadly at the consequences for everyone affected? The important ethical theory known as *utilitarianism* holds that an action or practice is morally justified if, and only if, it has better consequences for all affected than any alternative.[7]

Utilitarianism sounds like a relatively simple approach to ethics. Just do a cost-benefit analysis on the effects of the act or practice being evaluated. In fact, however, utilitarianism raises complex issues of theory and practice before it can even be applied to an actual problem. For example, what are we to count as a good or bad consequence? In economic analysis, costs and benefits often can be measured in terms of monetary profits and losses, but what is to count as a cost or benefit in ethics? Should pleasure and pain be the criteria, as classical utilitarians such as Jeremy Bentham and John Stuart Mill suggest? Are there other criteria, such as excellence in performance, achievement, or knowledge that should also count? For example, is a well-played game of greater intrinsic value than a poorly played game even if the participants experience the same levels of pleasure and pain in each case? If we say that only pleasure and pain count, our theory may be too narrow. If we add other goods, such as excellence of performance, how are we to aggregate them with pleasure and pain to get an overall total?

Moreover, even if we can agree on criteria of good and bad consequences, they may admit of different interpretations. For example, should we identify benefits with what actual participants seem to want or with what they would want if they were better informed and more rational? Suppose, for example, that Jones despises practices because of her coach's emphasis on teamwork, but that Jones would value the practices if she were better informed about the value of teamwork and more rational about her own abilities. Are the practices beneficial to Jones or not?

None of this totally discredits utilitarianism. All of us sometimes assess the consequences of behavior on our own lives and others. Any ethical theory that totally ignored the consequences of actions or practices for human life would be very hard to defend. How many of us, for example, would advocate an action, however noble, knowing that one of its consequences would the painful death of millions? But even though any satisfactory ethic must give some weight to the effects of acts or policies on human life, the choice of what framework we should adopt for evaluating the consequences often will be controversial.

In addition, if we are to evaluate the effects of competition in sports, another problem arises. Just what practices are we evaluating? Competition in sports can range from professional athletic contests to interscholastic competition to backyard contests among friends. Moreover, it is important to distinguish competition as *actually* practiced and as it *ought to be* practiced. Thus, even if actual competitive practices often have bad consequences, we should not necessarily conclude that competition in sports is morally indefensible. Perhaps competition in sports as actually carried out has harmful consequences that would be avoided if the practice were properly organized.

Accordingly, any utilitarian evaluation of competition in sports will rest on a number of perhaps unstated and often controversial assumptions. In assessing the significance of such an evaluation, we should identify just what presuppositions have been employed. For example, if a study shows that participation in sports has little positive effect on character development, we need to be clear at least on what traits of character are regarded as positive, what forms of competition have been studied, and whether the study has considered only competition as actually practiced or the likely effect on character of an ethically defensible form of athletic competition.

An exhaustive analysis of the consequences of competition in sports is beyond the scope of this study and would involve extensive empirical research, but it is important to keep in mind the philosophical and methodological assumptions underlying such work. Given that the presuppositions of any proposed utilitarian analysis are likely to be controversial, it is doubtful if utilitarianism by itself can provide a decisive evaluation of competition in sports. In any case, we need to be cautious in assessing broad consequentialist generalizations in this area.

For example, proponents of competitive sports frequently claim, as we have seen, that participation promotes such desirable character traits as loyalty, discipline, commitment, a concern for excellence, and a "never say die" attitude. These views often are expressed by well-known slogans, sometimes posted on locker room walls, such as "a winner never quits, a quitter never wins," and "when the going gets tough, the tough get going." Strongly stated generalizations such as the assertion that athletics offer virtually unique opportunities for character development are common.

Unfortunately, even if we restrict ourselves to actual effects upon competitors, such claims are difficult to document. Thus, with regard to altruism, one recent study concludes: "Most athletes indicate low interest in receiving support and concern from others, low need to take care of others, and low need for affiliation. Such a personality seems necessary to achieve victory over others."[8] More generally, the authors reported: "We found no empirical support for the tradition that sport builds character. . . . It seems that the personality of the ideal athlete is not the result of the molding process, but comes out of the ruthless selection process that occurs at all levels of sport. . . . Horatio Alger success—in sport or elsewhere—comes only to those who already are mentally fit, resilient and strong."[9]

Although no single study is by itself decisive, this passage does have a number of significant methodological implications. In particular, even if participants in competitive sports do manifest desirable character traits to an unusual degree, it does not follow that participation in sports *caused* such traits to develop. Rather, it may have been prior possession of those traits that led to successful participation. *Correlation* should not be confused with *causation*.

On the other hand, if we must not take for granted that positive character traits associated with participation in sports are caused by such participation, we must be equally cautious in assuming that negative character traits associated with participation are caused by it as well. Thus, it has been suggested that "athletes whose sense of identity and self-worth is entirely linked to athletic achievement often experience an identity crisis when the athletic career has ended, and it becomes necessary to move on to something else."[10] However, this may be true generally of hard-driving individuals who face significant career changes in other fields as well. Would anyone be surprised at the claim that "executives whose sense of identity and self worth is entirely linked to achievement in business often experience an identity crisis when their career has ended and it becomes necessary to move on to something else"? Perhaps anyone sincerely committed to a field of endeavor would feel a sense of loss at such a time of change, which, incidentally, is not necessarily a bad thing to feel.

Even though there may be no direct and demonstrable connection between participation in competitive sports and desirable character development, there may be more subtle and indirect connections. Harry Edwards, while acknowledging that sports do not build character from scratch, suggests that participation in competitive sports may reinforce and encourage the development of preexisting character traits.[11] Perhaps persons with certain character traits do tend to participate in competitive athletics, but then have those traits reinforced by participation to a greater extent than otherwise would have been the case. This suggests that it is not easy to show either that participation does or does not promote specific character traits in participants. (Similarly, it is not easy to show that exposure to a liberal arts education has an effect on the values of students, but we do not thereby conclude either that there are no effects or that there are none we *ought* to try to bring about.)[12]

Moreover, even if competitive sports have less impact on character development than many have claimed, they still may play a major role in *expressing* and *illustrating* our values. This might be called the expressive function of sports.[13] For example, athletic competition may illustrate the value of dedication and teamwork by publicly manifesting the degree of excellence the cultivation of those traits can enable us to attain. Closely contested contests can provide opportunities for the exhibition of such personal virtues as courage and loyalty. By welcoming challenges in sports, participants and spectators can affirm and exhibit such virtues.

Critics of competitive sports may reply that athletic competition can also illustrate indefensible values, such as the commitment to win at all costs. When applied to actual competitive practices, this response may have force. In addition, if competition itself is inherently immoral, competitive sports may express that inherent immorality as well.

Perhaps then, especially in view of the difficulties in evaluating the consequences of participation in competitive sports, it is competition itself that is at issue. Competition by its very nature, the critics contend, cannot satisfy legitimate ethical requirements.

Competition, Selfishness, and the Quest for Excellence

Perhaps the most important criticism of the moral worth of competition is that it is inherently selfish and egoistic. Because competitive activities are zero-sum games, one person's victory is another's defeat. As we have seen, the internal goal of competition is to defeat an opponent and win the contest.

According to some critics of competition throughout society, such as political theorist John Schaar, the competitive society is a very unattractive place. It reduces human interaction to "a contest in which each man competes with his fellows for scarce goods, a contest in which there is never enough for everybody, and where one man's gain is usually another's loss."[14] This position is defended by Michael Fielding, a thoughtful writer on educational philosophy, who identifies competition with "working against others in a spirit of selfishness."[15]

The argument of the critics, then, is roughly this. The goal of competition is enhancement of the position of one competitor at the expense of others. Thus, by its very nature, competition is selfish. But since selfish concern for oneself at the expense of others is immoral, it follows that competition is immoral as well.

Critics of competitive sports do not direct their argument only against clearly debased forms of competition, such as obvious cases of cheating. After all, virtually everyone acknowledges that competitive sports can be morally objectionable when players are taught to cheat in order to win or when teams are so unequally matched that participants risk injury or are intentionally humiliated by opponents. The critics, however, object even to competitive sports at their best. Even supposing that the participants are playing fairly in the best spirit of the game, is competition in sports still not ultimately selfish and egoistic?

The argument that competitive sports are selfish by their very nature is not without some intuitive force for in athletic competition, if X wins, then Y loses. Moreover, if they are good competitors, X and Y each try to win. Nevertheless, even if the argument that competition is essentially selfish turns out to be justifiable when applied to economic competition in the market, which is hardly self-evident, it faces special difficulties when applied to sports and athletics.

For one thing, the idea of competition in sports as a virtually unrestricted war of all against all seems grossly inaccurate. To begin with, even though team sports involve competition between opponents, they also involve cooperation among members of the same team. Moreover, in many sports, even at the professional level, it is common for opponents to provide encouragement and even instruction to each other in the off-season or even between contests. In fact, this can even be overdone. Thus, one widely cited explanation for the slump of professional golf star Ben Crenshaw during the early 1980s was the over-solicitiousness of his fellow touring golf professionals, who bombarded him with remedies that many believed only confused him still further. Critics might reply that such examples only show that even professional athletes find it morally impossible to live according to a strict competitive ethic. However, as we will see, such cooperative behavior can be regarded as part of a defensible competitive ethic, based not on the idea of a war of all against all but on the value of meeting the challenges provided by competition in sports.

As we have noted, competition in sports takes place within a context of constitutive rules binding on all the participants. The ideal of good competition requires competitors to forgo momentary advantages that might be secured by violation of the rules. Commitment to this ideal is perhaps best illustrated by the behavior of athletes in individual sports, ranging from weekend tennis players to professional golfers, who call penalties on themselves in the heat of competition, sometimes at great financial cost. In other sports, rules often are enforced by officials. But while it is considered legitimate to question the calls of officials, no one can legitimately protest that officials ought not to apply the rules in the first place or only apply them selectively to some competitors and not others.

Finally, in addition to obligations to obey the constitutive rules of the sport, there are obligations of competitive fairness that also restrict selfishness in sports. Thus, competitive success seems insignificant, or even unethical, if it is obtained against vastly inferior opponents or under competitive conditions where the deck is stacked against one side. Thus, John Thompson, coach of the nationally ranked Georgetown Hoya basketball team, was widely criticized for scheduling a series of early season games in 1989 against weak opponents, from Division II and Division III schools which do not offer the kinds of athletic scholarships or emphasize athletics to the extent that Division I institutions such as Georgetown do. This scheduling of inferior opponents culminated in a noncompetitive rout of the University of the District of Columbia, a game which many believe provided little if any benefit to either team. Similarly, whatever the formal legality the San Diego Yacht Club's action, the club is open to ethical criticism for choosing to race a catamaran in the 1988 America's Cup race, since such a multihull vessel normally will always defeat the single-hulled vessel used by the challenging New Zealanders.

Finally, selfishness in competitive sports often is criticized. The basketball player who is overly concerned with how many points she scores rather than with whether her team wins is criticized for being selfish, a practice that seems inexplicable on the hypothesis that selfishness is the norm in competitive athletics.

At this point, critics might concede that there are some normative restrictions on selfish behavior in athletic competition. However, they might still argue that just as limited war is still war, so minimally constrained selfishness still is selfishness.

To answer this point, a fuller account of competition in sports needs to be provided. Let us begin by considering the following description of a Yale-Princeton football game played in 1895. Princeton was winning 16–10 but Yale was right on the Princeton goal line with a chance to turn the tide on the very last play of the game.

> The clamor ceased once absolutely, and the silence was even more impressive than the tumult that had preceded it. . . . While they (Yale) were lining up for that last effort the cheering dies away, yells both measured and inarticulate stopped and the place was so still . . . you could hear the telegraph instruments chirping like crickets from the side. [16]

Yale scored to win the game on a brilliant run. "It is not possible to describe that run. It would be as easy to explain how a snake disappears through the grass, or an eel slips from your fingers, or to say how a flash of linked lightning wriggles across the sky."[17]

Is the important point here simply that Yale won and that Princeton lost? Edwin Delattre, former president of St. John's University of Annapolis, has drawn a different lesson from this episode and the many like it that take place in all seasons and at all levels of competition.

> Such moments are what makes the game worth the candle. Whether amidst the soft lights and sparkling balls of a billiard table, or the rolling terrain of a lush fairway, or in the violent and crashing pits where linemen struggle, it is the moments where no letup is possible, when there is virtually no tolerance for error, which make up the game. The best and most satisfying contests maximize these moments and minimize respite from pressure.[18]

According to Delattre, it is these moments of test rather than victory or defeat that are the source of the value of competition in sports.

> The testing of one's mettle in competitive athletics is a form of self-discovery. . . . The claim of competitive athletics to importance rests squarely on their providing us opportunities for self discovery which might otherwise have been missed. . . . They provide opportunities for self-discovery, for concentration and intensity of involvement, for being carried away by the demands of the contest . . . with a frequency seldom matched

elsewhere.... This is why it is a far greater success in competitive athletics to have played well under pressure of a truly worthwhile opponent and lost than to have defeated a less worthy or unworthy one where no demands were made.[19]

Delattre's comments suggest that although it is essential to good competition that the competitors try as hard as they can to achieve victory, the principal value of athletic competition lies not in winning itself but in the process of overcoming the challenge presented by a worthy opponent. In fact, good competition presupposes a *cooperative* effort by competitors to generate the best possible challenge to each other. Each has the obligation to the other to try his or her best. Although one wins the contest and the other loses, each gains by trying to meet the challenge that each has voluntarily agreed to face.

If this view has force, competition in sports should be regarded and engaged in not as if it were a zero-sum game, but as a *mutually acceptable quest for excellence through challenge*. Underlying the good sports contest, in effect, is a hypothetical social contract according to which both competitors accept the obligation to provide to the best of their abilities a challenge for opponents according to the rules of the sport in question. Competition in sports is ethically defensible, in this view, when it is engaged in voluntarily as part of a mutual quest for excellence.

This is not to say that all instances of actual competition in sports are ethically defensible; actual practice may not satisfy the requirements of the mutual quest for excellence. It is to say that competition in sports is ethically defensible when it does satisfy such requirements.

The view of competitive sports as a mutual quest for excellence not only emphasizes the cooperative side of athletic contests and the acceptance of the challenge from the point of view of all the competitors, it also explains much of our society's fascination with competitive sports. The late A. Bartlett Giamatti, former president of Yale and Commissioner of Baseball (although not necessarily in that order of importance) emphasized the quest for excellence when he reminded us:

When ... a person on the field or fairway, rink, floor, or track, performs an act that surpasses—despite his or her evident mortality, his or her humanness—whatever we have seen or heard of or could conceive of doing ourselves, then we have witnessed ... an instant of complete coherence. In that instant, pulled to our feet, we are pulled out of ourselves. We feel what we saw, became what we perceived. The memory of that moment is deep enough to send us all out again and again, to reenact the ceremony, made of all the minor ceremonies to which spectator and player devote themselves, in the hopes that the moment will be summoned again and made again palpable. [20]

At this point, critics of competition in sports may become impatient. Sports events, conceived as part of a mutually acceptable quest for excellence, may indeed be ethically defensible, they might reply, but such a view does not justify competition in sports. Rather, they might claim, what it does is replace competitive sports with something else. What has been done, in their view, is a verbal trick. "Competition" has been so redefined that it no longer refers to true competition at all, but rather to the quest for excellence, self-improvement, and self-knowledge through exposure to challenge. By emphasizing the quest for excellence, we have changed the aim of the sports contest from that of defeating opponents to the quest for self-development and achievement. The aim is no longer to defeat opponents but to reach certain standards of performance or to gain self-knowledge and development through trying to satisfy those standards. Competition in sports has not been defended but instead has been replaced by the ideal of personal development in the pursuit of excellence. The ideal of competition with others has been merely replaced with so-called "competition with oneself."

Has competition in sports really been justified as a mutual quest for excellence or has it merely been replaced by a different noncompetitive ideal of the mutual quest for excellence? Let us consider this issue further.

Self-Development and Competition with Self

The expression "competition with self" calls up the image of athletes playing against ghostly images of their earlier selves. Because there are no ghostly images and no presently existing earlier selves with whom to compete, this expression, if not incoherent, is at least potentially quite misleading. It will be clearer and less paradoxical to speak of individuals striving for self-development or improvement rather than speaking loosely of individuals competing against themselves.

Should participants in sports strive mainly for self-development or personal improvement? Is such improvement a more important or more ethically defensible goal than competitive success? After considering such questions, we will then consider whether competition, conceived of as a mutual quest for excellence, really is only a disguised way of talking about the quest for self-improvement.

The claim that improvement is an ethically better or more defensible goal than competitive success in sports presupposes there is an ethically relevant difference between the two. What might that difference be? Perhaps the difference is that in aiming at improvement, we do not necessarily aim at beating others. We can all improve together, so the element of the zero-sum game is missing. Since all can improve together, to aim at improvement does not appear to be selfish in the same way that intending to beat others seems selfish and egoistic to critics of competitive sports.

However, there are two defenses against such an approach. The first, as we have seen, is that competition thought of as a mutual quest for excellence is not necessarily selfish or a total zero-sum game. Although only one party can win, each cooperates in providing a mutually acceptable challenge to the other. Moreover, although not all competitors can win, there is a sense, as we will see, in which all the competitors in a well-played contest can meet the challenge and achieve excellence.

Second, and perhaps most important, we can question the extent to which the quest for self-improvement actually differs from competitive sports in an ethically relevant way. At the very least, the two approaches share some central features. For one thing, an especially significant criterion of improvement is change in one's competitive standing when measured against the performance of others. A major way, perhaps the best way, of finding out if one is improving is to see if one does better against opponents than one has done in the past.

In fact, doing better against opponents is not merely a contingent sign of improvement. In many contexts in sports, what counts as playing well will be logically determined by what counts as an appropriate competitive response to the moves of opponents. For example, it would be incorrect to say that Jones is playing well in a tennis match if what Jones did was hit crisp ground shots in a situation where intelligent play called for charging the net. Similarly, it would be incorrect to say Jones is improving if Jones continues to make such competitively inappropriate moves in match after match.

The conceptual point, then, is that evaluation of achievement, improvement or development cannot easily be divorced from comparison with the performance of others. Robert Nozick provided a pertinent illustration: "A man living in an isolated mountain village can sink 15 jump shots with a basketball out of 150 tries. Everyone else in the village can sink only one jump shot out of 150 tries. He thinks (as do the others) that he's very good at it. One day along comes Jerry West."[21]

The example clearly illustrates that what counts as a significant achievement requires reference to the performance of others. What may not be so obvious is that judgments about what counts as significant improvement also presupposes comparative evaluations about the performance of others. Before the arrival of a great professional basketball player such as Jerry West, the village star may have thought that improving his average to 17 out of 150 shots would constitute improvement of a significant order. After the visit, even if it is acknowledged

that no villager can ever match West's skill, the very criterion of significant improvement would have radically changed. At the very least, the
more expert villagers should expect that, after reasonable practice, they
should make at least 50 shots out of 150 tries. Before the visit, the
"30-shot barrier" must have seemed as impossible to reach as breaking
the 4-minute mile must have seemed to runners of an earlier era.

Does this imply that an athlete seeking to improve really is implicitly ·
competing with others? Such an athlete is striving to reach standards set
by an appropriate reference group of others, at least if the improvement
is thought of as an achievement. Thus, success or failure is partially
determined by how others perform or are capable of performing.
Accordingly, those who value "competition with self" because it seems
not to involve (possibly negative) comparisons with the performance of
others may need to rethink their position.

Thus, it is at least arguable that self-improvement as a goal of athletics
is not ethically more defensible than the goal of competitive success,
because they share several ethically relevant features. In particular,
improvement often is difficult to measure apart from competitive
success, and the competitive moves of an opponent often determine
what the proper response is in specific sports. Most important, what
counts as improvement, or at least significant improvement, presupposes
a comparative judgment about the performance of an appropriate reference class of other participants. Accordingly, even in judging our own
performance, we are evaluating it in terms of how it compares to a group
with whom we believe it appropriate to compare ourselves.[22]

On the other hand, there are important differences between striving
for improvement and striving for competitive success. In particular, the
significant improvement of some participants does not preclude
the similar improvement of others and may even facilitate it, as when the
level of play of the whole group is raised. The attainment of victory by
some, however, does preclude its attainment by the opposition. Although
this difference may not be as important as critics of competition allege,
since everyone can meet the challenge of competition, it remains the case
that although all participants can improve, not all participants can win.
Moreover, competition emphasizes meeting the challenge set by an
opponent, but improvement emphasizes the development of one's own
skills. Even if one can only measure development by examining competitive performance, the two goals are conceptually different. One can meet
the challenge of an opponent without necessarily improving on one's
past performance.

Our discussion, then, suggests two conclusions. First, since there are
differences between striving for improvement and striving to meet the
challenge set by an opponent, our defense of competition as a mutual

quest for excellence is not a disguised defense of a noncompetitive ideal of self-development in sports. Second, because the defense is of competition as a mutual quest for excellence, it avoids many of the objections to competitive excess that may have made "competition with self" seem more attractive. As we have seen, athletic competition, conceived of as a mutual quest for excellence, is significantly cooperative, in that each competitor, in effect, contracts to provide a challenge to the opponent. Finally, emphasis on improvement, development, or "competition with self" does not avoid comparisons with the performance of others; rather, such comparisons are presupposed by evaluations of personal performance in the first place.

Finally, one last point needs to be considered. Suppose that dancers were given the following advice: "it's unimportant whether you are good or bad dancers. Just try to get better and better every day." Surely it is important whether dancers improve their performance, but isn't the level of achievement they actually have attained also important? In the dance, we appreciate personal development, but we also value achievement and the production of a skilled performance as well. If athletic performance is regarded as significant, skilled performance is important and valuable in sports as well. Competition is the mechanism by which achievement is measured and determined. Improvement surely is a desirable goal, but there is no reason to assume a priori that concern for achievement is any less important or noble.

Competition, Selfishness, and Inequality

Keeping these points in mind, let us return to the arguments of the critics of competitive sports. As we have seen, one major charge of the critics is that competitive sports are inherently selfish. However, this criticism seems to ignore the significantly cooperative elements of competition in sports, conceived of as a mutual quest for excellence through challenge. According to this conception of competitive sports, opponents are cooperating in generating mutually acceptable challenges that each has voluntarily chosen to face.

It is true that winning will normally be in a competitor's self-interest. However, it need not always be so. Winning may breed egotistical behavior or generate excessive self-confidence that may ultimately lose friends or lead to dangerous risk taking. It can cause a young athlete to neglect academic work and overemphasize athletic success. Whether or not winning is in one's overall self-interest in particular cases is an empirical question, depending upon the particular circumstances at hand.

However, even if victory is in one's self-interest, it does not follow that the pursuit of victory is selfish. Of course, if we define selfish behavior as self-interested behavior, then the pursuit of victory will be selfish, because we have stipulated it to be so by definition. But is such a definition or characterization of selfishness acceptable?

Consider the following examples:

1 Jones is playing in a touch football game with friends. Jones says, "I'll be the quarterback." The others declare that they too want to be quarterbacks and suggest the position be shared. Jones replies, It's my football! If you don't let me play quarter back, I'll take my ball and go home!"

2. Jones is in a spelling contest between two teams in her fifth grade class. She correctly spells a difficult word. As a result, her team wins and the other team loses.

The concept of selfishness simply is stretched too far if it is applied to both kinds of cases. Isn't there a significant difference between the first case, in which Jones *disregards* the interests of others in favor of his own, and the second case, in which each student is given a fair chance to succeed? If there is an important difference between trying to defeat an opponent within a mutually acceptable framework of rules and simply disregarding the interests of others, then there is a significant, ethically relevant difference between athletic competition and selfishness.

To summarize the discussion of competition and selfishness, the charge that competition in sports and athletics is intrinsically selfish faces several weighty objections. It does not take into account the cooperative elements in competition, and in particular, does not appreciate the ethical significance of competition conceived of as a mutual quest for excellence. In addition, it rests on a far too broad conception of selfishness itself. Accordingly, unless the critic can reply satisfactorily to these objections, we are entitled to reject the claim that competition in sports, by its very nature, is just another example of selfish acquisitiveness in action. This is not to deny that competitors in sports sometimes act selfishly. Rather, it is to deny that action within competitive sports *must* be selfish because of the nature of the activity itself.

However, even if competition is sports is not intrinsically selfish, it has another feature that may worry critics. Competitive sports, according to this second critical view, generate *inequalities*. It divides us into winners and losers, successes and failures, stars and scrubs. Many of us are all too familiar with the slogans, popular with some coaches, that equate losing with failure, and that virtually assign "losers" to an inferior branch of the human race.

In practice, competition is too often used for making invidious distinctions. Making an error in a crucial game or situation is equated with lack of drive or lack of courage. In the early stages of his career, Tom Watson, who later developed into one of the greatest golfers of all time, was referred to as a "choker" because he couldn't seem to hold leads in tournaments. One of the sadder features of organized sports for children is the emphasis sometimes placed on winning by the adults involved. As a result, young players often become more concerned with avoiding errors, and the criticism or even ridicule that follows, than with enjoying competition or developing fundamental skills.

Thus, there is something to the claim that competitive sports generate inequalities and that these sometimes are harmful or unethical. But before we accept too broad a version of the criticism, a number of considerations must be examined.

First, we need to distinguish between whether a rule or practice generates a factual *inequality* or *difference* and whether that difference is unethical, unfair, or *inequitable*. Some inequalities may well be fair or equitable, as when an instructor gives a high grade to an excellent paper and a low grade to a poor paper in a course. Whether inequalities or differences exist is one thing, and whether or not they are morally defensible normally is quite another. Accordingly, it doesn't follow that every inequality generated by competitive sports is unethical, unfair, or inequitable.

It can be conceded, then, that competitive sports generate inequalities, and even that some of these inequalities, such as those generated by excessive emphasis on winning and losing in children's sports, are ethically objectionable. On the other hand, it may not be the case that *all* inequalities generated by competitive sports are ethically objectionable.

It will be useful here to employ a distinction made by legal scholar Ronald Dworkin between the right to *equal treatment*, "which is the right to an equal distribution of some opportunity of resource or burden, " and the right to *treatment as an equal*, which is the right "to be treated with the same respect and concern as anyone else."[23] Unlike equal treatment, equal respect and concern do not require identical distribution of a good, such as playing time on a basketball team. Thus, if one of my children is ill and the other isn't, treatment as an equal does not require that I divide the available medicine in half. Rather provision of all the medicine to the sick child is compatible with and may even be required by equal respect and concern for both children.[24]

This suggests, as Dworkin himself maintains, that the right to treatment as an equal, or the right to equal respect and concern, is more fundamental ethically than the right to equal treatment. This is because, as we have seen, factual inequalities in distribution, or what Dworkin calls unequal treatment, may or may not be defensible depending upon whether they are compatible with the showing of equal respect and concern to all affected.

Accordingly, even though competition in sports may lead to unequal treatment, such as different assignments of playing time to better and worse players on a team or to a distinction between winners and losers of a contest, this is not sufficient to show that competition in sports is inequitable or unjust. The critic must show, for example, not just that there is a distinction between winners and losers but, in addition, that this distinction violates the right to treatment as an equal.[25]

Contrary to such a supposition, it is arguable that if people are treated with equal concern and respect, justified inequalities in distribution naturally will emerge. This is because part of treating persons with respect surely is treating them as beings "who are capable of forming and acting on intelligent conceptions of how their lives should be lived."[26] But different people will have different conceptions of how their lives should be led and make different choices accordingly. For example, if critics respond more favorably to one novel than another, the author of the first novel may make more money in royalties than the author of the second novel. But how can such an inequality be avoided without prohibiting persons from making and acting upon their critical judgments? In other words, certain inequalities of outcome can be avoided only by failing to treat and respect others as the persons capable of critical choice that they are.[27]

A similar point can be made about many of the inequalities of result which emerge from competitive sports. For one thing, most participants are participating because they want to be competing. They themselves find the challenge posed by competitors worth trying to meet and the competitive sport they play worth their commitment. If respect for persons requires that we respect their conception of how their life should be led—as long as it involves no violation of the rights of others—the inequalities generated by competition in sports seem no less justified than those other inequalities arising from the uncoerced autonomous choices of those involved.

Critics might object that treating people as equals involves more than simply respecting their choices. In addition, the choices must at least be reasonably informed and not made under conditions that undermine clear thinking or the competency of the agent, such as mental illness, depression, or mood-altering drugs. For example, suppose Jones chooses to continually humiliate himself in order to gain Smith's affections. Surely, Smith does not treat Jones with respect if she continually heaps extreme humiliation after extreme humiliation upon him, even though he chooses to leave himself open to such treatment. Rather, Jones is degrading himself, probably because of some psychological problem of which he is not aware, and Smith is contributing to that degradation rather than providing help. Similarly, just because participants in sports agree to compete, it doesn't follow that their choice is of the kind that ought to be respected. In addition, it must be shown that the competitive relationship itself is not inherently degrading or incompatible in some other way with respect for persons as equals.

Indeed, competitive relationships often are characterized in derogatory terms. Competitors often are seen merely as obstacles to be overcome rather than as fellow participants and persons. They are to be "destroyed," "humiliated," and "run off the court." Persons are reduced to mere things or barriers standing in the way of competitive success.

For example, in a major college football game, a star running back, playing again for the first time after experiencing a serious knee injury, reported that during a pileup, he felt the opposing players trying to twist his injured knee. Thinking quickly, he yelled out, "You've got the wrong knee! You've got the wrong knee!"[28]

If the competitive attitude required that we set out to injure our opponents in order to win, it clearly would be ethically indefensible. It should be clear from our earlier discussion, however, that the ethics of good competition prohibits the intentional infliction of injury. Indeed, if competition is understood as a mutual quest for excellence, competitors should want their opponents to be at their peak so as to present the best possible challenge. Victory, if it is to be significant, requires outplaying worthy opponents, not deliberately injuring them to prevent them from competing.

Accordingly, in evaluating competition in sports, it is crucial that features that are central to competition be distinguished from those that are not. Many features of competitive sports that are ethically objectionable are not necessarily part of competitive sports. In particular, the reduction of opponents to mere things, while unfortunately too often a part of high-pressure athletics, is not a central element of competitive sports and can consistently be condemned by proponents of a defensible competitive ethic.

Inequalities generated by competitive sports, then, need not be ethically indefensible. Participants in competitive sports presumably prefer a life including competition, with the possibility of winning or losing, to a life that does not. If treating individuals as equals requires us to react appropriately to the life plans of persons—to treat them as agents "capable of forming and acting on an intelligent conception of how their lives should be led"—inequalities that arise from their decisions in athletics are presumptively fair and equitable.[29]

In fact, an even stronger conclusion is supported by our discussion.

Because each competitor in an athletic contest must respond and react to the choices and actions of fellow competitors—actions manifesting the skills the participants have chosen to develop and the decisions they have made during play—competition in sports, conceived along lines of a mutual quest for excellence, is a *paradigm case* of an activity in which the participants treat each others as equals. The good competitor does not see the opponent merely as an obstacle to be overcome but as a person whose activity calls for an appropriate response. Rather than being incompatible with equal respect for persons, competition in athletics, at its best, may presuppose it.

Is Winning Important?

If we view competitive sports and athletics as a mutual quest for excellence in the face of challenge, what importance should be assigned to winning? Is simply playing well in an attempt to meet the opponent's challenge all we should strive for? Why should who wins or loses matter at all?

Can't it be argued, however, that winning is significant precisely because it is a criterion of the challenge being met? To lose is to fail to meet the challenge; to win is to succeed. If competition in sports is justified in terms of attempts to meet challenges, it surely is important whether or not we succeed in meeting them. After all, isn't the principal point of deliberately embarking upon a difficult task to see if we can accomplish it?

Although there is much to this position, perhaps it is overstated. Winning is not necessarily a sign of competitive success, and losing is not necessarily a sign of competitive failure. If winning were the only criterion of success, it would be sensible to take pride in consistently defeating far weaker opponents by wide margins. One could achieve competitive success merely by consistently playing vastly inferior opposition. Conversely, if losing were necessarily a sign of competitive failure, a weaker opponent would have no cause for pride after having extended a far superior opponent to the limit before going down to ultimate defeat.

This suggests that winning is far from everything in competitive sports. Not everyone can win, but each competitor may well meet the challenge set by an opponent, although one wins and one loses.

However, it is not unimportant who wins or loses. If winning is not everything, it is something. For one thing, if the competition is not one-sided, winning will certainly be an important criterion, sometimes *the* criterion, of having met the challenge of the opposition. Because one is trying to meet the challenge set by the opponent, it seems perfectly appropriate to feel elated at victory or disappointed at defeat. Even when opponents are mismatched, pride in victory often may be appropriate. The victors rightly may be proud that they played to their potential without having the incentive of strong opposition.

Moreover, it is often far too easy in sports to take pride in defeat on the grounds that the opponents really were better. It is easy enough to make excuses, such as "we played well but lost to a clearly better team," but one may suspect that the truth is "if we had played to our potential, we could have beaten them." Of course, sometimes it is appropriate to take pride in a well-played defeat, but often the scoreboard is an important indicator of whether the play was really good after all.

Finally, we should remember that playing well in some aesthetic sense is not necessarily playing well in the sense of meeting the competitive challenge presented by an opponent. Remember the earlier example of the tennis player who hits ground strokes with beautiful form yet loses because the competitive situation called for aggressive play at the net. Similarly, a 3-point shot from twenty feet may look good but may make no competitive sense if the team with the ball has a 2-point lead and fifteen seconds left on the clock. What may look like good play from an aesthetic standpoint may be poor play given the competitive situation.

Thus, for a variety of reasons, although winning may not be a necessary criterion of competitive success, it often is the most reliable indicator of it. In many competitive contexts, it won't do to separate winning and losing from how well one played the game, because the outcome of the game is an especially significant indicator of how well one actually played.

But why should success and failure matter at all? After all, "it's only a game." Isn't concern for competitive success overemphasized, given the nature of the activity in question?

There is no question that competitive success can be overemphasized, especially at the level of children's sports. Certainly, if the slogan "it's only a game" means that extreme depression, abusiveness to others, extended withdrawal from family and friends, spouse beating, and existential anxiety are inappropriate responses to losing, it surely is correct. Sports normally are not matters of life and death.

On the other hand, if "it's only a game" means that success in competitive athletics shouldn't matter at all, it is far more dubious. Competitive sports provide a context in which we can stretch our bodily skills and capacities to the limits in the pursuit of excellence. The pursuit of excellence in the use of the body is hardly trivial. On the contrary, the meeting of the demands athletes place upon their talents often involves beauty, courage, dedication, and passion. If these things don't matter, what does? Would the critics say to the artist who botches a significant project or to the dancer who fails to perform well in a major perform-ance, "well, it's only art!"? Finally, at the professional level, concern for professional success, which may involve winning, seems no less appro-priate than similar concern in other professions.

Our conclusions do not imply that all sporting activity should always be intensely competitive. Not everyone wants or needs a challenge all of the time. At many levels of play, the trick for coaches and educators will be to balance an emphasis on achievement and competitive success with participation and instruction in developmental skills. On the other hand, insofar as an activity is a sport, then even if played with little emphasis on competition, it will still involve a degree of competitive challenge because the goal of the participants, as players, will be to make correct moves or plays, which in turn will be defined by the moves of the opposing players. If standards of good and bad performance did not apply, the participants would merely be exercising, not engaging in sports.

This point suggests that critics of overemphasis on winning and competitive success may take their points too far by ignoring the perhaps equally deleterious effects of underemphasis. Thus, if participants normally are told that "it doesn't matter how you do, just go out and have fun," the subtle message being conveyed may be that doing well is unimportant. If participation in competitive sports can be a form of human excellence, if it can contribute to self-development and self-expression, and perhaps reinforce desirable character traits, perform-ance may well matter after all.

It is worth considering here former Secretary of Education William Bennett's description of a rigidly noncompetitive softball team he refers to as The Persons:

> The team is coed, they have no "discrimination" and no "rules.". . . Occasionally, they let one of their dogs . . . "play a position" . . . and the Persons laugh and try to look loose and non-competitive. . . . In the end, the Persons must be judged in their own terms to be insensitive both to the game and to one another as "players"—the cost no doubt of each one's being sensitive to himself exclusively as a Person. [30]

Bennett concludes that

> Charles Reich's ideal in *The Greening of America*—a laughing generation playing football in bell bottom trousers—is one of sheer aimlessness, of distraction pure and simple, doing nothing. Serious playing and watching, on the other hand, . . . are rarely if ever doing nothing, for sports is a way

to scorn indifference, and occasionally, indeed, one can even discern in competition those elements of grace, skill, beauty, and courage that mirror the greatest affirmations of human spirit and passion.[31]

The sarcasm Bennett devotes to noncompetitive play may be overdone, but his suggestion that competitive sports, at their best, involve application of standards of excellence to challenges people regard as worthwhile in themselves should be taken seriously. If competitive sports are understood on the model of a mutual quest for excellence through challenge, they not only can be activities of beauty and skill, but they also represent a striving for human excellence, and in so doing are a paradigmatic way of respecting each other as person—of taking our status as persons seriously.

Conclusion

This chapter suggests that competition in the context of sports is most defensible ethically when understood as a mutual quest for excellence in the intelligent and directed use of athletic skills in the face of challenge. Athletic competition of this sort, under appropriate conditions, may have such beneficial consequences as expressing important values and reinforcing the development of desirable character traits. Perhaps more important, competition in sports may have intrinsic worth as a framework within which we express ourselves as persons and respond to others as persons in the mutual pursuit of excellence. Although other such frameworks also exist, few are as universally accessible and involve us so fully as agents who must intelligently use their bodies to meet challenges we have chosen for ourselves.

Competition as the mutual quest for excellence, it must be emphasized, is an *ideal*. Actual practices may not conform to its requirements. In the real world, winning may be overemphasized, rules may be broken, athletes may be exploited, and unfair conditions for competition may preclude genuine challenge. If so, the ideal provides grounds for moral criticism of serious deviations from it. In the remainder of this book, the ideal will be applied to the moral evaluation of actual practices in sports.

The ideal of competition in sports as a mutual quest for excellence itself needs to be examined, refined, clarified, criticized, or even replaced with a better conception if sufficiently powerful objections are raised against it. However, without some defensible standards against which actual play can be measured, the valuable aspects of sports cannot be distinguished from the harmful or unfair aspects. Without reasoned standards of evaluation, criticism and acclaim alike would rest on purely emotive reactions rather than upon the results of perhaps the most important quest—the quest for justification through meeting the challenges of open discussion and critical inquiry.

3

Cheating and Violence in Sports

In early October 1990, the highly regarded University of Colorado Buffaloes were playing a home football contest against the University of Missouri. Top national ranking was at stake. The final seconds saw Colorado, trailing 31-27 at the time, driving toward the Missouri goal line. Somehow, in the confusion on the field, the seven officials on the field as well as the "chain gang" working the sideline markers, and the scoreboard operator, lost track of the downs. On what should have been the fourth and deciding down, Colorado failed to score, in part because the Colorado quarterback, mistakenly thinking he had another play left, intentionally grounded a pass. In fact, the officials signaled that Colorado had another chance, unaware that the Buffaloes already had used the four chances to score allowed by the rules. Colorado scored on the illegal but unnoticed fifth down to eke out a 33-31 "victory."

Did Colorado really win? Should the final score have been allowed to stand? It was decided that the officials' mistake was not the sort of error that can be overruled. But should the University of Colorado have accepted the victory? Is such a "win" meaningful in any important ethical sense?

Consider another example. Two top college basketball teams are struggling for a conference championship. The score is tied with five seconds to go and the team with the ball calls time out. The noise in the gym is deafening and, in the pandemonium, the defending team does not hear the buzzer signaling the end of the time out. Before they can regroup, the referees, as required by the rules, give the ball to the offensive team. The offensive team drives the length of the court to score the winning basket before the defenders can even leave their huddle to get on the floor. Did the offensive team behave as they should have? Is their "win" something in which they may properly take pride?

Take a third example. A championship basketball game is tied, with

37

only a few seconds remaining. A player on the defensive team steals the ball and breaks away for the winning basket. Only one player can catch the streaking guard heading for the winning bucket. The defender realizes she cannot block the shot but also knows the opponent is that team's worst foul shooter. She pretends to go for the ball but in fact deliberately fouls her opponent. Is deliberate fouling ethical? After all, fouling is against the rules. Was committing a deliberate foul in this way a form of cheating? Should one take pride in the resulting victory? Why or why not?

Finally, consider a boxing match for a major championship. Both boxers are skilled but each inflicts physical damage on the other. Is this violence in sports? Is it unacceptable? After all, more than 350 boxers, amateurs as well as professionals, have been killed in the ring since 1945.

If violence is unacceptable in boxing, what about football? Is football a violent sport? Should violence be permitted in sports? Are violent activities like boxing really sports at all? What is violence anyway? When, if ever, should it be permitted in sports?

These examples raise questions, not about the general issue of whether competition in sports is ever ethical, but about how to ethically conduct competition. They raise issues of sportsmanship, cheating, and violence in sports. By examining them, we can better understand the values that may be used in assessing the behavior of competitors within the athletic contest itself.

Sportsmanship and Fairness in the Pursuit of Victory

What values ought to govern the behavior of competitors in athletic competition? Sportsmanship is one value that often is appealed to in such contexts. Sportsmanship has received relatively little attention by moral thinkers, and probably suffers today because of associations with the morality of an elite "uppercrust" and perhaps by concerns about a male bias being built into the meaning of the term.[1] Nevertheless, sportsmanship is a value frequently cited by coaches, players, and commentators on sports, and ought not to be dismissed without a hearing.

But what is sportsmanship? Does it apply equally to intense athletic competition as well as to informal games among friends?

Perhaps the most influential recent analysis of sportsmanship has been provided by James W. Keating. Keating properly warns us, first of all, not to make our account of sportsmanship so broad as to make it virtually identical with virtue.[2] Not every virtue is an instance of sportsmanship and not every vice is unsportsmanlike. Thus, one dictionary defines "sportsmanship" rather unhelpfully as "sportsmanlike conduct" and continues by listing conduct appropriate to a sportsman as exhibiting "fairness, self-control, etc." Keating tells us that a formal code of sportsmanship promulgated earlier in this century included such diverse injunctions as "keep yourself fit," "keep your temper," and "keep a sound soul and a clean mind in a healthy body." The trouble with such broad accounts of sportsmanship is that they do no specific work. We cannot say conduct is ethical *because* it is sportsmanlike, for "sportsmanlike" has just become another way of saying "ethical." The idea of sportsmanship has been characterized so broadly that there is no particular aspect of morality that is its specific concern.

Keating believes that a more useful account of sportsmanship will develop the rather vague suggestion of the dictionary about behavior expected of a sportsman or sportswoman. To develop this idea, he introduces a crucial distinction between *sports* and *athletics*:

> In essence, sport is a kind of diversion which has for its direct and immediate end fun, pleasure, and delight and which is dominated by a spirit of moderation and generosity. Athletics on the other hand, is essentially a competitive activity, which has for its end victory in the contest and which is characterized by a spirit of dedication, sacrifice, and intensity.[3]

Sportsmanship, then, is the kind of attitude toward opponents that best promotes the goal of sports as defined by Keating; namely, friendly, mutually satisfactory relationships among the players. "Its purpose is to protect and cultivate the festive mood proper to an activity whose primary purpose is pleasant diversion, amusement, joy."[4] In Keating's view, then, the supreme principle of sportsmanship is an injunction to "always conduct yourself in such a manner that you will increase rather than detract from the pleasure found in the activity, both your own and that of your fellow participant."[5]

Sportsmanship, Keating argues, is a virtue that applies to recreational activity of sports, as he understands it, but not to the more serious and competitive activity of athletics. To Keating, sportsmanship and athletics do not fit together easily. "The strange paradox of sportsmanship as applied to athletics is that it asks the athlete, locked in a deadly serious and emotionally charged situation, to act outwardly as if he was engaged in some pleasant diversion."[6]

Sportsmanship only applies to athletics in an attenuated way, then, involving adherence to the value of *fair play*, which to Keating implies adherence to the letter and spirit of equality before the rules. Since the athletic contest is designed to determine which competitor meets the challenge best, fair play requires that competitors not intentionally disregard or circumvent the rules. Broadly understood, perhaps more broadly than Keating would recommend, fair play requires that victory be honorable. So fair play can be expected of the serious athlete in intense competition, but to also require sportsmanship—the attempt to increase the pleasure of the opponent in the contest—normally is to ask too much.[7]

If sportsmanship can be distinguished from fair play, what is cheating? It is natural to identify cheating with violation of the rules of the game but that surely is not enough. Thus, one who *unknowingly* violates the rules is not a cheater. At the very least, the violation must be intentional, and designed to secure an advantage for the cheater or for some other participant for whom the cheater is concerned.

What makes cheating wrong? There is a tendency to assimilate the wrongness of cheating to promise breaking or to deception. Someone who cheats in tennis, for example, by calling an opponent's serves out when they actually are in, deceives the opponent and can be regarded as breaking an implicit promise binding all competitors to play by the rules.

However, as philosopher Bernard Gert has pointed out in a perspicuous analysis, cheating does not necessarily involve either deception or promise breaking.[8] A competitor who has power over the other competitors may cheat quite openly. Similarly, a revolutionary who cheats on a civil service examination in order to to attain a powerful position, which can then be used for purposes of betrayal, may deny that he has ever promised, even implicitly, to obey the rules laid down by the very government he despises. More generally, the idea of an "implicit" promise simply may be too vague to support charges of cheating.[9]

Cheating probably is best identified with intentional violation of a public system of rules in order to secure the goals of that system for oneself or for others for whom one is concerned.[10] Cheating is normally wrong, not only because it deceives or violates a promise or contract, although deceit or violation of a promise may contribute to its wrongness in most cases. However, the distinctive element that accounts for the general presumption that cheating is wrong is that the cheater acts in a way that no one could rationally or impartially recommend that everyone in the activity act. Thus, cheaters make arbitrary exceptions of themselves to gain advantages and in effect treat others as mere means to their own well-being. Cheaters fail to respect their opponents as persons, as agents with purposes of their own, by violating the public system of rules that others may reasonably expect to govern the activity in question. Thus, a golf tournament would not be an athletic contest if everyone cheated because it would not determine who was the best player. The rules of golf are the public system under which it reasonably can be presumed that the participants expect to compete. By violating the rules, cheaters arbitrarily subordinate the interests and purposes of others to their own, and so violate the fundamental moral norm of respect for persons. It may be going too far to say that all competitors have implicitly promised to abide by the rules, but the rules nevertheless are part of the publically acknowledged requirements governing the competition, and all competitors have the right that others abide by them.

We now have provisional accounts of sportsmanship, fair play, and cheating. Perhaps they will be helpful in allowing us to analyze the morality of the actions in sports with which we began our discussion. Alternately, perhaps examination of such cases will suggest the need to revise our accounts of these values. Let us see.

Winning Versus Sportsmanship and Fair Play

Consider the example with which we began this chapter. It involved a top-ranked university football team winning a game on a "fifth down" play, which was run because officials lost count and didn't notice that the allotted number of downs already had been used up. Should the winning team, the University of Colorado, have accepted the victory or, as many critics of the university suggested, have refused to accept a tainted win?

Proponents of one view might begin by appealing to Keating's distinction between sports and athletics. They might argue, first, that since a major intercollegiate football game is clearly an example of athletics, neither team is under an obligation to make the experience pleasurable or enjoyable for the other. Moreover, generosity should not be expected either. After all, no one would expect the opponent, Missouri, if a referee, say, had made an incorrect pass interference call in their favor, to not accept the penalty.

Second, Colorado did not cheat, at least as we have defined cheating above. There was no *intent* to violate a public system of rules to gain an advantage. Moreover, it probably is unclear just what is required in the situation that occurred, simply because of its rarity. There are unlikely to be even informal conventions that apply to the situation.

Finally, one might argue, it is at best unclear whether principles of fair play apply. Colorado did not intentionally violate either the letter or spirit of the rules, and in fact was unaware of the true situation. Tapes reveal that on the fourth-down play, the Colorado quarterback looked to the sideline, noticed that the play was officially marked as a third down on the official scoreboard, and intentionally grounded a pass to stop the clock. Had the quarterback believed the play was his team's last down, he surely would have gambled by attempting a touchdown pass, perhaps successfully.

But while these arguments cannot just be dismissed, other individuals may think that they rest on an indefensible conception of ethics in competition. To begin with, they might reject Keating's distinction between sports and athletics as misleading. In particular, if it is taken as *descriptive*, it may set up a false dichotomy. Activities need not be classified exclusively as athletics or exclusively as sports but may share elements of each.

More important, we need to ask the normative question. Which conception *should* apply to a particular activity?[11] Thus, to assume that the Colorado-Missouri football game should be regarded as an example of athletics rather than sports, in Keating's sense, is to beg the question about whether or not Colorado should have accepted the victory. By assuming the contest *ought* to be like what Keating calls athletics, we would be assuming the very point that is being debated—namely, whether Colorado ought to have accepted the victory.

Second, critics might maintain that sportsmanship, while certainly not an all-encompassing value, covers more than simply generosity towards opponents. In particular, if athletic contests ought to be regarded as mutual quests for excellence, along lines argued in Chapter 2, implications follow for sportsmanship. Thus, opponents ought to be regarded as engaged in a cooperative enterprise designed to test their abilities and skills, and whether or not they are owed generous treatment, should be treated as partners in the creation and execution of a fair test. To treat them differently is to reject the presuppositions of the very model of athletic competition that ought to be observed.

Arguably, the Missouri team was not treated in such a fashion. The play that won the game was not allowed by the rules of the game. The fact that the officials were mistaken about how the rule applied does not alter the fact that Colorado did not win the test as defined by the rules.[12] By accepting victory, Colorado did not treat its opponents as partners or facilitators in a common enterprise but instead treated them as a means for attaining the kind of rewards that go with victory in big-time college games.

If this point has force, it suggests that the distinction between sportsmanship and fair play may not be as sharp as Keating's account suggests. If by "fair play" we mean adherence to criteria of fairness implied by the idea of a mutual quest for excellence, it is at best unclear if Colorado's decision was truly fair. If its team did not truly demonstrate superiority by the public code of rules that all parties agree applied to the game, in what sense was the assignment of a victory fair?

Indeed, it is worth noting that in a famous game played forty years before the contest between Colorado and Missouri, a similar incident led to a dissimilar resolution. In the late fall of 1940, an undefeated Cornell team, also in contention for the national championship and a Rose Bowl bid, played a Dartmouth team that was hoping for a major upset. Although trailing late in the fourth quarter, Cornell apparently pulled out a victory with a scoring pass on the game's last play. But did Cornell really win? Film of the game indicated without a doubt that the referee, who admitted the error, had allowed Cornell a fifth down! The game should have ended a play earlier and Dartmouth should have pulled off a major upset.

Although no rule required that Cornell forfeit the victory, soon after the game film's release, "Cornell officials (including the Director of Athletics) telegraphed Hanover formally conceding the game to Dartmouth 'without reservation . . . with hearty congratulations . . . to the gallant Dartmouth team. . . .' Another loss the following Saturday to Pennsylvania helped the Cornell team drop from second to 15th in the Associated Press polls, its season ruined but its pride intact."[13] Should Colorado take pride in its victory? Should Cornell be proud of its loss?

What our discussion suggests so far is that some of the distinctions with which we began our discussion may need to be rethought. If we take fair play as a central value, and understand it, as perhaps Keating also would, to encompass commitment to the principles supported by the idea of athletic competition as a mutual quest for excellence, it has implications for sportsmanship. Sportsmanship would involve treating opponents in a way fitting their status as partners in a partially cooperative enterprise, namely, the provision of a challenge so that skills and abilities may be tested. Finally, we can question whether even intense competition at high levels of performance *ought* to be regarded as pure cases of athletics in Keating's sense. Although some activities, such as major intercollegiate and professional sports, might justifiably tend more in that direction, a strong case can be made that sportsmanship and fair play should both apply, although perhaps with different emphases, at all levels of sports and athletics. "Athletics," in Keating's sense, arguably ought not to exist at all in its pure form, because unless fair play is understood broadly enough to encompass sportsmanship in the wider sense developed above, "athletics" and the ethic of the mutual quest for excellence are incompatible. Accordingly, the terms "sports" and "athletics" will be used interchangeably in what follows, unless otherwise indicated.

We also need to consider the role of officials and referees in sports. Should we conclude that since opponents in many forms of organized competition delegate responsibility for enforcement of the rules to officials in full knowledge that officials sometimes make mistakes, the decisions of officials should be accepted as ethically final? Alternately, do participants have obligations not to accept unearned benefits arising from particularly egregious official errors, especially those that involve misapplication of the rules rather than "judgment calls" about whether a rule was violated?

We can test our intuition on these issues by considering another kind of case: one where the rules are followed rather than broken but so as to give what many would regard as an unearned advantage to some competitors over others. An example of this is provided in basketball, where the rules of some college and interscholastic organizations require that, after a time-out ends, the referee give the ball to the offensive team, even if the defensive team is not yet ready to continue the competition. Presumably, the intent of the rule is to insure that time-outs are equal in length for each team by eliminating delays caused by coaches taking too much time in the huddle. However, the rule can have unintended consequences. For example, suppose it is applied to a team that is late coming out of its huddle, not because of any intent to gain extra time, but because in the excitement of the moment and noise of the crowd, the buzzer signaling the end of the time-out simply was not heard. Should the other team take advantage of this lapse and, as is allowed by the rules, score even before the other team is on the court?

Here, a much stronger case can be made that the behavior of the offensive team is defensible than in the case of the fifth down discussed earlier. After all, the behavior in question is allowed by the rules. Both teams should be aware of the rules and their implications before the contest starts and should take steps to insure that the noise and confusion in the arena where a major contest is played does not affect their poise or analytic acuity during a time-out. After all, it is not one team's business to insure that the other performs efficiently, but rather to take advantage of inefficiencies as allowed by the rules of the game.

But while such points are not unconvincing, they may not be determinate either. Ask yourself the question, "Is a victory earned in this way significant, one I should take pride in?" I suggest the answer is negative. Presumably, one wants to take pride in being the better basketball team, not being better at noticing the end of time-outs.

Again, the model of athletic competition as a mutual quest for excellence through challenge can be helpful here, although admittedly, it is controversial how it might apply in the kind of case under discussion. Scoring when the opposing team isn't even on the floor is not particularly challenging and does not demonstrate excellence at the activity in question. Arguably, then, such behavior is not "fair play," understood as adherence to the implications of the model of the quest for excellence. Neither does it involve sportsmanship, understood as treatment of opponents as required by their status as partners obligated to present a challenge to one another. One group of competitors, those that come out of their time-out late, are not even given the opportunity to present a challenge. Their opponent in effect is allowing the rules to be used to avoid the challenge the other team otherwise would present. Attainment of victory is seen as more important than what should be the point of the contest: testing oneself against the challenge presented by other competitors.

Such an analysis, critics might retort, needs to take into account the level at which the contest is played. Here Keating's distinction between "sports" and "athletics" may have a point. Although it may be inappropriate for a team in an eighth-grade contest to win a game by scoring before the opponents are ready, it surely is equally inappropriate for a professional team or a major college team that has worked hard all season to qualify for postseason play, to simply toss the ball in bounds and wait for the opposition to get ready. Surely, that is too much generosity to expect, given the opportunities for success and achievement at stake.

Reasonable people of good will may well disagree over this kind of example. Before making up our minds, however, we should ask what "achievement" and "success" mean in this context. If they mean that the winning team has succeeded in meeting the challenge set by an opponent and has deserved to advance, then it is far from clear that taking advantage of the situation to score is the right option. After all, would anyone—players, coaches, or fans—really want an important championship settled in this way? If not, even if it is controversial whether or not we are morally *required* not to score in such a situation, wouldn't it morally be *better* if all teams, at all levels, adopted the qualities of sportsmanship implied by the idea of a mutual quest for excellence and voluntarily refrained from winning a game by such a tactic?[14]

Cases such as those discussed here are likely to be controversial, and discussion of them may generate disagreement, but it is important to remember that such disagreement occurs against a general background of deeper agreement on sports ethics. None of the parties to the discussion endorse cheating or blatant examples of unfair play or unsportsmanlike behavior. Rather, the disagreement concerns "hard cases" that help us define the boundaries of the values we are exploring. Sometimes disagreement over controversial cases is used as a justification for overall moral scepticism, since it may seem as if no rational resolution is possible. This overall drift to moral scepticism should be resisted, however, for often rational adjudication is possible (as application of the model of the mutual quest for excellence to our cases may suggest) or, if it is not, there still remains deeper agreement on the moral fundamentals that are not at stake in the controversies at issue.

Cheating, the Strategic Foul, and the Illegal Pitch

Although moral sceptics often appeal to disagreement on controversial moral issues, not all moral issues are controversial. Thus, there is widespread agreement that cases of straightforward cheating, cases where no moral justification for the act can be provided, are to be condemned. Such standard cases might include a golfer who fails to count all her strokes in an important tournament or a basketball coach who, in the confusion of a last-second foul call, intentionally deceives both referees and opponents by directing his best foul shooter to go to the line even though another player, a particularly poor foul shooter, actually has been fouled.

Different ethical theories may give different reasons for their condemnation of cheating. For example, some utilitarians might emphasize the bad consequences that are likely to ensue, particularly the harmful effects on the character of the cheater, that are likely to result in harm in the future. Other utilitarians, more concerned with the utility of rules and practices than of individual acts, may emphasize the beneficial consequences of general or universal observance of the rule against cheating.

However, other theorists might find the utilitarian justification of the prohibition against cheating unsatisfactory, perhaps because it rests on contingent empirical calculations about the consequences of acts, rules, or policies. These calculations may seem too speculative to justify a categorical moral prohibition.

On the view developed in Chapter 2, which is perhaps more congenial to the Kantian than to the utilitarian tradition in ethics, cheating normally is wrong because it disrespects persons as moral agents. On this view, the cheater in sports is someone who intentionally violates the public system of rules, which all competitors are entitled to have applied to the contest, for personal advantage. The cheater is acting unjustly or unfairly by behaving as if he or she occupied a privileged position, one outside the rules, even though there is no justification for such a claim. The cheater treats the other competitors as if they are mere means to be used for personal advantage, even though they too are moral agents, persons whose purposes and plans should count equally from the moral point of view.[15]

Although there is widespread agreement that cases of straightforward cheating are wrong, controversy often occurs over just what counts as cheating in unusual cases or when the conditions are straightforward.

We cannot consider a great variety of cases here but we can illustrate by examples the difficulty in identifying cheating and in determining whether or not it is wrong under certain conditions of competition in sports.

Consider the following examples:

1. In the last five seconds of an important basketball game, a player on the losing side, pretending to try and steal the ball, intentionally commits a strategic foul stopping the clock and forcing the leading team to make foul shots to hold the lead.
2. In an important football game, a team is forced to punt from its own forty-five yard line. The team believes it would be advantageous topunt from further back, giving it a larger target. It therefore deliberately incurs a delay-of-game penalty by taking too long to run off the next play, thereby being penalized five yards but gaining a larger target at which to aim.

Is the commission of such strategic fouls *deliberate* violation of the rules designed to procure a strategic advantage for the violator, and therefore cheating? Is it morally wrong?

Many philosophers would unequivocally assert that strategic fouling for advantage is cheating. For example, one commentator analyzes our basketball example by maintaining that: "intentional holding, tripping, and so on are not part of the game or within the rules of basketball. . . . (Therefore) the 'good' foul is a violation of the agreement which all participants know that all participants make when they agree to play basketball, namely, that all will pursue the . . . goal of basketball by the necessary and allowable skills and tactics and will avoid use of proscribed skills and tactics."[16]

These remarks suggest that players and teams committing strategic fouls violate an implicit social contract according to which players agree to play by the rules in order to see which opponent is best in the particular contest at hand.

However, there are at least two problems with this argument. First, and least important for our purposes, if the idea of a contract or agreement is taken literally, it is unclear that such a contract exists or that all players signed it, even implicitly. What if one competitor enters a contest with the intent of cheating? Is it plausible to think that player implicitly signed a contract not to cheat?[17]

More important for our purposes, it is far from clear that the common understanding among players of a game such as basketball does exclude the strategic foul. Thus, one can even argue that the strategic foul is part of the game because an explicit penalty—foul shots—is provided for in the rules.

This reply is not sufficient for critics, however, who may retort that "the obvious rebuttal to this position is that penalties for breaking the law are contained within the law books, but no sensible person concludes, therefore, that all acts are within the law."[18] For example, we surely would not say that murder is allowed by law simply because penalties for murder are prescribed by law. Similarly, we should not say that the strategic foul is allowed by the rules of basketball simply because the penalty is prescribed in the rule book.

Should we conclude that use of the strategic foul is a form of cheating? Such a question may not admit of a conclusive answer, but we should not accept the affirmative response too quickly. In particular, the parallel drawn between sanctions in law, such as punishment for criminals, and penalties for strategic fouls needs to be more closely examined.

Penalties as Sanctions and as Prices

Some penalties in sports do not play a role analogous to criminal sanctions in law. A jail sentence for a crime should not be thought of as the price the law charges for a particular act, such as a felony. That would make the felony a *permissible* option for those criminals who are willing to bear the cost of a jail sentence if caught. Rather, a felony is a *prohibited* act, and a jail sentence is not the price for allowable commission of the act, but rather is a punishment for committing it.

However, not all penalties in sports are sanctions for prohibited acts. For example, in golf, when shots come to rest in a position from which players judge they cannot be played, golfers may invoke the *unplayable lie* rule. According to this rule, the player either may replay the shot from the original location, or hit a new shot from two club lengths from either side of the location of the unplayable ball, or hit a new shot from as far behind the location of the ball as the player wishes (so long as the location is on the golf course!). The *penalty* for exercising any of these options is one shot. Here, the penalty clearly is not intended to be a sanction, prohibiting the exercise of any option. Rather, the options are there for the player to use. The penalty, in this case, is the price of exercise of the option rather than a sanction for doing what is forbidden.

Once we distinguish between two kinds of penalties, sanctions for prohibited acts and prices for options, we can see that it is far from clear that strategic fouling is cheating. This is because the penalties for the fouls can be regarded as prices for exercise of a strategy rather than sanctions for a prohibited violation of the rules. Indeed, this does seem to be the common understanding of intentional fouling to stop the clock in basketball. It appears to be simply false that players and coaches regard a commitment not to strategically foul as "a violation of the agreement which all participants know that all participants make when they agree to play basketball."

To be sure, sometimes it is difficult to tell whether a penalty should be regarded as a sanction or as a price. But while some situations may be inherently ambiguous, the notion of a fair price might help us distinguish the two. The intuitive idea here is that if a pricing penalty is fair in sports, violation of the rule should invoke a penalty that in fair compensation.[19] Thus, the penalty for intentional fouling in basketball is best regarded as a price rather than as a sanction if the foul shots awarded are fair compensation for the violation. Sports authorities can more clearly distinguish sanctions from prices by making the penalty for prohibited acts more severe than mere fair compensation would require. Thus, recent rule changes in college and high school basketball awarding extra foul shots and possession of the ball to the team that is intentionally fouled can be regarded as a step towards making intentional fouling prohibited rather than a strategy with a price. (The distinction between prices and sanctions may remain ambiguous, however, if referees fail to call intentional fouls because they believe the punishment is too severe.)

There are many other cases in sports where it is unclear whether certain actions are cheating. Is a tennis player who changes the tempo of her game to upset an opponent who prefers a faster pace cheating? Is a groundskeeper who wets down the home team's baseball field to slow down the opponent's base stealers cheating? Is the pitcher who slips an illegal spitball past the batter in a crucial game cheating?

Although we cannot explore all these examples here, they do suggest that the line separating cheating from permissible play may sometimes be difficult to draw, and that we sometimes may have to appeal not only to explicit rules of the game but to informal conventions for interpreting them.[20] For example, not all body contact in basketball is regarded by referees as a foul, and it seems plausible to think that different conventions or interpretations are applied by referees at different levels of play, so that what counts as a foul in a high school game might not count as one in the NBA, even if the formal definition of a foul is identical at each level.

Is It Ever Permissible to Cheat?

Is cheating always morally wrong? If our suggestion that cheating normally takes unfair advantage of other competitors is sound, then cheating is morally prohibited *except* in contexts where there are weightier conflicting factors that might be overriding. For example, if gamblers have kidnapped your family and will kill them unless your team wins, you would seem to be morally justified if you cheated to ensure the victory and save their lives.

Recently, it has been suggested that cheating is not always wrong, even if we restrict the kinds of factors at issue to sports. In fact, on this view, cheating, while it may undermine fair play, might make for good sports. As one commentator maintained,

> many competitions . . . would be more interesting if cheating takes place within it or if several players try to stretch the rules. Such deviant behavior adds a new dimension to the game which can also add to its interest. . . . Insofar as the contest is one of wits as well as one of skill and strategy, it can be exciting to compete with and against someone who uses his wits to try to cheat and it can be exciting for an audience to observe such intelligent behavior.[21]

For example, if the use of the illegal spitball pitch in baseball by a Gaylord Perry can make the game more fascinating and exciting, isn't its use justified?

However, this position seems open to the objection that cheating undermines the idea of the sports contest as a test of skill, a mutual quest for excellence by the participants. This, of course, is not to deny that sports serve other purposes in our society, such as provision of entertainment or the opportunities for professionals to secure financial gains. But these other purposes are parasitic in that what *ought* to be entertaining about our sports, and what makes them sometimes worth paying to see, is the test of excellence they provide. Gladiatorial contests or the throwing of the politically or religiously unpopular to the lions also *may* be entertaining to some people. Whether they *ought* to be entertained by such behavior is another issue.

Perhaps what is being endorsed are not solitary acts of cheating that deceive opponents or in some other way violate the public system of rules that players are entitled to have apply to the game. Thus, "if . . . cheating is recognized as an option which both sides may morally take up, then in general the principles of equality and justice are not affected."[22] Perhaps the practice of strategic fouling in basketball fits such a description, in that players expect other players to foul strategically in appropriate situations.

However, if the practice is acknowledged and expected, it is far from clear that it is a case of cheating at all. That is, once we realize that the rules of a game must be understood in terms of a set of conventions or interpretations, and that all penalties are not sanctions for prohibited activities, it is not clear that all intentional rule violations are cases of cheating. If all players acknowledge that other competitors will engage in the action at issue, and if the rules contain just compensation for violation, why is the act one of cheating? The difficulty for the proponent of the thesis that cheating in sports sometimes is justified because it makes for better sports, is to find behavior that clearly is cheating and that also is morally permissible. Insofar as such activity is acknowledged to be part of the rules, as interpreted by conventions known by participants and officials, it arguably is not cheating, and insofar as it is not part of such rules, as interpreted by conventions known by participants and officials, it arguably is not permissible.

We can conclude, then, that although it may sometimes be hard to determine what counts as cheating, cheating in sports, as elsewhere, is wrong, although the wrongness sometimes can be overridden by competing moral considerations of greater weight. More important, our overall discussion suggests that ethical reasoning does not support a sharp normative distinction between "sports" and "athletics." Although different levels of sports quite properly call for different levels of intensity and commitment, and hence behavior that is appropriate at one level may not be appropriate at other levels, basic values such as sportsmanship—understood as respect for fellow competitors as mutual participants in the quest for excellence—and fair play should apply to the good sports contest. Respect for opponents as fellow competitors and for the integrity of the sports contest apply at all levels of the game.

Violence in Sports

On Lincoln's Birthday, 1982, . . . Benjamin Davis and Louis Wade walked into the Civic Auditorium in Albuquerque to fight each other in the semi-finals of the New Mexico Golden Gloves. . . . You could not hope to meet two nicer boys. One would help kill the other in the ring that night.[23]

Benjamin Davis, known as Benjii, and Louis Wade had never met before that tragic night in 1982. Although they came from different ethnic backgrounds—Benjii, who was 22, was a Navaho and Louis, only 16, was Anglo—they had much in common. They both loved sports, were hard-working students, were loved by their families, and regarded as fine young men by those who knew them. They participated in boxing not because they wanted to become professionals, but because they wanted to work out and because they enjoyed the competition.

The tragedy happened in the second round. Benjii received a number of hard blows and seemed dazed, but the referee did not stop the fight. After another series of hard blows, Benjii crumpled and fell in a heap on the canvas, never to recover. Apparently, no one in Benjii's family blames Louis. "To this day, they only have compassion for him and everyone keeps assuring Louis that it was not his fault. Sometimes he believes that."[24]

Surely Louis is not to blame for playing by the rules of an activity in which both he and Benjii were involved, an activity that carried elements of risk to both participants. But is the activity, boxing, itself acceptable? Should our society permit young men and boys to participate in boxing, let alone make wealthy heroes out of the most successful? Hundreds of boxers have been killed in the ring. Moreover, the risks are borne not only by seasoned professionals but by boys and young men such as Louis and Benjii. Even boxers who survive the ring frequently suffer various degrees of brain damage, as the stumbling walk, halting speech, and poor memory of the "punch drunk" fighter attest.

The problems raised by violence in sports are not restricted to boxing. Football is regarded as a violent sport, and neck injuries in football can lead and have led to paralysis and death. Moreover, violence, in the form of hard body contact, and even intimidation and physical attack is hardly unknown in other sports. For example, the joke "I went to a fight the other night and a hockey game broke out" says something significant about the level of violence in professional hockey.

Violence in sports is an increasing problem in America and around the world. According to many observers of American sports, it is on the rise not only on the field but among spectators as well. The nature of violence raises many questions about its place, if any, in sports. Is boxing immoral? Is fighting in hockey permissible ("boys will be boys") or should it be more severely punished? Is football a violent and, therefore, a morally objectionable sport? What is violence anyway?

In this section, we will examine certain ethical questions about the role of violence in sports. As we will see, the issues raised apply not only to sports but also concern the meaning and scope of individual liberty, the relationship between society and the individual, and the significance of respect for persons.

Conceptions of Violence

Examples of violence unfortunately are all too frequent. Clearly, if one person assaults another, a violent act has taken place. But how is "violence" itself best characterized? Are brushback pitches or hard tackles just as much instances of violence as an assault?

Violence generally involves the use of force, but not every use of force is violent. For example, a tennis player uses force in serving, but few of us are even tempted to characterize the act of serving in tennis as violent. Moreover, perhaps some acts, such as intense verbal abuse, should be characterized as forms of (psychological) violence, even though they do not involve the use of force. So violence and the use of force cannot be equated. Moreover, it sometimes is argued that there can be forms of institutional violence which, while not intended or carried out by any one person, are the effect of unjust institutions upon the oppressed.

Can violence be characterized as the *wrongful* use of force? Leaving aside possible cases of psychological violence, which might not involve the use of force, other difficulties arise.

In particular, the proposed account of violence is morally loaded. That is, before we can determine whether any act is one of violence, we first must determine if the act was morally wrong. This has the unfortunate consequences that what we characterize as violent depends upon our moral views. Thus, if we regard the use of force by the Allies against Hitler in World War II as justified, we would not be able to call that use of force violent, since it was not wrongful.

What the proposal ignores is that sometimes it is far clearer that behavior is violent than whether it is right or wrong. Indeed, we may regard behavior as wrong precisely *because* it is violent, which would be pointless if we first had to decide an act was wrong before we could properly describe it as violent. For example, we might decide an assault was wrong because of the violence inflicted on the victim rather than deciding it was violent because we thought it wrong on some other grounds.

It will be useful to keep our account of violence as morally neutral as possible. Although it sometimes is impossible or undesirable to fully disentangle the normative and nonnormative elements of a concept, e.g. "heroism," doing so in this case will help us distinguish importantly different issues. One issue concerns which acts are properly characterized as violent. A second distinct issue concerns whether such acts are right or wrong. Nothing is gained in this context by blurring the two issues together.[25]

Rather than try to formally define "violence," a task that, even if it can be satisfactorily carried out, would take up far too much space for our purposes, it seems more useful to provide a rough explication instead.[26] An explication will fall short of supplying necessary and sufficient conditions for an act being violent but will pick out central features of clear cases of violence. It will be useful in allowing us to examine moral evaluations of behavior exhibiting the central or paradigmatic features of violence.

Typically or paradigmatically, violence involves the use of physical force with the intent to harm persons or property. Thus, assault, war, rape, fighting, and armed robbery clearly involve violence or the threat of violence. This is not to deny that it sometimes may be justifiable to speak of psychological violence or that unintentional violence is possible but only to suggest that special argument is needed to establish those points. Sports, to the extent that they involve violence at all, generally involve the use or threat of use of physical force to harm opponents, so it is upon physical force intended to harm opponents that we will mainly focus.

Perhaps the most controversial use of violence in sports involves boxing. Should boxing be prohibited because of its apparently violent nature?

The Case Against Boxing

What is the case against boxing? Actually, there are several arguments for the conclusion that boxing ought to be prohibited. A not atypical point of departure for our discussion is the following passage from an editorial in *The New York Times*:

> Some people watch boxing to see skill, others just for the blood. Far worse than the blood is the unseen damage. Retinas are dislodged, kidneys bruised and . . . the cerebral cortex accumulates damage to the higher functions of the brain, leading to loss of memory, shambling walk: the traits of the punch drunk boxer. Can a civilized society plausibly justify the pleasure it may gain from such a sport?[27]

This passage suggests two kinds of reasons for prohibiting boxing. The first is the protection of the boxers themselves. The violence inherent in boxing may make it too dangerous for the participants. In this view, society ought to protect boxers from harm by banning the sport. The passage also suggests a second line of argument. Might we somehow become less civilized, or morally more insensitive, if boxing is permitted to continue? The question concerning what civilized societies ought to permit implies that the practice of boxing may have social consequences that are harmful, not just to boxers, but to others as well. Do either of these lines of argument justify the prohibition of boxing?

Paternalism and Mill's Harm Principle

There is little question that boxing can be harmful to the participants. Every boxer who enters the ring faces the real possibility of serious injury. Doesn't society have the right as well as the duty to legally prohibit boxing in order to protect boxers themselves from harm and even death?

Before we agree too quickly, however, we should consider the following examples. Should your friends prevent you from ordering ice cream and fatty meats when you go out because such foods contain too much cholesterol? Should your friends prevent you from trying out for the basketball or football team because other sports you might play, such as golf, are much safer? On a broader level, suppose the state passes legislation requiring that reasonably healthy adults who do not exercise for at least thirty minutes a day must pay substantial extra taxes. This legislation is justified as an attempt to save the sedentary from themselves by requiring participation in a healthy life style.

The issue at stake here is one of *paternalism.* Roughly stated, paternalism refers to interference with the liberty of agents for what is believed to be their own good. A major objection to paternalism, however, is that it wrongly disregards the liberty and autonomy of those very agents who are interfered with for their own good.

Perhaps the most influential case against paternalistic interference with the liberty of competent agents was presented by the British philosopher John Stuart Mill (1806-1873) in his eloquent defense of personal freedom, *On Liberty*. Mill himself claimed to be a utilitarian in ethics, committed to the view that the sole criterion of right and wrong is the social utility of acts or practices. At first glance, utilitarianism does not seem to be particularly hostile to paternalism or especially protective of the freedom of the individual. It seems that paternalistic interference with liberty would be justified on utilitarian grounds whenever it produced better consequences for all affected than the available alternatives. Utilitarians might turn out to be interfering busybodies on the individual level and benevolent versions of Big Brother on the state level, interfering with freedom whenever necessary to bring about the best results.

However, in *On Liberty*, Mill advanced important arguments against applying utilitarianism so crudely. Even if, as many suspect, Mill was unable to consistently remain within the utilitarian framework, he did advance important arguments against paternalistic interference with the individual based on respect for the liberty and autonomy of the individual.

In one of the most widely discussed passages of *On Liberty*, Mill declared that

the sole end for which mankind are warranted individually or collectively in interfering with the liberty of action of any of their number is

self protection. . . . The only purpose for which power can be rightfully
exercised over any member of a civilized community, against his will,
is to prevent harm to others. His own good, either physical or mental,
is not a sufficient warrant.[28]

According to Mill, as long as another person's acts are self-regarding, so
long as they do not harm or constitute a threat to the welfare of others,
interference with them is unjustified.

Why did Mill reject what would seem to be the position most in
harmony with utilitarianism, namely, that paternalistic interference with
freedom is justified whenever it produces better consequences than
alternatives? Perhaps the line of argument Mill advances that is most
compatible with his official utilitarianism is one of efficiency. Paternalistic interference is likely to be inefficient. After all, agents generally know
their own interests better than others do. Moreover, paternalists may
often be influenced by their own values and prejudices or by fear for the
safety of others, and so are unlikely to properly calculate the consequences of interfering. As a result, allowing paternalism will create a
society of busybodies who, in their efforts to do good, will interfere in
the wrong place at the wrong time for the wrong reasons. In a sense, Mill
can be read here as advancing a *rule utilitarian* argument. A society
following a *rule* prohibiting paternalistic interference will actually
promote utility more efficiently than one adopting a rule allowing it, for
in the second society, the good produced by the few cases of justifiable
paternalism will be swamped by the harm promoted by unjustifiable
paternalistic interferences constantly carried out by utilitarian busybodies.

Although this argument is not implausible, it may not accomplish as
much as Mill thinks. After all, wouldn't paternalism still be justified in
those few cases where we are convinced it would do more good than
harm?

In fact, Mill advanced a second line of argument, not easily reconciled
with utilitarianism, which has perhaps been more influential than the
approach sketched above. Even if paternalistic interference would
produce more good than harm, constant interference with our liberty
will stunt our moral and intellectual growth and eventually make us
incapable of thinking for ourselves. As Mill maintained,

the human faculties of perception, judgment, discrimination, feeling,
mental activity, and even moral preference are exercised only in making
a choice. . . . The mental and the moral, like the muscular powers, are
improved only by being used. . . . He who lets the world. . . choose his
plan of life for him, has no need of any other faculty than the ape-like
one of imitation.[29]

Here, Mill seems to be appealing more to the value of the idea of autonomy than to social utility understood in the sense of a balance of pleasure or satisfaction over pain or frustration of desires. Arguably, the appeal to autonomy is more fundamental than the appeal to utility, since one must first be autonomous in order to evaluate any moral argument at all, including utilitarian arguments. Autonomy is a fundamental value, it can be argued, precisely because it is presupposed by the practice of moral argument itself.[30]

Finally, one can reinforce Mill's case by arguing that paternalism interferes with the fundamental moral right of individuals to control their own lives. Although moral rights may themselves be sometimes justified by the degree to which they promote utility, or as protections for autonomy, they also can be justified as basic moral commodities which protect individuals from being regarded as mere resources to be used for the good of the greater number. In a sense, rights function as political and social "trumps" which individuals can play to protect themselves from being swallowed up in the pursuit of the social good.[31] Individual rights to liberty protect the ability of persons to live their lives as they choose rather than as someone else, however benevolent, thinks such lives should be led.

Accordingly, supporters of boxing can appeal to the arguments suggested by *On Liberty* to reject the claim that boxing ought to be prohibited. In particular, they can maintain (a) it is unclear whether prohibition really will promote the most utility, (b) even if it does, it prevents both boxers and spectators alike from making the moral choice of whether to engage in and support the sport, and finally (c) it ignores the rights of the boxers and spectators to live their own lives as they themselves see fit. Are such arguments decisive?

Exceptions to the Harm Principle

Is it possible to accept the Harm Principle and still maintain that paternalistic interference with boxing *sometimes* is justified? For one thing, Mill himself acknowledges that the Harm Principle "is meant to apply only to human beings in the maturity of their faculties."[32] Thus, interference with the behavior of children and the mentally incompetent for their own good would be allowed by the Harm Principle. This surely is a plausible restriction because such persons are not in a good position to rationally evaluate their desires so as to determine their real interests, and they are not (yet) capable of making rational and autonomous choices.

However, such a restriction would not allow interference with the behavior of competent adults, some of whom can and do choose to box. Of course, one could argue that the mere fact that some persons choose to box demonstrates their irrationality and lack of competency and thus disqualifies them from protection by the Harm Principle. However, if the only reason for thinking such people are irrational is that they make a choice others of us don't like, such an argument must be rejected. The very point of the Harm Principle is to protect individuals from having the values of others imposed upon them, so we must have independent reason to think that agents are incompetent or immature before we are justified in interfering with their behavior; the mere fact that we don't like their choices is not enough.

A second kind of exception to the Harm Principle might allow interference with the choice of competent adults to participate in boxing. That is, perhaps paternalism is acceptable when its goal is not simply to benefit the people being interfered with but rather is to protect their status as rational and autonomous agents.[33] For example, suppose a person of sound mind and body is about to take a drug which, while causing pleasurable experiences, is highly addictive and will eventually destroy her capacity to reason. Aren't you justified in interfering to remove her supply of the drug, even against her will? After all, your goal is not to impose your conception of happiness upon her but to preserve her capacity to choose her own conception of the good life for herself.

How does this argument apply to the prohibition of boxing? In particular, repeated blows to the head produce brain damage, leading to the symptoms associated with the behavior of the "punch drunk" fighter. Long before those symptoms become evident, however, irreversible brain damage, and gradual diminishment of rational capacities, might have taken place.[34]

Although this sort of argument does provide grounds for interference, whether these grounds are sufficiently strong or weighty to justify interference with liberty is controversial. In particular, unlike the case of a mind-destroying addictive drug, the effects of boxing on mental capacity are long term and uncertain. Moreover, the rewards that some professional fighters can obtain are potentially great. Why is it less justifiable to risk one's capacity for rational choice to secure a great gain than it is, say, to risk shortening one's life span by following an unhealthy but pleasurable diet, or putting oneself under unhealthy stress in order to succeed in business?

Perhaps a third ground for making exceptions to the Harm Principle provides a stronger justification for interference with boxing. We have been assuming that athletes freely and autonomously choose to engage in boxing. But there are grounds for doubting the truth of that assumption.

For one thing, many boxers may be ignorant of the risks of engaging in their sport. Hence, they no more freely consent to run those risks than the person who drives over an unsafe bridge in the mistaken belief that it is safe consents to being thrown into the raging river below.

Of equal importance, many of the participants in professional boxing come from severely disadvantaged backgrounds. These men see boxing as their main chance of escape from the economic and social disadvantages of the ghetto, many of which are due to the injustice of racial discrimination. In this view, the athlete who chooses to box is not responding to an offer or opportunity, i.e., "you can better yourself by becoming a boxer," but rather is reacting to a threat, i.e., "if you don't become a boxer, you will continue to be a victim of social injustice and neglect." Accordingly, since boxers are not autonomous freely choosing agents, but rather are victims of societal coercion, they are not covered by the Harm Principle in the first place.

However, proponents of individual liberty will regard such a view as too extreme. Carried to its logical limits, they will point out, it implies that the poor and deprived should have less liberty to direct their own lives than the rest of us because they are not "truly free" to begin with. In other words, in the name of protecting them from themselves, we would be depriving the disadvantaged of one of the most basic element of human dignity, the ability to have some control of their own lives. By viewing them only as victims, we would no longer see them as persons in their own right. Would we go so far as to paternalistically deprive them of taking any risks to better themselves since they are, we are told, not able to freely choose to begin with?

This point does have force, but it also must be remembered that poverty and deprivation can lead people to take risks that no one would take unless desperate. The *justice* of a system that presents people with such cruel choices can be called into question. Thus, a proponent of prohibition might agree that the poor and deprived are not mere victims and can make choices but might regard the choice between becoming a boxer and living a life of deprivation as itself unjust. Perhaps a prohibition on boxing could be justified to prevent the imposition of such unjust choices upon the disadvantaged.

The evaluation of this point will depend upon whether one regards the athlete from a disadvantaged and perhaps minority background as having a reasonable set of available choices in our society. If one believes that the alternative to boxing is not starvation, or even welfare, but that educational opportunities are available for those who want to take advantage of them, then one will view the chance to become a boxer as an opportunity. If one regards alternate opportunities as shams, one will be inclined to see boxers as the victim of societal coercion. In any case, to the extent that alternate opportunities are available, it is the responsibility of coaches and parents to inform young athletes of them and of the relatively infinitesimal chances of being successful in professional sports.

Be that as it may, it is doubtful if the current argument supports an across-the-board ban on participation in boxing, even if one makes highly pessimistic assumptions about the range of opportunities available to disadvantaged youth in our society. This is because not everyone who chooses to participate in boxing need be from a disadvantaged background. At most, the argument justifies closing boxing only to certain classes of people, namely, (a) those for whom it is a last resort and who may be "forced" into it because of social or economic pressure, and (b) those who lack the education or have not had the opportunity to fully understand the risks of participation.

We can conclude, then, that although paternalistic arguments in favor of prohibition of boxing are not without force, they are not conclusive either. On the contrary, concern for individual liberty and autonomy justifies us in placing the burden of proof on the paternalist. Although further discussion might warrant us in revising our opinion, it appears from what we have seen that the burden has not yet been met where participation in boxing (and other risky activities) is at issue.

Boxing and the Protection of Society

So far, we have been assuming that the only grounds for prohibition of boxing are paternalistic. But what if the participation in boxing is not simply self-regarding but has harmful effects on others? The Harm Principle permits interference with the individual liberty of some to prevent them from harming others.

But how can boxing harm others? At first glance, it may appear that the only ones boxers can harm are themselves.

However, first glances can be deceiving. To see how boxing can harm society, consider the imaginary sport of Mayhem. The rules of Mayhem are simple. Adult volunteers, who have given their informed consent to participate, are placed in an arena with swords and spears and are divided into two teams. They then fight until only members of one team are left alive. The players on the winning, i.e., surviving, team then get to divide $10,000,000.

Does it follow that if there are no paternalistic reasons strong enough to justify prohibiting Mayhem, there are no reasons at all to justify prohibition?[35] Isn't it plausible to think that even though there is no direct harm to spectators—the gladiators refrain even from attacking those fans who boo—the indirect harm is substantial. Children might come to idolize (and imitate) trained killers. (Would youngsters collect gladiator bubble gum cards with kill ratio statistics on the back side?) Violence would be glorified and the value of human life inevitably would be cheapened. Such effects may not be inevitable, but the likelihood of eventual harm to others seems sufficient to justify a civilized society in banning Mayhem.

Can't a similar argument be applied to boxing, for as one newspaper editorial exclaimed, "the public celebration of violence cannot be a private matter."[36] After all, although many sports involve the use of force and risk of injury, only boxing has violence in the sense of intentional attempts to injure opponents at its core. Do we want our society to glorify such an activity in the name of sports?

How powerful are these sorts of considerations? In fact, they can be understood as supporting two distinct kinds of arguments. According to the first, public exposure to boxing causes nonparticipants to be influenced adversely and as a result to be more violent or tolerant of violence themselves, thereby increasing the risk for others. In this way, exposure to boxing contributes to the rise of violence throughout society. According to the second kind of argument, adulation of the violence inherent in boxing undermines the standards constituting our community. The public glorification of violence debases our society and changes it into one that is more vulgar and less civilized.

The difference between these two arguments is that the first is more *individualistic*, the second more *communitarian*. That is, the first stresses harm to individuals. The second emphasizes that the social context in which individuals are formed is adversely affected, and so a new and less worthy kind of individual will emerge from the debased social context that results.

The first argument needs to be supported by empirical evidence, which is likely to be inconclusive. In fact, many psychologists have maintained for some time that we can be and often are influenced by models, and, accordingly, if society presents persons engaging in violence as its heroes, toleration of violence and the tendency to commit it will increase.[37] On the other hand, it is unlikely that the normal boxing fan is going to act violently after watching a match. Thus, it is unlikely that any *direct* and *immediate* tie between boxing and broader social violence exists.

However, conceptual and moral issues are at least as important as empirical ones. Thus, even if participation in or observation of boxing does have subtle long-term effects on the amount of violence committed elsewhere in society, does it *follow* that boxing ought to be prohibited? In answering this question, we must consider its implications for regulation generally if our overall moral view is to be systematically consistent.

Suppose, for example, that a book advocates a kind of undisciplined secondary-school education, which, contrary to the author, would actually be educationally harmful to most youngsters. The book's author is highly respected and it is likely that the book will be widely read and will influence many educators. Are we justified in banning the book because its publication is believed to have harmful effects? On the contrary, it seems that if we prohibit activities, like boxing or reading a controversial book, because they might have harmful long-term effects, our right to liberty is drastically restricted. We would have ceded to others the ability to make up our own minds for us and to interfere with our lives in a broad range of areas where direct and immediate harm to others is not at issue.

However, to communitarians, advocates of the second argument sketched above, the role of individual liberty has been misrepresented in our whole discussion. We have proceeded, according to this criticism, as if the individual is an autonomous atom who can step back from social institutions and make choices in isolation. It is this individualistic choosing self who is seen as the locus of value, yet, according to the communitarian, such a self is in many ways a fiction. Rather, selves are formed within communities and are constituted or defined by their relationships with others in their social settings. Thus, one is a parent, teacher, coach, member of a religious group, and citizen rather than an isolated individualistic pure agent, allegedly capable of stepping aside from all roles and autonomously evaluating them. What would such an abstract individual be but a mysterious "0" stripped of all distinguishing human characteristics?[38]

What has this roughly sketched communitarian picture of the self have to do with the critique of boxing and with violence in sports? Although the specific implications for policy of theoretical communitarianism are not always clear, the communitarian approach at least emphasizes the need to preserve the common values that bind society together. Boxing and the public celebration of violence undermine the standards of the community and hence transform the kind of individuals it produces. There is no asocial individual who can stand outside his or her community to evaluate boxing. If we tolerate boxing, as well as violence in other areas, we will end up with individuals who no longer share the standards and traditions that lead to the condemnation of violence. Our community will gradually be replaced by one that tolerates and may even welcome behavior that the previous community would have regarded as degrading, threatening, and blatantly immoral.

Although all aspects of the debate between communitarians and what they regard as their liberal individualistic opponents cannot be touched on here, two important points should be kept in mind.[39] First, if the communitarian's major point is that we are so tightly situated within specific communities and traditions that free, rational, and autonomous choice is impossible, we cannot freely, rationally, and autonomously choose to believe communitarianism. That some of us accept a communitarian approach would be just another social fact, to be explained by reference to our social situation, rather than by the truth of communitarianism or the strength of the rational justification for it.

Presumably, the communitarian would not want to accept such a conclusion. But, then, some weight must be given to free, rational, and autonomous choice within communitarianism, even if the account of such choice differs in substantial ways from that of more individualistic approaches to political theory.

However, and this is the second critical point that should be kept in mind, what weight should be given to liberty by communitarians? If their reply is "It's up to the standards of one's community," then they must be reminded that many communities are oppressive, racist, intolerant, and fanatical. On the other hand, if they are to avoid giving weight to the standards implicit in the practices of immoral communities, they seem to be committed to some standard, such as Mill's Harm Principle, or liberal rights to free choice, which is relatively independent of the standards of particular societies. Thus, they cannot settle the issue of whether boxing ought to be prohibited by appealing to the standards of the community, for even assuming there is just one community in our society, the moral question of why its standards *ought* to be obeyed still remains to be answered. (In fact, it can be argued plausibly that many communities in the United States do find the violence in boxing acceptable. Does that settle the moral question of whether it is acceptable?)

Boxing, Morality, and Legality

Our discussion has not provided any conclusive reason for thinking boxing ought to be *legally* prohibited. Paternalistic arguments do not seem strong enough to justify a general prohibition, the link between boxing and individual violence is too tenuous and indirect to support such a general prohibition, and the standards of the community are an insufficient guide to action. On the other hand, while most of us regard individual liberty as of the greatest value, we probably would agree that society does have the right to prohibit such practices as professional gladiatorial contests (such as Mayhem), perhaps on communitarian grounds or perhaps because we doubt that the choice to participate can be truly free or informed. The trouble is that boxing seems to be a borderline case. It is not quite as dangerous as Mayhem, the harm is not as certain or direct, and we can at least begin to understand how a participant can voluntarily accept the risks involved. Thus, the arguments both for and against prohibition seem to be at something of a standoff. Given the dangers of interfering with liberty, perhaps the best policy would be one not of legal interference but of moral sanction and reform.

Thus, whether or not the case for legal prohibition is determinative, many reasons have been given for moral concern about boxing. It is perfectly appropriate for those who share such moral concerns to refuse to support boxing, to urge others to refrain from supporting it, and to advocate strong reforms in the practice of boxing. For example, reformers may want to direct boxing in the direction of becoming an example of the constrained use of force rather than of violence. On this view, boxing as a sport should be distinguished from boxing as a form of violence, just as we now distinguish fencing from actual dueling. Reforms that work in this direction include mandatory use of helmets by fighters, prohibition of blows to the head, and emphasis on scoring points through skill rather than on inflicting damage to opponents. Although boxing probably never will be sedate, it can be modified so it bears a much closer resemblance to fencing than to Mayhem.

To conclude, even if boxing should be immune to legal prohibition on grounds of respect for individual liberty, radical reform of the sport seems to be morally justified. Boxing, as presently constituted, has the goal of infliction of harm by one opponent on another at its core, and so makes violence central. If society should not glorify violence, and if violence in sports might contribute however indirectly to greater tolerance and commission of violence throughout society, or to the erosion of *defensible* community standards, we can be led by such considerations to freely, rationally, and autonomously choose to reduce the level of violence in sports.

Violence and Contact Sports

Can arguments concerning violence in boxing be carried over to contact sports? For example, if it can be successfully argued that boxing morally (if not legally) ought to be eliminated or at least reformed in part because it is inherently violent, shouldn't the same conclusion(s) be drawn about football?

Critics of football maintain that it is a violent sport. Coaches and fans sometimes urge players to "smash," "smear," or "bury" the opposition. On this view, football is a miniaturized version of war. Even players who claim to compete within the rules acknowledge that physical intimidation is part of the game. As former Oakland Raider safety Jack Tatum puts it in his perhaps aptly named book, *They Call Me Assassin*, "My idea of a good hit is when the victim wakes up on the sidelines with the train whistles blowing in his head and wondering who he is and what ran him over."[40] Unfortunately, one of Tatum's hits in a game against the New England Patriots resulted in what appears to be the permanent paralysis of the Patriots' receiver, Darryl Stingley.

Tatum claims that although he hits hard when he tackles, he plays within the rules and does not take illegal "cheap shots" at opponents. On his view, he is paid to make sure that pass receivers don't make catches in his territory. A good way to achieve this goal is to make receivers aware that they will get hit hard when running pass patterns. Then, the next time a pass is thrown, the receivers may think more about getting hit and concentrate less on doing their job and catching the ball. As Tatum puts it, "Do I let the receiver have the edge and give him the chance to make catches around me because I'm a sensitive guy or do I do what I am paid to do?"[41]

It is understandable, then, why to its critics, football is a sport which, like boxing, glorifies violence, encourages militaristic attitudes, and amounts to a public celebration of many of our worst values. In effect, these critics hold that football is to our society what bloody gladiatorial contests were to Rome: distraction for the masses through the presentation of violence as entertainment.

Thus, Paul Hoch, author of *Rip Off the Big Game*, a highly ideological critique of American sports but one which raises many serious issues for consideration, sees football as an expression of suppressed violence in the American psyche. He suggests that because violence in football is rule governed, as opposed to the less organized violence of racial disorders or radical political protest, it "provides powerful ideological support for the officially sanctioned, rule-governed violence in society, in which judges have the final say. In short, the fans are supposed to identify with the distorted framework of law and order, both on the football field and in society, irrespective of what that law and order is supposed to protect."[42]

Ethics, Football, and Violence

The charges against football suggested in the comments above can be understood in diverse ways, but two sorts of claims seem especially worth discussing. First, football is held to be a violent sport. Second, football is thought to express or encourage acceptance of officially sanctioned violence while discouraging external criticism or struggle against the official rules themselves. In other words, football, in our society at least, is not ideologically neutral but expresses a conservative bias against social change.

Are these charges justified? In considering them, we need to keep some distinctions in mind. The first concerns whether violence is necessary to football or merely contingently attached to it. The second is between violence and the use of force.

Clearly, violence in the sense of force aimed at harming an opponent normally is indefensible in sports as it is elsewhere. Such violence treats the opponent as a mere thing to be used for one's satisfaction or gratification. Thus, it violates the morality of respect for persons, expressed in the ethic of competition as a mutual quest for excellence. But is violence in this strong sense *necessarily* part of football in the first place?

Football clearly is a contact sport requiring the use of bodily force against opponents. It does not follow, however, that football necessarily is violent. As we have seen, the use of force is quite distinct from violence since only the latter covers the intent to harm others. In particular games, or on particular teams, players may indeed act violently towards opponents, but it does not follow that football itself is a violent game.

But how is the line between violence and the use of force to be drawn? When Jack Tatum attempts to intimidate an opponent through hard hits, is he being violent or is he merely using force efficiently? Tatum would say that since it is not his intent to injure his opponent, he is using force but not ethically indefensible violence. How is this claim to be evaluated?

To begin with, it is clear that many sports often involve the use of physical force applied to opponents so as to achieve strategic goals. The use of the brushback pitch in baseball, the hard smash directly at the opponent in tennis, and the hard drive to the hoop in basketball, can all involve the use of force against opponents. Not infrequently, this use of force carries some risk of injury with it. Presumably, players are willing to bear the risk in order to secure the benefits of participation. The key ethical question in fair competition may be whether the use of force takes advantage of an opponent's physical vulnerability. Thus, major league batters are supposed to have the reflexes that can enable them to avoid a brushback pitch.[43] However, the same pitch may be indefensible when thrown against an out-of-shape older businessman who hasn't played ball in years.

If this suggestion has force, it supports what might be called the *Vulnerability Principle*, or VP. According to the VP, for the use of force against an opponent in an athletic contest to be ethically defensible, the opponent must be in a position and condition such that a strategic response is possible and it is unlikely injury will ensue. Thus, attempting to block a shot from the front of an opponent in basketball conforms to the VP while "undercutting" an opponent already in the air from behind does not.

Normal play in football does conform to the VP as long as opponents are able to respond with strategic countermoves reflecting the basic skills of players of the game. On the other hand, a tackle from the receiver's blind side when the receiver is in a position of vulnerability is ethically dubious. Indeed, defensive backs such as Jack Tatum have argued that the rules be redesigned to give more protection to receivers.

Our discussion so far suggests that football can be (although not necessarily always is) played without players intending to harm opponents. On the other hand, it is often difficult to draw the line between defensible and indefensible uses of force in contact sports, although the VP may represent a useful first step in that direction. Perhaps football can be criticized because violence is too prevalent in the sport or because the use of force creates too much risk for the players, but it does not seem that football by its very nature must be violent.

Sports and Ideology

If football is not necessarily violent in a pejorative sense, the charge that football functions as an ideological defense of officially sanctioned violence is open to serious question. This is because not all instances of football are violent to begin with.

However, the thesis that football (and perhaps other sports) are ideologically biased deserves fuller consideration. Just what does such a charge amount to?

Perhaps it means that the attention given to big-time football, and perhaps other major sports, *causes* people to tolerate unjust situations and oppose disruptive protest, perhaps because sports create identification with the values of those in power. Alternately, perhaps what is claimed is that the values *expressed* by a sport such as football are inherently objectionable; football is warlike or football requires unquestioning acceptance of officially sanctioned violence.

The causal thesis ultimately must be confirmed or disconfirmed by empirical data. The existing data, although sketchy and difficult to interpret, can perhaps be read to provide for a modest association of interest in sports with adherence to conventional values.[44] Nevertheless, key philosophical points must be kept in mind in interpreting empirical studies.

Suppose, for example, that empirical evidence shows that football players and coaches adhere more to conventional values than a control group not associated with or interested in football. Can we conclude that football produces such value commitments? We cannot. As noted in Chapter 2, it is entirely possible that people with certain values tend to become football players and coaches, rather than it being the case that participation in football generates specific values among participants. Even more likely, some third factor, such as socioeconomic background, may tend to promote both participation in football and adherence to certain values.

Even leaving this point aside, there is a deeper philosophical point also at issue. If what we are looking for is whether football and other major sports promote such traits as "unquestioning obedience to authority," "acceptance of official violence," "uncritical toleration of injustice," and "unwillingness to challenge the system," we need to be careful that we do not beg the question in favor of certain values over others. What one investigator may see as blind obedience, another may regard as admirable loyalty or discipline. What appears to some as "unwillingness to challenge the system" or "toleration of injustice" may be considered by others as rational allegiance to a defensible set of rules. Accordingly, although critics of football are quite right to raise the issue of the social significance of sports, they themselves may smuggle in assumptions that have not been adequately defended. For example, they may assume that violence rather than the controlled use of force is a necessary element of football or that the relationship of players to coaches is more like one of robots to programmers rather than pupils to teacher. Thus, in assessing the effects of sports such as football on participants and spectators alike, we need to be careful to specify just which effects are being looked for rather than jumping to interpret the data so as to confirm our own biases.

What about the idea that regardless of its effects, football expresses or illustrates such values as conformity, toleration of violence, and blind obedience to authority? Again, while it probably is true that some players, coaches, and teams accept or attempt to promote such values, they do not seem to be necessary constituents of the game.

Consider, for example, the claim that excellence in football requires blind submission to the dictates of the coach, and hence teaches a hidden agenda of uncritical acceptance of the dictates of those in power. Although some coaches might well encourage such blind loyalty, there is nothing in the profession of coaching that requires such a conception of the role and much that goes against it. A good coach, it can be argued, prepares his or her players to think for themselves in the context of the game. The coach, as do other teachers, provides a framework within which players must make decisions for themselves in the context of play.

Such a conception of the coach as teacher seems not only possible but required if players are to reach their full potential in the quest for athletic excellence. Of course, a good coach may insist on discipline and hard work, but it is hard to see why this makes the coach any more of an authoritarian or any more conservative than the philosophy professor who insists that her students work to their best potential as well.

Thus, our discussion undermines the view that football *necessarily* is violent, as well as the claim that football expresses a bias in favor of conservative political values. Of course, in practice, football and other major sports sometimes may do all of the above. But as properly practiced, football and other contact sports should express the values of a mutual quest for athletic excellence, which include respect for opponents, a sense of fair play, and intelligent and critical application of the skills of the game. Even though football in particular involves the use of a good deal of physical force, and hence may be criticized because of danger to the participants, it need not involve the intention to harm opponents or the support of a particular partisan political ideology.

The Actual and the Ideal in Philosophy of Sports

At this point, some critics of violence in sports may be exceedingly impatient with the course of the discussion. On their view, the exercise has been an example of the philosopher's futile interest in the ideal, a focus which allows the theorist to conveniently ignore real abuses. "It is all too easy to say football is not *necessarily* violent," such a critic might exclaim, "when the important task is to show what *actually* is wrong with sports, and then change it."

However, although much of our discussion has been concerned with standards that should apply to sports, that hardly makes it impractical. It is difficult to understand how we could even identify abuses in sports unless we had some grasp of the ethical principles that were being violated in the first place. Besides, without some standards at which to aim, we would not know the proper recommendations to make for moral change.

Moreover, moral reform involves more than simply implementing ethical principles whatever the cost. At a minimum, ethical principles must be implemented and applied in a fair and just way. For example, even if boxing ought to be prohibited, it doesn't follow that we should simply prohibit boxing without consideration for the fate of those boxers who might suddenly find themselves unemployed. Sometimes, the moral and political costs of implementing some principles may be so great that considerations of justice or utility require us to adopt a "second best" solution. Be that as it may, unless we knew what ideals should apply in sports, how could we tell what reforms are needed in current practice?

In any case, the views developed in this chapter do have implications for policy. They indicate that while it is difficult to always draw the line between what sportsmanship and fair play permit and what they forbid, those values are not vacuous and do apply to the behavior of competitors in sports. And although our discussion does not indicate that the case for legal prohibition of boxing is compelling, it does provide ground for the condemnation of many forms of violence in sports. For example, those who defend the constant fighting in professional hockey as "part of the game" make the very same error as those who see football as essentially violent. Some uses of force, such as bodychecking, may be part of the game of hockey, but fighting involves the use of force with intent to harm and hence is in a different ethical category entirely. If such violence truly is part of the game, the game is not morally defensible to begin with.

However, we should not confuse the factual thesis that violence often is a part of sports, and even is sometimes exploited for commercial reasons, with the stronger thesis that contact sports are essentially violent. It is because the latter thesis is so questionable that we have reason for condemning violence and its exploitation in the name of good sports.

If competition in sports is thought of as a mutual quest for excellence, then violence, cheating, and bad sportsmanship are in different ways violations of the ethic that should apply to athletic competition. A defensible sports ethic, one that respects participants as persons, should avoid the twin errors of, on one hand, leaving no room for the clever strategic foul or the intelligent use of force, while, on the other hand, assuming that players in the pursuit of victory can do no wrong.

4

Enhancing Performance
Through Drugs

It is the 1988 Summer Olympics at Seoul, Korea. The long-awaited race between Canadian Ben Johnson and American Carl Lewis is about to be run. The muscles on Johnson's almost sculptured body stand out as the gun fires, and the runners are off. In a hard-fought race, Johnson defeats Lewis and apparently wins the gold medal.

However, urinalysis tests subsequently reveal that Johnson has been taking the steroid stanozolol to enhance his performance. To the shock of Canadians, to whom Johnson has become a national hero, and to the rest of the sports world, Johnson is disqualified. He forfeits his medal from the race against Lewis and all his other medals from the 1988 Olympics. Other athletes are also found to have been using performance enhancers as well. Indeed, it is alleged such use is widespread among top athletes in many sports even though such use is prohibited by the rules.

Is the use of performance-enhancing drugs such as anabolic steroids really unethical? Why shouldn't athletes be allowed to use them if they want to? Does their use somehow undermine competitive sports conceived of as a mutual quest for excellence? Did Ben Johnson *cheat*, or had he simply found a more effective way to compete, just as some athletes may use more effective programs of weight training than others? Let us consider these questions further.

Performance Enhancers and the Quest for Excellence

Competition in sports, it has been argued, is ethically defensible when it involves participants in a mutual quest for excellence through challenge. In effect, competitors should view themselves as under moral obligations to their opponents. Each competitor is obligated to try his or her best, so that opponents can develop their own skills through facing a significant test. On this view, sports can be of interest and significance because, at their best, they involve both our minds and bodies fully in meeting a challenge, a challenge regarded as worth meeting for its own sake.

Although there are different levels of competitive intensity, even the recreational athlete playing in a relaxed and informal atmosphere tries to play well and often fantasizes about making great plays. Whether one is a recreational softball player imagining himself or herself as a major leaguer or a hacker on the golf course who for once hits a perfect shot, participants in sports all take part in the quest for excellence, although with various degrees of intensity. What distinguishes the fun we have through sports from mere exercise is the presence of standards of excellence and the challenge presented by the play of others.

At the professional level, the primary goals of many players and coaches may be financial. However, regardless of the personal goals of the competitors, to the extent that professional sports capture the imagination of players and fans alike, it is because professional athletes are involved in the mutual quest for excellence at the highest level of attainable skill.

Many athletes at the most skilled levels of professional and amateur competition love the challenge provided by sports and seek constantly to improve their level of performance. Some seem to compete as much for the love of competition as for financial reward. Indeed, could anyone rise to the top in a highly competitive sport without love of the game and dedication to excellence providing the motivation for the hours of practice, drills, and preparation that are required?

The danger here is that the drive for excellence will lead dedicated athletes to use dangerous and arguably unethical means to achieve success. Losing becomes identified with failure and anything that promotes winning is also seen as promoting success. But is winning achieved by *any* means always a success worth having?

Accordingly, we need to ask about the means by which excellence might be achieved. In particular, is the use of drugs, such as anabolic steroids, an ethically permissible method for achieving excellence in sports, or, as most sports authorities argue, should the use of performance-enhancing drugs be prohibited in organized athletic competition?

Understanding the Problem

The relatively wide use of such drugs as anabolic steroids to enhance athletic performance dates back at least to the Olympics of the 1960's, although broad public awareness of use of such drugs seems compara-tively recent. Anabolic steroids are a family of drugs, synthetic deriva-tives of the hormone testosterone, that stimulate muscle growth and repair of injured tissue. Although not everyone would agree that the controlled and supervised use of steroids to enhance performance is dangerous, the American College of Sports Medicine, as well as other major medical organizations, warn against serious side effects. Some of these are, at least at high levels of dosage, liver damage, artherosclerosis, hypertension, a lowered sperm count in males, and masculinization in females. The regular use of steroids also is asserted to produce such personality changes as increased aggressiveness and hostility.[1]

Although the degree to which steroids are used by top amateur and professional athletes is unclear, most observers would acknowledge that their use is not infrequent, particularly at elite levels of some amateur and professional sports. Users range from weight lifters to football linemen to track and field stars. The Summer 1983 Pan American games were disrupted, for example, when several gold-medal winners, includ-ing Americans, were disqualified for the use of performance-enhancing drugs. In addition, other athletes withdrew from events rather than take tests that might have revealed drug use. What is particularly frightening is that world-class athletes are reported to be taking steroids at many times the recommended dosage, at dosages so high that it would be illegal to administer them to human subjects in an experiment to deter-mine their effect on health and performance. Some athletes are said to "stack" various forms of steroids in attempts to find the most effective combination. Moreover, many athletes who use steroids to enhance performance do so without medical supervision. Such athletes are unlikely to be influenced by claims that steroid use has little effect on performance, when such claims are based on studies where only low doses of the relevant drugs were administered.

What Is a Performance-Enhancing Drug?

Before we can turn to a discussion of the ethics of the use of performance-enhancing drugs in sports, we need to be clearer about what counts as a performance enhancer. Are vitamins performance-enhancing drugs? What about a cup of coffee stimulating a sleepy athlete before a match? What about medication that alleviates allergy symptoms, thereby allowing an athlete to compete more effectively? If we want to forbid the use of performance enhancers, what exactly defines the class of substances that is the target of our prohibition?

Unfortunately, there does not seem to be any clear and simple definition that distinguishes the kind of performance-enhancing drugs that officials of major sports organizations want to prohibit from the legitimate use of vitamins or remedies for symptoms caused by allergies. The situation is complicated further by the fact that a substance that might enhance performance in one context or sport may fail to do so, or even harm performance, in another context or sport. Thus, moderate use of alcohol normally would affect performance only adversely, but can be a performance enhancer in riflery. This is because alcohol is a depressant and therefore slows the heartbeat, which in turn allows for a steadier shooting hand on the rifle range.

Moreover, it is of little help to say that athletes should be permitted to take only what is "natural"; steroids are derivatives of the hormone testosterone, which does occur naturally in the human body, but many legitimate medications, which athletes ought to be allowed to take, are synthetic and clearly not present in the normal or natural diet. In any case, the term "natural" is too vague and opentextured to be of much help in this area.

In addition, what of practices such as blood doping, where athletes reinject samples of their own blood that were stored earlier, in an attempt to boost their oxygen-carrying capacity? It is doubtful if one's own blood can be classified as "unnatural," yet the practice of blood doping is regarded as an unethical form of performance enhancement by major sports organizations.

Rather than search for a precise definition to distinguish the substances we intuitively believe are illegitimate performance enhancers from those that are not, it seems more useful to examine the case of anabolic steroids, the use of which to enhance performance is prohibited by major sports organizations. We can then ask what factors, if any, *morally* justify this prohibition. If the prohibition is justified, and if we can isolate the moral reasons for it, then any other substances to which the same reasons apply also should be prohibited. In other words, rather than search for an abstract definition, we should first decide what sort of factors *ought* or *ought not* to be allowed to affect athletic performance. Then, any substance whose use involves factors that ought not to affect performance should be included on our list of prohibited substances. Let us consider the case of anabolic steroids to see whether any such factors can be discovered.

Evaluating the Use of Performance Enhancers

Different kinds of reasons are cited as justifications of the claim that competitive athletes ought not to be allowed to use steroids to enhance their performance in sports. Among the most frequently cited are the following: (a) use of steroids to enhance performance is harmful to athletes, who need to be protected; (b) use of steroids to enhance performance by some athletes coerces others into using steroids; (c) use of steroids to enhance performance is unfair, or a form of cheating; (d) use of steroids to enhance performance violates justifiable norms or ideals that ought to govern athletic competition. Let us examine each kind of justification in turn.

Why shouldn't athletes be allowed to use drugs such as steroids that enhance their performance in sports? One argument against allowing athletes to use steroids is that such use, particularly at the high dosages believed necessary to enhance performance, can be seriously harmful to the athletes who use them. Let us accept the factual claim that use of steroids as performance enhancers can be seriously harmful and consider whether the possibility of harm to the user constitutes a justification sufficient to prohibit their use.

The principal criticism of prohibiting the use of steroids to protect athletes from themselves is that it is illegitimately *paternalistic*. Such paternalistic interference violates the liberty of the athletes to make decisions for themselves. After all, would any of us want to have our liberty interfered with whenever some outside agency felt that our personal decisions about how to live our lives were too risky? If widespread paternalism were practiced, third parties could prohibit us from eating foods that might be harmful, playing in sports that carried even slight risk of injury, or indulging in lifestyles that were not sufficiently healthy. Our whole lives would be monitored, for our own good, of course. The trouble is that we might not conceive of our good in the same way as the paternalist.

As we saw in Chapter 3, the principal trouble with paternalism, then, is that it is far too restrictive of human liberty. Contrary to the paternalist, we may believe with John Stuart Mill, the great nineteenth-century defender of human freedom, "that the only purpose for which power can be rightfully exercised over any member of a civilized community, against his will, is to prevent harm to others. His own good, either physical or moral, is not a sufficient warrant."[2]

However, if each of us ought to be free to assume risks that we think worth taking, shouldn't athletes have the same freedom as anyone else? In particular, if athletes prefer the gains in performance allegedly provided by the use of steroids along with the increased risk of harm to the alternative of less risk and worse performance, what gives anyone else the right to interfere with their choice? After all, if we should not forbid boxers from risking their health in pursuit of their careers in boxing, why should we prohibit track stars or weight lifters from taking risks with their health in pursuit of their goals?

Although the antipaternalistic considerations advanced above have great force, we need to consider some difficulties before we can dismiss paternalism as a justification for a prohibition on the use of steroids as performance enhancers. As we have seen in our discussion of boxing, even Mill acknowledged that the kind of antipaternalism articulated in his Harm Principle had limits. Mill excluded children and young people below the age of maturity, and those, such as the mentally ill, who may require care by others from.[3] Moreover, Mill himself would clearly exempt those who are misinformed or coerced from immediate protection of the principle. To use one of his own examples, if you attempt to cross a bridge in the dark, in ignorance of the fact that the bridge has been washed away by a flood, I do not violate the Harm Principle by preventing you from attempting the crossing until I have had an opportunity to fully explain the situation to you.[4]

In particular, before accepting the antipaternalistic argument, we need to consider whether athletes who use steroids to enhance performance really are making a *free* and *informed* choice. If behavior is not the result of free and informed choice, it is not really action of a rational autonomous agent. If it is not informed, the person does not truly know what she is doing, while if the behavior is coerced, it is not what the agent wants to do in the first place.

Is there any reason to believe that athletes who use steroids to enhance their performance in sports are either uninformed about the effects of the drug or are coerced or are otherwise incompetent to make rational decisions?

First, those below the age of consent can legitimately be prevented from using steroids to enhance performance on paternalistic grounds. In the same way that parents can prevent children from engaging in potentially harmful behavior, even if the children want to take their chances on getting hurt, so sports authorities can prohibit the use of harmful performance enhancers by those who are incompetent because of age.

What about the requirement of *informed* consent? Are athletes who use steroids to enhance performance adequately informed about the serious potential side effects of the drug?

Some athletes, particularly teenagers may be uninformed or sceptical about the information available, but it is hard to believe that most adult users of steroids are ignorant of the risks involved. Even if H. L. Menken may have not been totally off the mark when he suggested that it was impossible to go broke by underestimating the intelligence of the American people, it is difficult to believe, in view of the amount of publicity devoted to the use of performance enhancer, that the majority of mature athletes are unaware that steroid use can be dangerous.

However, even if most or even virtually all athletes are uninformed in this area, total prohibition of steroid use still would not have been justified. At most, it might be required only that athletes show they are informed about the risks before they are permitted to use the drugs. Lack of information can be remedied by education about the risks. No paternalistic justification has yet been provided for prohibiting competent mature and well-informed athletes from using steroids to enhance their performance in sports.

Coercion and Freedom in Sports

What about the requirement of free choice? Are athletes really free *not* to use steroids? At least some analysts would argue that athletes are coerced into using steroids. Consider the case of professional sports. The professional athlete's livelihood may depend on performing at the highest level. Athletes who are not among the best in the world may not be professionals for very long. "Thus," one writer concluded, "the onus is on the athlete to continue playing and to consent to things he or she would not otherwise consent to. . . . Coercion, however subtle, makes the athlete vulnerable. It also takes away the athlete's ability to act and choose freely with regard to informed consent."[5]

However, while this point may not be without force in specific contexts, the use it makes of the term "coercion" seems questionable. After all, no one literally is forced to become (or remain) a professional athlete or participate at elite levels of amateur athletics. If we want to use "coercion" so broadly, are we also committed, absurdly it seems, to saying coaches coerce players into practicing or training hard. Do professors similarly "coerce" students into studying hard? Isn't it more plausible to say that although there are pressures on athletes to achieve peak physical condition, these amount to coercion no more than the pressures on law or medical students to study hard?

At best, then, it is unclear whether top athletes are coerced into using steroids, or whether they make a free decision, in light of various incentives and disincentives, that the gains of steroid use outweigh the risks. Surely, we are not entitled to assume that professional athletes as a class are unable to give informed consent to steroid use unless we are willing to count similar pressures in other professions as forms of coercion as well. And if we use "coercion" that broadly, it becomes unclear who, if anybody, is left free.

Of course, there may be specific cases where athletes clearly are victims of coercion. Perhaps an athlete who otherwise would not use steroids is threatened with a loss of job by an owner who requires such use. Apart from such specific cases, however, it appears doubtful that a general desire by the athlete to be successful at his or her profession can by itself undermine the capacity for free choice.

However, even if the athlete's own internal desires for success do not rule out free choice, what about coercion by other competitors? That is, even if we agree that *internal* pressures generated by the athletes are not coercive, we might suspect that there are *external* pressures created by their competitors that are coercive. Thus, it sometimes is argued that even if some sophisticated athletes do give informed consent, their drug use may force others, who would not otherwise do so, into taking steroids as well. Such athletes may believe that unless they take such drugs, they will not be able to compete with those who do. Athletes may believe they are trapped; don't take steroids and lose or take them and remain competitive.

Note that the argument here is no longer that we should interfere with athletes on paternalistic grounds—to prevent them from harming themselves—but rather that we should interfere with them to prevent them from coercing others. Such an argument is in accord with Mill's Harm Principle; liberty is restricted but only to prevent harm to others.

Do pressures generated by athletes who use drugs *coerce* other athletes into using performance enhancers too? One reason for doubting that they do is that it once again appears as if "coercion" is being used too broadly. One might just as well say that students who study harder than others "coerce" their classmates into studying harder too in order to keep up, or that athletes who practice longer hours than others "coerce" their competitors into practicing longer hours as well. The problem with such claims, of course, is that any competitive pressure becomes "coercive" in such an extended sense of the term. As a result, the term "coerce" is deprived of any moral force because virtually no competitive behavior is left over that would be *not* be coercive. If *anything* one does to gain an advantage in competition counts as coercion, the term "coercion" becomes vacuous because it lacks any intelligible contrast.

Unethically Constrained Choice

The appeal to coercion as a justification for prohibiting the use of steroids is vulnerable to the charge that it uses the notion of coercion far too broadly. Perhaps, however, the argument can be reconstructed or modified without unacceptably stretching the term "coercion."

Whatever the proper definition of "coercion," what seems to make coercion presumptively wrong is when it unduly, illegitimately, or in some other way, *improperly* interferes with the freedom of another.[6] Thus, we are reluctant to say that the student who studies harder than his peers, or the athlete who trains harder than her competitors, coerces them because we don't think the student or the athlete is acting illegitimately or improperly. Both have a right to work harder, so their working harder does not coerce others to do the same, or, if it does, it does not do so improperly or wrongly. Accordingly, we have no reason to prohibit the behavior of the student and athlete (and, in fact, have reason to encourage it since it leads to superior achievement).

But consider another case where competitive pressures arguably are imposed wrongly or improperly. Suppose you work in a firm where young employees compete for promotions to higher levels. Up to a point, if some work harder than others, no ethical issue is involved, because it is not wrong for some workers to try to perform better than others. But now, suppose that some workers work virtually all the time, including weekends. Everyone feels the pressure to keep up, and soon virtually all the workers give up their holidays and evenings for fear that they will lose their jobs if they do not. In this case, it looks a bit more plausible that the workers are coerced or, if not "coerced," at least unjustifiably pressured into putting in hours and hours of overtime.

Let us make the case a bit more extreme. Suppose some of the workers start taking stimulants—drugs with some harmful side effects— in order to be able to work even harder. Other workers feel that they too must take the stimulants in order to keep up. They complain to the employer, asking that limits be set on the amount of time they are expected to work, on the grounds that they are being coerced into taking the stimulants in order to keep their job.

In this case, it is at best unclear that the workers who take the stimulants are behaving properly. Arguably, they are unduly putting pressure on other workers to risk harming themselves in order to keep their jobs. If so, they are violating the freedom of the other workers and their behavior may be regulated in the interests of protecting the freedom of all.[7]

Is the practice of steroid use in competitive sports like that of our last example? Do users of dangerous performance-enhancing drugs behave illegitimately or improperly when they put pressure on others to keep up competitively? Some would say "No!" As one writer argues, "The ingestion of steroids for competitive reasons cannot be distinguished from the other tortures, deprivations, and risks to which athletes subject themselves to achieve success. No one is coerced into world class competition. . . . If they find the costs excessive, they may withdraw."[8]

But while such a rejoinder has force, it may not be decisive. Although the suggestion that steroid use is not strictly "coercive" has force, because athletes can always withdraw from the competition, the choice of either using a potentially harmful drug or being noncompetitive may be unethical to impose on others. Perhaps a prohibition on steroids can be justified as a means of protecting athletes from being placed in a position where they have to make such a choice. To the extent that we think it is wrong or illegitimate to face athletes with such a dilemma, then to that extent we will find the argument from coercion to have a point. Whether or not we want to apply the term "coercion" in such a context, we need to consider whether it is morally wrong to insist that athletes must be prepared to risk seriously harming themselves in order to compete. If so, a prohibition on steroid use may be justified as a means of protecting athletes against having such a choice imposed upon them and from competitive pressures which, if unregulated, are far too likely to get completely out of hand.

Such considerations may not satisfy those who think use of steroids is permissible. They would reply that athletes who engage in especially demanding and sometimes stressful forms of training also impose hard choices on other competitors, but their behavior is not considered unethical. How can we justifiably condemn the users of performance-enhancing drugs for confronting competitors with difficult choices when we do not make the same judgment in similar sorts of cases?

This rejoinder does need to be explored further. Perhaps we can distinguish the risks inherent in stressful training programs from those inherent in the use of steroids. Alternately, perhaps we should prohibit particularly dangerous kinds of practices elsewhere in sports, as was done with the method of tackling in football known as spearing.

Although we have not arrived at an uncontroversial justification for prohibiting the use of steroids in organized athletic competition, we have discovered a line of argument that is well worth further examination. Whether it will survive the test of further critical discussion remains to be seen, but perhaps the general case for a prohibition on the use of steroids can be reinforced by considerations of a different sort.

Fairness, Cheating, and the Use of Performance Enhancers

Many of those who object to the use of performance-enhancing drugs in sports do so not (or not only) because they believe users coerce others into also becoming users. Rather, they believe that use of such drugs is a form of cheating. What reasons, if any, can be given for regarding the use of drugs, such as steroids, to enhance athletic performance as an unfair competitive practice?

Those who assert that users of performance-enhancing drugs are cheating their opponents mean more than that users are breaking existing rules. Of course, if the existing rules prohibit the use of such drugs, then use is a form of cheating. Those who secretly violate the rules take unfair advantage of those who conform to the rules. The interesting philosophical issue, however, is whether the rules themselves should be changed to allow the use of performance-enhancing drugs. According to the approach we will now consider, a rule allowing the use of performance-enhancing drugs would be unfair even if such drugs were available to anyone.

Many of us share the intuition that use of performance enhancers provides an unfair advantage, but we need to ask whether this intuition can be supported by good arguments. One line of argument suggests an analogy with differences in the equipment available to competitors. For example, if one player in a golf tournament used golf balls that flew significantly further than balls used by opponents even when struck with the same force, the tournament arguably is unfair. One player is able to avoid one of the major challenges of golf not because of skill but simply because of use of a superior product. Perhaps the use of steroids provides a similar unfair advantage.

The problem with this line of argument, however, is that it is at best unclear that the golf tournament is unfair. If the ball is legal and available to other competitors, the user indeed has an advantage over players using ordinary equipment, but what makes the advantage unfair? In fact, there are all sorts of differences in equipment, background, training facilities, coaching, and diet that can affect the performances of athletes but are not regarded as unfair. Until we can say why the advantages provided by such performance enhancers as steroids are illegitimate, and advantages provided by other differences in background conditions are legitimate, the charge of unfairness must be dismissed as lacking adequate support.[9]

A similar difficulty affects the view that performance enhancers make sports too easy. Thus, we might say the trouble with the "hot" golf ball is not that it gives some competitors unfair advantages over others, as the same ball is available to them all, but rather that it makes golf significantly less challenging and interesting. Similarly, perhaps the trouble with steroids, we might claim, is that they reduce the challenge of sports by making achievement the result of taking a pill rather than skill. But as Roger Gardner points out, the same claim can be made about the introduction of new equipment, such as perimeter-weighted clubs in golf that expand the "sweet spot" of clubs and thereby reduce the level of skill needed to attain a desirable shot, as well as about diets promoting carbohydrate loading, high-tech running shoes, and top-of-the-line practice facilities, all of which are regarded as acceptable parts of athletic competition.[10]

The difficulty, then, is that of finding a principled way of drawing the line between the illegitimate use of steroids and other performance enhancers, on one hand, and factors that provide legitimate competitive advantages, on the other.

Even though it is doubtful that any one principle can do all the work needed in this area, the charge of unfairness should not be dismissed too quickly. Perhaps by expanding considerations mentioned in our discussion of potential coercive effects of steroid use, a different analysis of the unfairness involved can be developed. What was suggested earlier was that steroid use by some athletes created a situation of unpalatable choices for others. Either use steroids and risk harm or cease to be competitive. In a sense, the steroid user, if perhaps not like the robber who demands your money or your life, at least creates a dilemma like that facing the workers who must use harmful stimulants in order to keep pace with the drug-induced energy of colleagues. We may conclude that neither athletes nor workers should face such choices, and that therefore we should enact legislation to protect them from having such a cruel dilemma thrust upon them.

It is tempting to conclude that a similar line of argument also suggests that the use of steroids to enhance performance is unfair. Suppose we ask whether it would be rational for all athletes to support either the rule "use of steroids should be prohibited in athletic competition" or the rule "use of steroids should be permitted in athletic competition"? Let us stipulate one artificial but plausible and morally justifiable limitation on their choice, namely, the athletes vote as if in ignorance of how the use or nonuse of steroids would specifically affect them personally but with knowledge of the general properties of steroids. The use of this limited "veil of ignorance," suggested by John Rawls's theory of justice which we discuss in Chapter 5, forces the athletes to be impartial and unbiased rather than voting according to personal self-interest.[11] How would rational athletes vote?

Can it be established that a vote for the rule permitting steroid use would be irrational under such circumstances? One might argue for such a view by pointing out that all athletes would know of the general harmful effects of steroids, but, because of the requirement of limited ignorance, none would have any reason to believe steroids would be especially beneficial in his or her particular case. Widespread use would at best yield only minimal gains for any one competitor, since the advantages gained by some would be largely cancelled out by roughly similar advantages secured by others. However, the risk of serious effects on health would be significant for all.

Under such circumstances, a rule allowing the general use of steroids seems collectively irrational. Why would rational individuals choose to run great risks for minimal gains, gains which, from behind the veil of ignorance, they have no reason to believe will accrue to them rather than to their competitors? It seems that only way significant competitive advantage can be secured is if some athletes use steroids covertly, without the knowledge of others. The general practice of allowing steroid use would not be supported by an informed impartial choice of all athletes, and in any case provides only minimal gains relative to the risk of serious harm.

Unfortunately for those who oppose the use of steroids to enhance athletic performance, this appeal to what is in effect a hypothetical social contract among all athletes is hardly free from objection.[12] In particular, it assumes, perhaps incorrectly, that the only outcomes athletes would consider behind the veil of ignorance would be risks to health versus competitive gains over other athletes. Some athletes, however, might consider other issues. For example, some athletes might consider the value of a higher level of competition among all athletes generated by use of steroids, whether or not they gain advantages over others, more than compensates for risks to health. Other athletes may value being stronger as a result of steroid use, whether or not it yields a competitive gain over others. (Strictly speaking, athletes behind the veil will be ignorant even of their own values, but will have to take into account the possibility that in the real world they might have such values and vote accordingly.) Thus, it is not as uncontroversial as it first appeared that athletes behind the veil would collectively agree to prohibit steroid use in athletic competition. In fact, their deliberations behind the veil might be indeterminate because of conflicting views of the values at stake.

Accordingly, even though we have not been able to show the argument from fairness is decisive or free of reasonable objection, our discussion at least suggests an approach that is worth further development and examination. Perhaps further development of the argument would help undermine some of the objections to it. For example, we might consider whether the official rule-making bodies of sports, such as the NCAA (National Collegiate Athletic Association) or the International Olympic Committee, are obligated to ignore the idiosyncratic values of individual athletes and simply consider the issue of steroid use from the point of good competition. If we can justifiably rule out the preferences of those athletes who value increases in strength or in overall athletic achievement over risks to health, and only consider the issue from the point of competitive advantages and disadvantages (which arguably is the point of view that rule-making bodies should take), then our original conclusion seems to follow. From the standpoint of collective impartial choice about the conditions of competition, users of steroids are making exceptions of themselves from rules to which they themselves would not consent under conditions of free impartial choice.[13] Since they are making exceptions of themselves arbitrarily, can their behavior be regarded as justifiable or fair?

Performance-Enhancing Drugs and the Ethic of Competition

Even if the argument from fairness has force, it may seem to miss part of the issue raised by the use of performance enhancers. For one thing, it depends heavily on the fact that prolonged use of steroids can be harmful to the user. But we may believe that the use of performance-enhancing drugs in sports would be wrong even if the drugs were not harmful. If there were a "magic pill," which if taken properly would improve athletic ability significantly without risks to health, would use of such a pill be ethical? Doesn't the use of steroids run counter to the ethic of good competition outlined earlier? Steroid use seems a way of avoiding the challenges presented by sports rather than overcoming them. These sorts of intuitions do not rest on claims that the use of steroids is coercive or that such use is unfair but seem to arise independently from concerns about the basic ethic of athletic competition. Can such intuitions about the wrongness of the use of performance-enhancing drugs be justified?

If competition in sports is supposed to be a test of the athletic ability of *persons*, isn't the very heart of competition corrupted if results are affected by performance enhancing drugs? Presumably, we would not accept a new high-jump record if the winner wore special mechanical aids that added spring to her shoes. Similarly, home runs produced by use of a corked bat in baseball are disallowed. In all these cases, we are inclined to say that success does not reflect the skill of the athlete but in large part is the result of special equipment instead.

Isn't it the same with the use of performance-enhancing drugs? Where such drugs lead to improved play, it is not the person who is responsible for the gains. Rather, it is the drug that makes the difference. Isn't this similar to the examples of the mechanical track shoes and the corked bat? In all these cases, isn't the ethic of competition violated because the skills of the athlete are replaced by technological aids that turn the contest from one of competing persons into one of machines? The logical extension of such a route would be to replace flesh-and-blood athletes by robots especially designed to maximize performance in every category. What we would have, if such a nightmare ever became reality, might be enhanced performance, but would it be sport?

It is unlikely, however, that those who believe the use of performance-enhancing drugs should be permitted would be convinced by such an argument. In particular, they might suggest three important objections. First, we often do allow new equipment in sport, even if such equipment does enhance performance. The introduction of fiberglass poles for vaulting and the replacement of wooden golf shafts by steel ones are two examples of innovations that enhanced performance.[14] How does the introduction of performance-enhancing drugs differ? Second, changes in diet are widely believed to enhance performance. If runners can "load-up" on carbohydrates before a race to improve their times, why can't they take steroids as well? Finally, steroids and other performance enhancers are not magic bullets that immediately produce results; they yield improvement only in conjunction with hard training. Why isn't the decision to use steroids just as much a decision of a person as the decision to use weight training? Is there any reason for us to say that weight training reflects our status as persons and the use of steroids does not?

Let us consider the point about technological innovations in equipment first. Although there probably is no one principle that explains when an innovation in equipment is acceptable and when it isn't, some distinctions can be made nevertheless. For example, some technological improvements in equipment remedy defects in what was available earlier. Old wooden shafts in golf clubs twisted to varying degrees under the pressure of the golf swing, producing arbitrary inconsistencies in results. The same player could make two equally good swings but get different results because of too much torque in the wooden shaft. This defect was remedied by the introduction of more consistent steel golf shafts. Similarly, improved athletic shoes can be regarded as removing defects of unnecessary weight and faulty structure. Although both innovations made it easier to perform better, neither changed the character of the game and both can be regarded as removing handicaps created by faulty equipment that were extraneous to the real challenges set by the sports in question.

However, other changes in equipment that have been regarded as permissible cannot easily be seen as simply removing defects in materials used earlier. In golf, the sand wedge, a club with an especially designed flange, invented by professional Gene Sarazen, made it far easier to escape from sand bunkers than before. In fact, many skilled professionals would rather have a missed shot land in the sand than in a difficult lie on grass because the sand wedge has made highly accurate recoveries likely for the advanced player. Similarly, the introduction of fiberglass poles has made it possible for vaulters to achieve heights previously considered unreachable. Graphite and other composite materials have contributed to advances in play in golf, tennis, and other sports. In other words, it does not seem to be true that all technological advances in sports equipment simply are remedies for defects in earlier materials. Why should such advances be allowed and use of steroids prohibited?

This reply by the proponent of allowing use of performance-enhancing drugs may not be convincing to the critics who may feel that while technological improvements in equipment do yield advances in achievement, the equipment must still be used by persons. Performance-enhancing drugs, they believe, change the nature of those who use the equipment and so undermine the challenge presented by sports. Instead of meeting the challenge of the test, we change the nature of the test takers so as to minimize the challenge faced. But while such intuitions may be widely shared, are they supportable by good arguments? It appears that both the proponents and the critics of the use of performance-enhancing drugs in sports have advanced points well worth considering, but that the arguments presented by both sides are still inconclusive.

Perhaps we can make some progress by considering more fully the suggestion that the use of performance enhancers undermines the challenges presented by sports. In particular, if use of steroids and other performance-enhancing drugs were permitted, what would significantly affect outcomes would be the way particular athletes were affected by the drug. But this seems athletically irrelevant. Jones should not defeat Smith because Jones's body more efficiently utilizes steroids than Smith's. We want the winner to be the best athlete, not the individual whose body is best attuned to a performance enhancing drug! In other words, use of performance enhancers turns sport from a contest among persons in the direction of a contest among "designer" bodies that are manufactured, not by effort and hard training, but through a technological fix.[15] The winners are the individuals whose bodies react best to the available drugs, which hardly seems to be what is meant by sports as a mutual quest of *persons* for excellence through challenge.

However, a proponent of the use of performance enhancers might ask if the same thing isn't true of special diets. Thus, "carbohydrate loading," or consuming unusually large amounts of carbohydrates prior to competition, seems to be a common and accepted practice among long-distance runners, but clearly some competitors may gain more from the practice than others. Is this an example of outcomes being unfairly affected by athletically irrelevant qualities? Or if it is permissible to adhere to a performance-enhancing diet, why isn't it also acceptable to use performance enhancing drugs?

Even if this point is ignored, proponents of steroid use might charge that the case against use of performance enhancers is still inconsistent in another way. On one hand, competition in sports has been defended here because such competition is particularly expressive of our moral status as persons. But, by prohibiting athletes from using performance-enhancing drugs, it can be argued that we disrespect them as persons. That is, we deny them the control over their own lives that ought to belong to any autonomous, intelligent, and competent individual. In other words, aren't athletes persons? If so, shouldn't their choices, including the choice of using drugs to enhance performance, be respected?

While these points have force, they too may be no more decisive than forceful points made by the critics of performance-enhancing drugs. Thus, while the antipaternalistic arguments discussed earlier emphasized the importance of autonomy and free choice, they also permitted interference with free choice at one point in order to maximize possibility for choice at another. For example, it arguably is permissible to prevent someone from becoming addicted to a drug because, once addicted, that person might lose the capacity for free choice in the future. Similarly, in the *Odyssey*, Ulysses allowed himself to be tied to the mast of his ship by his crew so he would not give in to the lure of the song of the sirens. Ulysses gave up the freedom to pursue a particular desire at a particular time in order to maximize his capacity to pursue a greater variety of desires in the future.

Similarly, although the choice to use performance-enhancing drugs can, under appropriate circumstances, be autonomous and free, and so reflect our capacities as persons, that choice, once acted upon, can significantly restrict the area in which we can act as persons in the future. In particular, the critics of drug use fear that once steroid use is permitted, sports become less like an interaction among persons and more like one among machines. For example, if a point of weight lifting is to test the limits of human strength and endurance, how can it continue to fulfill such a function if what really is being tested are the limits of drug-induced strength and endurance? If that is what we are after, why not give each competitor a machine that would help lift an additional fifty pounds mechanically? Why not substitute well-designed robots for humans in athletic competition? (Perhaps such fears lie behind the claim that the use of steroids is unnatural.)

On the contrary, the goal of athletic competition should not be simply to achieve even greater heights of performance: lifting heavier and heavier weights, running the mile faster and faster, hitting more and more home runs, winning more than anyone else ever has. Rather, it is to do so in a particular way by meeting as a person the challenges set by opponents or by the qualities of an obstacle, such as a golf course. The good competitor does not see an opponent simply as a body to be beaten down but as another person whose acts constitute a mutually acceptable challenge and which calls for appropriate response. By making victory depend on qualities of bodies, the ability to efficiently utilize a drug, which have nothing to do with athletic ability or our status as persons, the use of performance enhancers moves sports in a direction that makes it less and less an expression of our personhood.

In order to assess this line of argument, we need to consider further whether using a performance-enhancing drug is a significant step towards turning oneself into a robot. There is a long slippery slope between one and the other. Moreover, even if the use of performance-enhancing drugs was permitted, the nightmare of teams of robot athletes competing at levels of excellence far beyond human attainment probably never will materialize. Finally, we need to remember that actual performance enhancers, such as steroids, are not "magic bullets" that guarantee results. The athlete still has to work exceptionally hard and develop finely tuned skills in order to derive any advantage from the drugs.

Summary

Our discussion of the ethics of the use of performance-enhancing drugs in sports suggests that although critics and proponents of their use have advanced important arguments, it is difficult to conclude that either side has provided a decisive justification for their point of view. Perhaps the debate can be rationally resolved through further critical inquiry.

In the meantime, however, sports authorities must promulgate rules about whether or not to permit the use of such performance enhancers as anabolic steroids. Policymakers often have to decide difficult issues over which reasonable persons of good will disagree. If we had to wait for the emergence of decisive arguments on controversial moral issues, we often would be paralyzed in circumstances demanding some action.

In fact, we often have to draw lines between what is permissible and impermissible in areas where reasons for making the distinction do not apply in as sharp a fashion as we would like. For example, the democratic state must distinguish between those who are sufficiently mature to vote and those who are too immature to be allowed to vote. Since the maturity of each person cannot be evaluated on the merits in individual cases, we attempt to draw a line reasonably. So long as the process by which the line is drawn is itself consistent with democratic values, and the boundary is reasonable, there are good grounds for regarding it as justified.

Given that there is sharp division in the world of sports over the morality of the use of performance-enhancing drugs, but that perhaps a substantial majority of those involved not only disfavor the use of performance enhancers but are repelled by the practice, we may want to give sports authorities the discretion to prohibit the use of performance enhancers if their best judgment supports such a policy. If sports authorities have reasonable grounds for making distinctions between impermissible performance-enhancing drugs and permissible diets, equipment changes and the like, and if they are not acting in an autocratic or dogmatic fashion, then even if no conclusive argument can be given for drawing the line in one particular place, their decision still has normative force. Official bodies, such as the NCAA or the International Olympic Committee, which have the responsibility of protecting the integrity of sport, arguably are preserving rather than limiting the domain in which we can interact as persons by prohibiting the use of drugs to enhance athletic performance. At the very least, our discussion suggests that although no conclusive argument may be available, reasons can be given for prohibiting the use of steroids as performance enhancers in sport and that, therefore, official governing bodies in sports have the authority to prohibit their use. Unless it can be shown that such decisions are arbitrary, dogmatic, or authoritarian, the fact that they are promulgated by legitimate governing bodies of sports gives them significant moral weight.[16] Rather than assigning the burden of proof to those who find the use of performance enhancers to be immoral, why not maintain instead that in cases where there is deep disagreement with the sports community itself, the decisions of the governing bodies of organized sports are morally binding where not unreasonable, undemocratic, or arbitrary?[17]

Moreover, there are lines of argument we have considered for prohibiting the use of performance-enhancing drugs which, while clearly not determinative, might well be strengthened by extended discussion and debate. First, it can be argued that either the use of such drugs by some athletes coerces others, or, if "coercion" does not strictly apply to such cases, wrongly imposes upon them the unhappy choice of competing under a significant handicap or risking serious injury. Second, it can be argued that the general use of performance enhancers would not be acceptable to athletes under suitably defined impartial conditions of choice. Finally, it can be argued that the use of performance-enhancing drugs arguably violates an important ethic of athletic competition.

None of these argument avoids serious objection, and each must be developed further if it is to withstand forceful criticisms, but it is far from clear that the objections are so decisive as to justify their total rejection. Perhaps they even are sufficient to at least vindicate the policies of those governing bodies of organized sports that prohibit the use of performance enhancers in their competitions, at least until the ethical issues involved are more satisfactorily resolved.

Enforcement

If the rules prohibiting the use of performance-enhancing drugs are to be effective, they must be enforced. Enforcement, however, raises a host of ethical issues. For example, drug use often can be detected by the use of urinalysis and other scientific tests, although some athletes have experimented with techniques designed to chemically disguise evidence of drug use. But assuming that tests often are effective, should athletes be *required* to take them? Does this amount to forcing users to incriminate themselves, violating constitutional guarantees against self-incrimination? Do drugs tests violate a right to privacy? Which methods of enforcement are ethical and which are not?

What is the principal ethical objection to requiring athletes to be tested for use of performance-enhancing substances? Clearly, it has to do with their liberty and privacy. One of the most cherished principles of Anglo-American law, and of the liberal political theories from which it derives, is that the presumption is on the authorities to prove the guilt of an individual. Individuals are to be left free and undisturbed unless a reasonable case can be made to show that particular persons are guilty of some infraction.

To see why this principle is so important, consider the alternative. Under a presumption of guilt, individuals could be detained, their homes searched, their lives disrupted simply because prosecutors decide they might find evidence of some infraction if they looked hard enough. Clearly, our liberty and our privacy would be minimal at best under such an arrangement. We would have them only to the extent that the authorities permitted us to keep them, which is to say we would not have them in any meaningful sense at all.

Requiring the individual to submit to drug tests seems to those concerned with our freedoms and liberties similar to requiring individuals to open their homes to searches, or to detaining individuals against their will, without there even being any evidence which, if it existed, might justify such intrusions. It was on such civil libertarian grounds that Stanford University swimmers challenged the constitutionality of NCAA regulations requiring athletes to submit to testing.[18] Accordingly, it seems that those of us committed to respect for the freedom of the individual must reject required testing of athletes for drug use.

But while this argument does have considerable force, it also may admit of exceptions. For example, shouldn't those persons directly responsible for the safety of others be required to show that they are not under the influence of mind-altering drugs while at work? Airline pilots, railroad engineers, surgeons, police officers, and firefighters are among those with special obligations to care for the safety of others. Accordingly, requiring them to take drug tests seems to be an exception permitted even by Mill's Harm Principle, since its purpose is to prevent direct injury to others.

This line of argument, it must be conceded, can be extended by gradual steps until it becomes dangerously broad in scope. Thus, although loss of worker efficiency due to drug use is a major national problem, could we justify required testing of all workers in order to prevent harm to fellow workers and to consumers?[19] What happens to our civil liberties then?

Although we cannot pursue this important question in depth here, we ought not to be driven down the slippery slope too quickly. Although drug use on the job by some workers may lead to indirect injury of consumers, lines can be drawn. The greater the threat of harm, the more serious the kind of harm at stake, and the more directly it is attendant upon drug use, then the greater the case for required testing. In most cases, the threat of harm will be sufficiently indirect or weak, or other methods of protection and detection will be available. It is doubtful, then, that making exceptions to the general principle of noninterference in cases of direct and serious harm to individuals will undermine civil liberties generally.

Is there another kind of exception that might apply to organized athletics? After all, unlike the case of airline pilots who use drugs, athletes who take steroids do not directly endanger the general public.

Perhaps the idea of a collection of individuals *voluntarily* taking part in a joint activity requiring the mutual observance of common rules applies here. Thus, in professional baseball, an umpire has the right to require a pitcher to empty his pockets so the umpire can check that the player is not carrying special prohibited substances which, when applied to the baseball, can alter its flight, making it more difficult to hit. Off the field, the umpire would have no right to search the player but does have such a right in the special context of the game. This is because the game is fair only if all players observe the same rules. The umpire, with the consent of the competing teams, is charged with enforcing the rules, thereby insuring a fair contest. As a result, the umpire *qua* umpire acquires rights he does not have as an ordinary citizen. The civil rights of the players, for example, the right to be free from unreasonable searches, have in effect been waived or limited in the context of the game because the players have committed themselves to accepting its rules and the enforcement procedures the rules provide.

A similar argument can be applied to testing for the use of performance-enhancing drugs in organized athletics. Participants consent to playing by publically acknowledged rules, such as the rule prohibiting the use of steroids and other performance enhancers. No one is forced to participate, but once consent is given to participation, players are owed protection from those who would intentionally violate the rules for their own advantage. Without enforcement, no protection would be provided. In particular, if effective means of detection were not used, athletes would suspect each other of breaking the existing rules by taking performance-enhancing drugs. Pressures would exist to use such drugs illegally in order to remain competitive.

Because participants voluntarily agree to participate and because they agree to play under the assumption that the rules will be applied fairly to all, they are owed protection against violators.[20] Drug testing of athletes, on this view, seems not a violation of their civil rights but a reasonable protection against being unfairly disadvantaged. To the extent that requiring athletes to submit to drug tests can be defended, it is because each participant in sports is entitled to play under the public conditions specifying the rules of the contest. If umpires in baseball can enforce such an entitlement by requiring pitchers to reveal if they are carrying illegal substances that can alter the flight of the ball, why don't sports authorities have a similar justification for drug testing to ensure that advantages prohibited by the rules are not obtained through ingestion of illegal substances of a different kind?

Conclusion

Our discussion in this chapter has explored important lines of argument for and against the view that the use of performance-enhancing drugs in sports is immoral. Although arguments for different positions on these issues need to be defended further in the forums of critical inquiry, our examination provides provisional but not conclusive support for a prohibition on the use of such drugs and supports drug testing as a principal means of detection and enforcement in certain kinds of cases. Critics of the use of steroids and other performance enhancers no doubt will wish for an even stronger verdict on their behalf. Perhaps such a verdict will be justified by further critical reflection on the issues we have discussed. However, as we have seen, there are important criticisms of the arguments for prohibiting steroid use, not all of which have yet been answered satisfactorily. In the meantime, while debate continues, rules prohibiting the use of steroids in competition in organized sports can be defended as permissible since they have not been shown to be arbitrary, unreasonable, or illegitimately imposed. To covertly violate those rules solely to gain a competitive advantage seems unjustifiable, whether or not the rules themselves ultimately should be revised.

5

Equality and Excellence in Sports

In Chapters 2, 3, and 4, an attempt has been made to develop, defend, and apply an ethic of competition in sports and athletics. In the next three chapters, our focus will shift from examination of ethical principles that should regulate competition in sports to an examination of the rights and responsibilities of participants. In this chapter, we will consider questions of just distribution in sports. Are there fundamental rights to share in the benefits of participation in sports? Does everyone, or at least everyone interested in playing, have a right to participate? Does the greater athletic ability of some entitle them to greater rewards, or at least more playing time, than others? In addressing these and related questions, issues involving the scope and nature of rights, the significance of equality, and the meaning of equity and social justice will face us. These questions will not only force us to confront issues of fairness and social justice in sports, but broader issues about the just and equitable society as well.

Throughout our discussion, it has been argued that competition in sports is not only ethical but also valuable when it involves a mutual quest for excellence among competitors. However, we have not yet considered issues of access to competitive sports, and distribution of the benefits and burdens of participation. In particular, do individuals have *rights* to participate in sports and to share in the benefits that participation promotes? Do communities have obligations to provide athletic facilities, such as swimming pools, so such rights to participation can be implemented? Are individuals entitled only to the use of whatever athletic facilities they can purchase on the open market? Are special rewards and opportunities that go to the athletically talented justified or are they in violation of justifiable norms of equal treatment?   *equality.*

Each of these questions involves the concept of *equality*. Do individuals have equal claims to participate in sports and share in the benefits? What significance should be attached to inequalities of talent and motivation? What are the requirements of equality in sports?

93

Although equality of treatment has to do with sameness or identity of treatment, there are different conceptions of the ways in which people ought to be treated identically.[1] "Equality," for example, can refer to the negative requirement that we should not discriminate on grounds of race, sex, and religion, or to the positive requirement that we should provide fair background opportunities, such as equivalent educational facilities, so that we all have a fair chance of developing our potential. "Equality," some would argue, requires us to show the same respect and concern for all, but others might maintain that in addition, it implies that everyone should receive an identical share of some burden or benefit. Accordingly, although the concept of equal treatment can be explicated in terms of identity or sameness of treatment, there are different conceptions of how the idea of identical treatment is to be understood.

There is a tendency to identify equal treatment with just, fair, or equitable treatment. However, it is important to keep in mind that since there are different conceptions of equality, as well as different theories of justice, fairness, and equity, mere verbal agreement that equality is a good thing may hide deep disagreement on substance. Two individuals may both claim to favor equality, but if all one means by equality is nondiscrimination and the other understands equality as meaning an identical division of resources, they are in radical disagreement over what social structures ought to be implemented. Moreover, unequal treatment is not always unjust or unfair. An instructor, for example normally should grade work of unequal merit unequally, giving the higher grade to the work of higher merit. In spite of the tendency to equate them, equal treatment is not always fair, just, or equitable treatment.

Questions about equality arise in sports as well as in other social contexts. In particular, three separate questions about equality will be pursued in this chapter:

1. Do individuals have rights to participate in sports and to the benefits such participation provides?
2. Should more equal participation in sports be a goal of sports policy in America?
3. Is it unjust to treat people unequally in sports on the basis of their unequal athletic ability?

Sports and Social Justice

In his provocative and readable book, *Sports in America*, James Michener argues that our society lavishes far too much attention on the star athlete at the expense of the ordinary person. According to Michener, "we place an undue emphasis on the gifted athletes fifteen to twenty-two, a preposterous emphasis on a few professionals aged twenty-three to thirty-five, and never enough on the mass of our population aged twenty-three to seventy-five."[2] Michener proposed instead that "the goals of American sports must be to provide every man or woman an equitable opportunity to develop his or her skills to the maximum capacity."[3]

There is much to be said for the charge of overemphasis on the performance of a highly talented elite. Top professional sports stars receive far more in salary than nurses, researchers, scientists, university presidents, and even the president of the United States. Large universities often devote far more resources to their intercollegiate varsity athletic programs than to providing a sound program of physical education for the majority of their students. At the high school and even elementary school level, greater attention may be spent on developing the skills of top athletes than to insuring that the greater number of students learn to enjoy participation in sports or to achieve good physical conditioning. Even in organized children's sports, the best young players often receive the most playing time at the most desirable positions while many less talented youngsters spend a disproportionate amount of time watching from the bench.

The result seems to be that in spite of a much publicized fitness boom, most Americans do not get sufficient exercise for good health. Moreover, rates of participation in some form of exercise or athletics may well vary along socioeconomic lines. As observers have noted, the current emphasis on jogging and exercise may be largely a middle-class and upper-class phenomenon.[4]

The costs of lack of fitness are both personal and social. Roughly one out of five American males has a heart attack by age sixty, a much higher rate than for most of the rest of the world. Although the statistics are better for women, many experts believe lack of exercise can contribute to heart attacks in females as well as males. Even though physicians disagree about just what causes many ailments, there does seem to be widespread agreement that lack of proper exercise can contribute to the inception and severity of many illnesses.

Moreover, participation in sports can contribute to the enjoyment of life in a variety of ways other than through direct effects on health. For example, studies of female athletes suggest that such women have a more positive self-image and a greater sense of well-being than nonathletes.[5] Perhaps most important, there is the pleasure of athletic activity itself, which too many of us only rarely experience in the daily course of our lives.

In the passage quoted earlier, James Michener suggests that America should have a *policy* towards sports. In particular, that policy should be one of encouraging mass participation in sports and athletics. Instead of overemphasizing rewards for the athletically talented elite, we should focus on involving a greater number of people in enjoyable and healthy athletic activity. Let us examine some of the implications of this claim.

What Michener leaves unclear is whether he believes our sports practices are merely *less good* than they ought to be, perhaps because they produce less benefit for the overall population than possible, or whether they are *unjust* in that they violate individual rights or entitlements. It is important to distinguish questions of individual rights and social justice, on one hand, from questions concerning what is desirable social policy, on the other. An injustice involves violation of a central facet of individual concern, personhood, or individual right, and therefore *wrongs* the victim in some particularly significant manner. Accordingly, an injustice is not morally tolerable even if it benefits the greatest number. Rather, justice, and the individual rights it protects, limits the methods we may use in pursuing overall social benefits. Thus, it normally would be wrong, because it is unjust, to discriminate against an unpopular minority even if such a policy produced the overall greatest good for the greatest number. As one writer has put it, rights function as political trumps that individuals can play to protect their fundamental concerns against encroachment, even when such encroachment is favored by the majority.[6]

Is Michener, in criticizing current emphasis on an athletic elite, making a claim about social justice and individual rights or is he making a claim about desirable social policy? Is he arguing that greater participation and more equality in sports is desirable because it would produce many benefits, such as a healthier and happier work force? Or is he implying that individuals have rights to participate in and benefit from sports and that a society which does not honor those rights is unjust? Michener himself, as we noted, is not explicit as to which claim he is making, but the difference is crucial. Although it is undesirable for a society to be inefficient, it is wrong, except perhaps in extreme emergencies, for it to fail to rectify injustice. Is sports policy in America seriously unjust?

Equality and Freedom in Sports

Basic and Scarce Benefits

What benefits arise from sports? Do all individuals have equal rights to such benefits? If not, how should the benefits be distributed?

It is useful to begin with a distinction suggested by Jane English, in her article "Sex Equality in Sports." English suggests that we distinguish the *basic benefits* of participation in sports from the *scarce benefits*. Basic benefits are available to all participants and their possession by some does not preclude their possession by others. Among such basic benefits are "health, the self-respect to be gained from doing one's best, the cooperation to be learned from working with teammates and the incentive to be gained from having opponents, the 'character' of learning to be a good loser and a good winner, the chance to improve one's skills and learn to accept criticism—and just plain fun." [7]

Scarce benefits, on the other hand, cannot be equally available to all. Their possession by some at least tends to preclude equal possession by others. The principal scarce goods of sports are fame and fortune. If everyone is equally well known or has equal wealth, then no one is famous or wealthy. Fame and fortune, by their very nature, are comparative. [8]

When Michener and other writers complain that sports in America overemphasize the achievements of an athletic elite, they can be read as claiming that the basic benefits of sports should be more widely distributed. In examining this claim, let us first consider whether individuals have rights to the basic benefits. If so, a society that does not provide such benefits to its citizens when it is able to do so is unjust.

Rights and Basic Benefits

Do all individuals have equal rights to the basic benefits of participation in sports?[9] Such a view seems at least initially plausible. Unequal merit might entitle better athletes to special rewards, but it does not seem to entitle them to extra shares of the basic benefits. Top players do not deserve to have more fun or better health simply because of their superior skills or performance in athletics.

However, before agreeing too quickly that all individuals have equal rights to the basic benefits, we had better consider just what having a right entails. Although philosophers disagree on the precise details about how rights are to be analyzed, there is wide agreement that rights impose obligations on others. For example, if I have a right to speak freely on a college campus, others have an obligation not to interfere with the legitimate exercise of my right. Similarly, if I have a right to adequate medical care, some person(s) or organization(s), such as the state, must be under an obligation to provide me with the required care. Thus, to understand the force of a rights claim, it is crucial to understand what obligations it imposes and upon whom the obligations are imposed. Even though rights normally are a benefit to the bearer, they may impose significant burdens on others.

Rights also may be understood *negatively* or *positively*. Understood as a negative right, the right to the basic benefits of sports requires only that people be left alone to pursue such benefits for themselves if they so desire. Negative rights obligate others only to refrain from interfering with our pursuit of the basic goods. Positive obligations, such as the obligation to pay taxes for construction and support of recreational facilities, are not imposed by negative rights.

If we interpret the right to the basic benefits of sports as a negative right, it is relatively uncontroversial. It would be only a special instance of our general right to liberty. That right obligates others only to refrain from interfering with legitimate exercises of our freedom; namely, it protects our free acts that do not violate the rights of others. But although such a right is relatively uncontroversial, it also is relatively undemanding. It obligates us only to leave others alone. As such, it provides little basis for the criticism of sports in America because it demands so little of us. The alleged negative right to the basic benefits of sports is simply the liberty to pursue them. It does not require either that anyone actually attain the benefits or that others help us do so.

However, the claim that individuals have a right to the basic benefits of sports can be understood in a different and more controversial way. On this second interpretation, it may impose positive obligations on others to actually provide the basic benefits to the rights bearer. If we construe the right to basic benefits as a positive right, we cannot say we are honoring it just by leaving others alone. Rather, we must be doing something specific to promote their actual enjoyment of the basic benefits. This is an important point for, as we will see, it is all too easy to use the rhetoric of positive rights while forgetting that such rights can impose onerous costs on others. This point is one foundation of the political position known as libertarianism.

Rights and Liberties

What sort of costs would the implementation of the positive right to the basic benefits of sports impose on others? Consider, for example, one of the basic benefits cited by Jane English, namely, the incentive to be gained from having opponents. Clearly, if one has a positive right to such a good, then someone else must have an obligation to serve as an opponent. But surely opponents are persons in their own right who should be left free to decide whom they wish to play against or whether they wish to play at all. A similar point applies to the alleged right to participate with coaches and teammates. They too are persons who cannot be "drafted" simply to please others. Here we need to keep in mind Robert Nozick's important reminder that "the major objection to speaking of everyone having a right *to* various things . . . is that these 'rights' require a substructure of things and materials and actions; and *other* people may have rights and entitlements over these."[10]

Carried to what many would regard as an unjustifiable extreme, this criticism of positive rights evolves into a position known as libertarianism. According to libertarianism, interference with the liberty of others is morally prohibited, except when necessary to preserve the right to liberty itself. Accordingly, while the libertarian accepts the police functions of the state, which are held to be necessary for the protection of negative liberty, libertarians reject the welfare state. In their view, such a state is an example of Orwell's Big Brother. It constantly interferes with our liberty to control our property by using the tax system to force us to benefit others.

Robert Nozick has used his widely discussed Wilt Chamberlain example to illustrate the libertarian complaint against redistribution of resources for purposes of securing a favored pattern of benefits, such as equality, throughout society. According to this example, we are to suppose that goods have already been redistributed throughout society according to whatever pattern of ideal justice we individually happen to favor. For example, we may suppose that goods have been distributed equally among all individuals. Suppose further that a talented athlete, such as former basketball star Wilt Chamberlain, sets up a series of professional games. Wilt is to get $.25 out of every $1.00 paid for admission, while the other players agree to split what remains. It turns out that 1,000,000 people turn out to see the games. Wilt becomes $250,000 richer, the other players profit somewhat less, and each spectator loses a quarter. As a result, the initial pattern of redistribution is shattered.

What is the point of this example? According to Nozick,

> the general point illustrated by the . . . example . . . is that no . . . distributional patterned principle of justice can be continuously realized without continuous interference with people's lives. . . . To maintain a pattern, one must either continually interfere to stop people from transferring resources as they wish to, or continually (or periodically) interfere to take from some persons resources that others . . . wish to transfer to them. [11]

Applied to sports, the Chamberlain example can be cited in support of the claim that implementation of rights to the basic benefits interferes unduly with the liberty of others.

Objections to Libertarianism

Is libertarianism an acceptable political philosophy? This question raises issues going well beyond the arena of sports, so a brief examination of some of the major issues facing libertarianism will help us focus more sharply on issues raised by rights claims to basic benefits of sports. Two central criticisms of libertarianism are particularly relevant to our inquiry. First, it is far from clear that either the Chamberlain example or Nozick's warning about the limitations of positive rights are sufficient to justify libertarianism. Secondly, as we will see, there is reason for believing that the libertarian rejection of positive rights is unjustifiably arbitrary, given the values of the libertarians themselves. Let us consider each point in turn.

A critic of libertarianism need not concede the force of the Chamberlain example. Such a critic can argue, with justification, that the example shows, at most, that maintaining a rigid distributional *pattern* requires continuous interference with individual liberty. But a proponent of the welfare state, who believes in positive rights to health care, welfare, education, and the like, need not support the implementation of such a rigid pattern. For example, one might hold that there are positive rights to the goods and services necessary for a minimally decent standard of living, but also maintain that as long as no one falls below such a welfare floor or safety net, other goods may be distributed according to individual choice within a free market. The tax system could then be used to keep the safety net in place but not to preserve any rigid distributional pattern across society.

Libertarians might reply that even preserving the safety net might involve appropriation of property to which other people have a right. Such appropriation would be unjust, in their view, since it would violate the entitlements of others. As we have already seen, no athlete can have a right to an opponent, for potential opponents have rights to determine for themselves whether and with whom they wish to compete.

However, even if this point applies to alleged rights to opponents in sports, it may not apply to *all* positive rights claims. The libertarian is not entitled to simply *assume* that every positive rights claims violates the entitlements of someone else. On the contrary, if some positive rights claims are justified, others are not entitled to everything they may possess but have obligations to contribute to the support of others. Thus, even if we have no right to a tennis opponent, we may have a right to a decent diet or to basic education. The libertarian may be correct to point out that some positive rights claims ought to be rejected because they intrude too greatly on the liberty of others, but it remains to be seen whether all positive rights claims can be rejected on such grounds.

Indeed, upon reflection, we may reject the libertarian's claim that the only fundamental moral rights are negative ones. In fact, the very same reasons that may lead us to postulate negative rights may also support positive rights claims as well. For example, negative rights to liberty from interference by others seem important because we view persons as centers of autonomy, entitled to make their own choices about how their lives should be lived. We don't believe rational, autonomous agents should be viewed as mere resources to be exploited for the benefit of the majority. Negative rights protect persons from such exploitation by insuring each of us a sphere of noninterference that others are prohibited from violating.

But if negative rights are necessary to preserve the independence and autonomy of persons, positive rights also may be needed to perform a similar function. How autonomous or independent can one be without an adequate diet, shelter, or education? Isn't it arbitrary, then, for the libertarian to accept negative rights as protections for the autonomy and integrity of persons but reject *all* positive rights, even though some positive rights might perform the very same function?

Again, the libertarian might reply that there is a crucial difference between positive and negative rights, namely, positive rights infringe on the liberty of others but negative rights do not. But even leaving aside the point made earlier, that if there are legitimate positive rights, enforcement of them does not *illegitimately* transfer resources from others, there is a further difficulty with this libertarian reply. To see this, consider that any libertarian, except perhaps libertarians who happen to be anarchists, concedes that the state might provide police protection to protect the safety of its citizens and a judicial system to fairly try and punish criminals. But in order to do this, the state must tax its citizens to support the police and the courts. So even the libertarian acknowledges that the just state must do more than merely leave its citizens alone. In addition, the good citizen has an obligation to provide a fair share of resources necessary to support the police and judicial functions of the state. But if the citizen can permissibly be taxed to support such functions, why can't the citizen permissibly also be taxed to support other state functions that also are necessary for the development of independent and autonomous citizens, such as provision of basic public education?[12]

Although a much fuller examination of these points would be necessary to justify an outright rejection of libertarianism, our discussion indicates at least that libertarianism faces significant difficulties. However, even if the objections to libertarianism that we have considered were decisive, we still could not conclude, without additional argument, that individuals have fundamental rights to the basic benefits of sports. Just because we may have some positive rights, it does not follow that

rights to the basic benefits are among them. Such rights may be too intrusive of the liberty of others. So even if libertarianism is not fully
acceptable as a political philosophy, libertarian objections that specific
rights to the basic benefits of sports intrude too greatly on the individual
may have considerable force. Accordingly, while we probably cannot
appeal to libertarian arguments to rule out all claims to positive rights,
the kinds of worries libertarians raise about some positive rights claims
being too intrusive on the rights of others do need to be taken seriously
where claims to entitlements to the basic benefits of sports are at issue.

Rights and Possibilities

There is a second difficulty with the idea of rights to the basic benefits
of sports. Some basic benefits, such as good health or fun, are not fully
or perhaps even largely subject to social control. Thus, it is not always
possible to provide health for all of us, for we all age and eventually die.
Moreover, whether we have fun due to our participation in sports may
depend as much upon our own personality and character as upon the
contribution of others. In addition, there are also limits of reasonableness of what others are expected to provide. If Jones is habitually mo-
rose, but Smith could get Jones to have fun playing tennis if she devoted
virtually all her time to trying, it does not follow Smith is obligated to
make such an heroic effort. Even if Jones does have a positive right to the
basic benefits of sport, including fun, it does not follow that others are
required to go to unreasonable lengths to carry out their responsibilities.
Others cannot be obligated to provide us with what is beyond their
control and should not be required to make heroic sacrifices to provide
us with the benefits of sport. Their obligations, and hence the extent of
any positive rights we might have, are limited both by what is possible
and by what reasonably may be required.

Rights and Opportunities

In view of these objections, should we give up the claim that there are
fundamental moral rights to the basic benefits of sports? Not necessarily.
Perhaps we should follow the wording suggested by Michener and
speak of equal *opportunity* to acquire the basic benefits rather than a right
to the benefits themselves. The right to equal opportunity, as understood
here, is more than the right to negative liberty. One can have the liberty
to fly from Boston to San Francisco if no one will interfere but have no
real opportunity to do so if no flights are available. A right to opportu-

nity differs from a negative liberty in that it may impose positive obligations on others, but it is less demanding than a right to positive liberty, since it does not require others to actually provide goods and services to us. Perhaps the right to the basic benefits of sports can best be understood as an opportunity right.

The exact content of such a right will surely be controversial, but one way to unpack the right which seems plausible is to require schools at a minimum to introduce children and young adults to the value of exercise, to promote fitness, to teach "carry over" sports such as tennis, golf, and swimming, which can be pursued for a lifetime, and generally to introduce students to the positive values of participation in sports. The emphasis in such physical education programs would not be on producing future star athletes but in giving each child a significant chance to strive for fitness through participation in some level of sport. Unfortunately, many school districts actually have cut back on physical education. Some of the remaining physical education programs, perhaps in an attempt to be attractive to the physically unfit, have tended to emphasize recreation rather than fitness. For example, one school attracted national attention when it was learned that its curriculum allowed students to play pinochle in physical education class.[13]

Critics might point out that rights to minimal levels of basic benefits need not be construed to include physical education programs in the schools, and in any case might clash with other, more important, priorities, such as provision of adequate salaries for teachers or purchasing needed science equipment. Nevertheless, if we do take rights to basic benefits seriously, physical education programs in the schools seem a reasonable place to begin implementing them, and need not be regarded as frills, the content of which is of no significant concern to the community.

A right to equal opportunity to secure the basic benefits might also require communities to provide such minimal facilities as parks, playgrounds, jogging paths, basketball courts, and ball fields. Understood somewhat more extensively, the right might require establishment of more elaborate facilities such as public swimming pools, tennis courts, and golf courses.

However, there may be grounds for refusing to extend opportunity rights quite so far. The more extensive such rights are, the greater the burden they impose on others. Even if we grant the existence of some positive rights, it can be argued that not even a relatively affluent society is *unjust* if it fails to provide public golf courses, swimming pools, and other amenities. People who want such facilities often will be able to pay for them themselves. Those who have no interest in sports will object that they should not be required to subsidize the play of those who do.

Before we accept such an argument, however, we need to remember that we already tax the public to support museums and libraries, even though some taxpayers never use such facilities themselves. If one point of living in communities is to collectively provide elements of the good life that we cannot always provide for ourselves, why can't as strong a case be made for provision of public athletic facilities as for provision of cultural ones? After all, such facilities promote health, a positive self-image, and expression of our status as persons through athletic competition.

Perhaps it would help to return to the distinction made earlier between the question of whether people have a *right* to opportunities to secure the basic benefits and the question of whether it is *good policy* to provide them with the basic benefits. We can then argue that perhaps there is an opportunity right to such minimally decent facilities for participation in sports as jogging paths, playgrounds and parks, and good physical education programs in the schools. These minimal facilities provide people with an opportunity to secure the basic benefits of participation for themselves, without imposing basic burdens on others. Provision of more extensive facilities can be regarded as an amenity, which may or may not be provided by various local communities as their members decide. Ideally, those who strongly object to being taxed to support what they regard as amenities should have the choice of moving to communities that don't provide them. Then, those who regard more extensive athletic and recreational facilities as significant elements of the good life can move to communities of like-minded people, without imposing their conception of the good on those who do not share it. (In practice, providing people with genuine opportunities to exercise such choice might require social progress in a variety of areas, including alleviation of poverty and expansion of employment opportunities.)

Why should we think there is any opportunity right to basic benefits of sports in the first place? Even if there are some positive moral rights, such as rights to education, welfare, or adequate medical care, what makes the alleged right to the basic benefits fundamental enough to be regarded as a basic moral entitlement? If we regard fundamental moral rights as entitlements necessary to guarantee those conditions under which we can develop and express our nature as persons, a plausible case can be made that minimally construed opportunity rights to the basic benefits of sports are among such basic moral commodities. For one thing, the exercise and relaxation such opportunities provide may be a prerequisite of good health for many people. More important, sports provides an especially accessible area where we can develop and express our status as persons. As we have seen, athletic competition, and participation in sports generally, provides a framework within which we can develop and express character and react to the choices and character of others. Finally, opportunities to participate in sports are a significant element of a minimally decent human life. Play, and particularly play in the context of sport, arguably is too important a part of a minimally decent human life to be left entirely to the private market for support.

Has the importance of sports been overemphasized by such remarks? Don't music and the arts, education, and a variety of other activities also provide practices through which we can develop and express ourselves as persons? The answer clearly is that they do. But while this reminder is well taken, it does not take away from the point that sports also play an important role in such an enterprise, one that is special because sports provide a common framework for men and women of all ages, with different ethnic, social, and religious backgrounds, and from different economic classes.

To summarize our discussion so far, although the libertarian is correct to warn us against inflating the notion of positive rights, libertarian arguments are not strong enough to show that all positive rights claims are ungrounded. Given a case for some positive fundamental moral rights, a plausible case can be made for including minimal opportunity rights to the basic benefits of sports among them. Even if such a case cannot be made, the libertarian fails to show that it is impermissible for communities to voluntarily provide opportunities to secure the basic benefits to their citizens, even where provision of relatively expensive facilities such as public golf courses and recreational centers are at issue. Even if people are not entitled to such extensive facilities as a matter of right, the good community may provide them as it wishes, just as it provides museums, libraries, and cultural centers as well. Thus, while the libertarian's a priori rejection of all positive moral rights seems too extreme, the claim that people have a basic right to all the basic benefits of sports may also be too extreme, confusing what the ideal society might choose to provide with what the reasonably just society is obligated to provide. But provision of minimal opportunities to acquire the basic benefits may be required by social justice, and more extensive opportunities to benefits from participation in sports may be important constituents of the good life that we might want our community to help us secure.

Equality Versus Excellence in Sports

Our discussion so far suggests either that every individual has a fundamental moral right to minimally decent opportunities to participate in sports or, if such a rights claim cannot be justified, that the good society should provide such opportunities, and perhaps more extensive facilities as well. Such a conclusion can be justified by appeal to each individual's claim to a minimally decent level of human existence, which includes opportunities to develop healthy living habits and to express basic human capacities and talents. Even though it is debatable how extensive opportunities to participate must be, afflue... societies surely have greater responsibilities in this area than do less developed ones.

The opportunities in question involve chances to acquire basic benefits of sports. However, in addition to the *basic* benefits, there also are *scarce* benefits, such as fame and fortune. In our society, these scarce benefits go disproportionately to the talented and highly motivated.

To many, this unequal distribution of the scarce benefits seems almost self-evidently fair and just. After all, who should get the greatest rewards but the best and hardest working individuals among us? But although such a view probably commands widespread support, it hardly is free from significant criticism.

In the discussion that follows, two different sorts of criticism need to be distinguished. The first, suggested in the passage quoted from Michener, appeals to the alleged *bad consequences* of adulation of an athletic elite. These include discouragement of the less talented, a resulting drop in participation, a less healthy population, a lower level of satisfaction throughout society than might otherwise be achieved, and reinforcement of harmful inegalitarian status distinctions between high and low achievers. In other words, one line of criticism is that unequal distribution of the scarce benefits to an athletically talented elite lacks social utility.

The second kind of criticism is that the practice of unequally rewarding an athletically talented elite is not merely undesirable, but is positively *unjust*. For example, some writers have argued that it is unjust to reward individuals for gifts and talents with which they were born and for which they deserve no credit.

It will be useful to begin our discussion with consideration of organized sports for children. The critique of athletic elitism has considerable force in such a context. Whether it also has such force where higher levels of competition are at issue remains to be seen. But if it has weaknesses, even at the level of sports for children, these weaknesses also are likely to be even greater where discussions of interscholastic, intercollegiate, and professional athletics are of concern.

Should John and Jane Warm the Bench?

According to many critics of such organized sports for children as Little League Baseball and Pop Warner Football, too much emphasis is placed on the performance of the superior players and not enough on equal participation. Critics maintain that an overemphasis by parents and coaches on winning puts far too much pressure on young children. Because adults want to win, they assign highly skilled youngsters to the more demanding positions and give them the bulk of their coaching. Younger, smaller, and less skilled players spend a disproportionate part of the season watching from the bench. When they do play, they seldom are given a chance to fill key roles or positions.   *never improve*

As a result, it is charged that talented and untalented youngsters alike suffer harm, or at best derive fewer benefits from participation than would be possible otherwise. Less mature youngsters do not receive an adequate opportunity to develop skills, which might eventually come to surpass those of early bloomers if only given a chance to develop. Even worse, bench warmers may become so discouraged or humiliated that they lose interest in participating in sports or develop an actual fear of participation, and never experience the basic benefits that participation in sports might provide. On the other hand, the more skilled and developed children can be placed under pressure too great for them to handle. Sports, under such circumstances, can cease to be play and turn into work, carried on mainly to please adults. Young players may "freeze up," trying to avoid making mistakes in front of parents and other spectators, rather than enjoying the competition or working on improving skills. No wonder that a number of professional athletes have warned against overemphasis on competition and winning in organized children's sports.

This critique has considerable merit. The overbearing Little League parent and the coach who makes inappropriate demands of children have become national stereotypes. However, the criticism can also be exaggerated. National organizations, such as Little League, as well as parents' groups, have become aware of the dangers of excessive competition for children, and many have instituted rules requiring participation for all children (although not necessarily *equal* participation).

Rather than debate exactly how much competition for children is too much, a question about which reasonable people can be expected to disagree, it will be more useful to clarify some of the conflicting values at stake in children's sports so that coaches, officials, parents, and youngsters can make more informed decisions on their own.

We already have discussed some of the dangers of overemphasis on competition and winning in children's sports. However, some of the critics of competition tend to go to the opposite extreme and advocate complete equality of participation along with complete deemphasis of achievement and competition. Because they fear the effects of overemphasis, they recommend virtually disregarding differences in athletic ability and achievement. We will consider an admittedly extreme version of such a view, for we can gain an appreciation of the value of competition and achievement, even at the level of children's sports, if we consider what sports might be like in their absence.

Although the suggestion that every youngster in organized children's sports should have an *identical* chance to play may seem attractive, because it appears to give every child an equal chance to attain the basic benefits, it can be seen upon reflection to have significant weaknesses. For example, in baseball, not every child is physically capable of playing all positions. It would be dangerous to assign a child who has difficulty even catching the ball to the position of catcher or first baseman. If a child with no control was made pitcher, every batter would walk while fielders could avoid boredom only by chasing butterflies.

There are also more subtle difficulties with the position we are considering. Thus, we need to consider the well-being of the athletically skilled child as well as those of the beginner or the less talented player. Just as academically gifted children may need special challenges in the classroom if their capacities are to be developed to the maximum, athletically gifted children may need special challenges on the playing field. In both academics and athletics, it would seem inappropriate to treat more talented individuals as if their special abilities did not exist or were of no significance.

It also is important to remember that sports are more than mere exercise. In particular, standards of skillful performance have special weight in sports that they do not have in exercise. An important part of learning to enjoy and appreciate sports is to learn to recognize and appreciate acts of skill by players. To the extent that identical treatment requires us to pretend that differences in skill and excellence do not exist, it requires us to ignore qualities that should be recognized and appreciated. If this point is sound, one of the major goals of participation in sports for children should be not only to teach skills and encourage future participation but also to develop the kind of appreciation of excellence that will promote enjoyment of sports throughout a lifetime for both players and spectators alike.

Proponents of identical levels of participation for all might reply that equal participation does not actually require that we ignore differences in skill, only that all players get equal chances regardless of their differences in skill. However, if one of the goals of participation should be to promote skillful play and to teach appreciation of it, it is important that some emphasis be given to athletic success. Sometimes it is important that the most skilled players learn to play together and to test their talents against those of the opposition, and it may be of benefit to all children that they be encouraged to do so.

Thus, equal respect for each child does not require that each child be treated identically in sports. On the contrary, equal respect for individuals will often require recognition of and appropriate response to individual differences. Critics are quite right to reject a dominant emphasis on winning and development of star athletes in organized children's sports. But the other extreme, which denies the importance of recognizing and responding to different degrees of excellence also goes too far. Rather, the adult who works with children in sports will have to show sensitivity and ability to weigh the many competing values at stake. As in many other areas of moral complexity, the trick is to do justice to a variety of often conflicting values, rather than to assign exclusive weight to any one, whether it be winning or identity of treatment, at the expense of the other values that also apply.

A Nation of Spectators

We have seen that while Michener's warning about overemphasis on an athletic elite is well taken, particularly where children's sports are concerned, it should not be taken so far as to lead to identical treatment of different individuals or to submerge concern for excellence in performance. A second aspect of Michener's position, although also worth considering, can be taken too far as well.

Thus, the line of criticism suggested by Michener that we are a nation of spectators rather than participants needs to be considered. Critics of American sports point out that millions of us spend our weekends glued to the television screen, watching football, baseball, or golf rather than playing a sport ourselves. Moreover, most of us watch sports in relative isolation, as networks such as ESPN bring more and more major games into our homes, rather than in the communal setting of a local high school game. The time devoted to observing sports rather than participating in them is seen by critics as unfortunate, not only because of ill effects on the health of those who only sit and watch, but also because spectators miss out on the other basic benefits of participation. According to this view, the true result of the "star" system is to drive people from participation on the playing field to the grandstand, or more often the living room couch, instead.

Is this aspect of the critique of American sports justified? Note that it rests on at least two hidden assumptions, neither of which is clearly correct.

First, it is assumed that watching sports tends to preclude participation; that spectators tend not to play precisely because they are spectators. But this assumption hardly is obvious.

In fact, it is far from clear that being a fan has a negative effect on participation. On the contrary, many fans, particularly youngsters, may be motivated to try to emulate the moves of the successful athletes they see on television. What schoolyard basketball player has not tried to copy the moves of a Michael Jordan or a Dr. J? Similarly, fans, particularly in such sports as tennis and golf, often watch top players in order to observe the techniques of the best professionals in order to apply them to their own games. In such cases, watching sports events may promote participation rather than lowering it. In essence, stars such as Jack Nicklaus and Steffi Graf not only are watched but also are imitated.

What about the fan who is not a participant? Here we must be careful not to jump to the conclusion that such individuals are not participants *because* they are fans. Perhaps they wouldn't be participants even if they weren't fans. Maybe they enjoy watching skilled performers but would not be motivated to play themselves even if there were no top athletes to watch. Or perhaps there are inadequate facilities for participation in their area, as is the case for many golfers in metropolitan areas. Accordingly, the simple assumption that emphasis on big-time sports and on the skills of an athletic elite reduces mass participation is, at the very least, open to serious question.

A second assumption about the relationship between participation in sports and watching sports is open to even more serious question. According to this second assumption, being a participant in sports is of greater value than being a spectator. Playing is better than watching. In its most extreme form, this view characterizes watching sporting events as a passive, almost slothful activity, requiring minimal intellectual and emotional capacities. The stereotype of the beer-drinking, overweight football fan who spends the whole weekend in front of the television set watching games expresses the disdain in which mere fans sometimes are held.

This second assumption also is questionable. First of all, none of us can participate in everything. Most of us are spectators of some practice or other; sports, music, and dance come immediately to mind. After all, we don't sneer at spectators, commonly known as audiences, at the ballet or theater, even though few members of the audience are also participants in the activities they are observing.

Moreover, spectators of sports, like audiences in other areas, are often called upon to exercise critical judgment and apply standards of excellence. Consider, for example, a fine double play executed at a crucial point in a pressure-packed baseball game. An observer unacquainted with baseball might appreciate the grace and fluidity of the players' movements. However, such a spectator could not see the movements as examples of excellence at baseball. To such an uninformed spectator, a botched double play would be indistinguishable from a well-executed one, since the failure of the fielder to, say, touch second base would be unappreciated.

Thus, it is unclear that watching games is of less value than playing in them, just as it is unclear that appreciating a ballet is less valuable than dancing it. But even if there is less value in watching than participating, it is far from clear that intelligent observation of sports, or other human activities in which excellence is demonstrated, is without value at all. Spectators at sporting events can be rude, ignorant, or passive, but so too can audiences of other kinds. On the other hand, appreciation of a competitive athletic contest involves use of intelligence, powers of observation, and the critical application of standards of excellence.

A critic might respond that while such points have force, we have been presented with an overintellectualized account of what it is to be a sports fan. Spectators don't just appreciate good performances, they also root for their teams to win. Indeed, the atmosphere at an important college basketball game often far more resembles the atmosphere at a revival meeting than that of a seminar on excellence in sports.

Loyalty to our favorite team and players, and the expression of emotion in support of them, surely do and should play a major role in sports. As in other areas of life, we develop special relationships with those we care about. If we were not loyal to those we cared about and did not take a special interest in their success, life would be far less rich and interesting.

Nevertheless, loyalty and emotion should not get out of hand. The behavior of soccer fans in many countries who go on rampages, destroying property and threatening life, should not be tolerated. Violence and abusive behavior by sports fans increasingly is becoming a problem in the United States.[14] Even where overt violence is absent, the partisan, hostile character of crowds at many sporting events threatens to intimidate visiting players and referees alike.

Thus, while the critical perspective towards sports, which was attributed to fans, is only part of the story, and undoubtedly idealized at that, it serves as a moral and intellectual constraint on the kind of emotionalism generated by excessively provincial fan loyalty, or just plain bad behavior. That is, a moral requirement of good sportsmanship for fans is that they retain their critical perspective. Even though we need not be ashamed of caring about our team's fate and wanting them to win, when we care so much that we become unable to appreciate good play by the opposition, not only are the opposing players disrespected as persons but the justification of athletic competition also is undermined. If competition in sports should be conceived of as a mutual quest for excellence, we should retain enough detachment to appreciate who best meets the challenge. Otherwise, sports is reduced to a mere means for satisfying our own egos rather than constituting an area where spectators and athletes alike can learn and grow by understanding and meeting ever increasing challenges to their athletic and critical skills.

We can conclude, then, that if avid interest of fans in observing sports events lowers participation, a debatable claim at best, watching athletic contests may have value of its own. Sporting audiences, no less than other audiences, are called upon to appreciate excellence and to apply critical standards of judgment. Emotional bonds to favorite teams and players, when constrained by the norms of respect for persons and appreciation of excellence, can enrich our existence and motivate us to do our best.

The Internal Goods of Sports

We have considered the claim that too much emphasis has been placed on the star athlete and too little on participation by the many. While it may remain controversial just how much emphasis is too much, some principles of evaluation have emerged from our discussion. In particular, while our discussion commits us to supporting efforts to encourage greater participation, it also indicates that emphasis on participation should not commit us either to identical treatment of all athletes or blindness to excellence in athletics.

This focus on excellence suggests that our earlier analysis of the basic and the scarce benefits of sports sets up far too narrow a framework for discussion. The posing of issues in terms of the distribution of only the scarce and basic benefits immediately suggests tension between the athletic elite and the greater bulk of the population, who often lack adequate opportunity to pursue the basic benefits. But this emphasis on opposition between an elite and the rest of us, though not wholly inaccurate, may obscure an important part of the picture. In philosophy, the questions we ask may determine what sorts of answers we end up considering. In restricting ourselves only to questions about scarce and basic benefits, we may have cut ourselves off from considering the relationships that exist *between* outstanding performances by the few, and the enjoyment and appreciation of the many.

In particular, both scarce and basic benefits are *external* to sports. That is, each logically can be conceived and obtained apart from sports themselves. Goods, such as health, fun, fame, and wealth can be understood and obtained by those who have no understanding of or relationship to sports.

However, in addition to such external goods, there also are goods which are *internal* to sports.[15] Goods are internal to a practice or activity when and only when they logically cannot be understood or enjoyed independently of that practice or activity itself. For example, the concept of a "home run" is unintelligible apart from the practice and rules of baseball; the elegance of a winning combination in chess cannot be understood or enjoyed without an understanding of the rules and standards of strategy that characterize the game of chess.

The distinction between internal and external goods of sports is central to our concerns in this chapter because the conformity to standards of excellence implicit in various sports creates shared internal goods available to the whole community. Spectators appreciate and share in the enjoyment of the internal goods created by top performers at all levels of athletic competition. Thus, a point often ignored by those who fear overemphasis on an athletic elite is that skilled participants in sports are just as capable of creating internal goods, shared by large numbers of people, as are skilled participants in other practices, such as dance or theater. By creating such goods, which can be widely shared, skilled athletes benefit everyone who appreciates their achievements.

Rewards, Merit, and Athletic Ability

Even allowing for creation of internal goods, however, the distribution of scarce benefits in athletics, particularly fame and wealth, can be called into moral question. After all, top professional athletes routinely earn millions of dollars each year; nurses, teachers, cancer researchers, and assembly line workers may not make that much for a lifetime of service. Consider also the attention lavished on top intercollegiate sports stars compared to that focused on the best students at the same universities. What, if anything, justifies the distribution of scarce benefits in athletics, where a relatively few top performers reap rewards that most of us only can dream about?

One important type of defense of inequalities in distribution is based on their social utility. If such utility is lacking, the inequality is unjustified because it does no good. Conversely, if the kind of inequality in question results in better consequences for everyone affected than available alternatives, it is justified on utilitarian grounds.

However, even if inequalities in the distribution of the scarce benefits of sports (or of any other goods) promote social utility, it does not follow that they are fair or just. Promoting the greatest good is one thing, but conformity to the norms of fairness and justice, as we have seen, is quite another. Accordingly, even though the issue of the overall justification of unequal distributions is too broad to be covered in depth here, considering one aspect of the debate as it applies to scarce benefits in sports will prove interesting. This issue concerns whether the scarce benefits can be *deserved*. Philosophical critics of the whole idea of personal desert have questioned whether any rewards can be deserved, for the natural abilities determining success are mere "gifts" that the individual has done nothing to deserve in the first place.

In his important book *A Theory of Justice*, John Rawls maintained: "It seems to be one of the fixed points of our considered judgments that no one deserves his place on the distribution of native endowments any more than one deserves one's initial starting place in society."[16] The talents we are born with and the environment we are born into are not of our making; we deserve no credit or blame for them. Therefore, the Rawlsian argument continues, we also deserve no credit or blame for what we do with what we have fortuitously inherited. For example, since Michael Jordan was born with a body better suited for basketball than I, this accident of birth cannot be a justification for the claim that he deserves more fame and fortune than I do. One cannot deserve something on the basis of mere accident or luck.

Here, one is tempted to object that in athletics, as in many other endeavors, natural talent is only part of what determines success. We all are familiar with both the "natural" athlete who never achieves success commensurate with ability due to lack of motivation or intelligence and with the less naturally gifted player who attains peak performance because of overwhelming drive, dedication, courage, and desire. Hours of hard work in practice, coolness under pressure, intelligent analysis of personal weaknesses, good tactical sense, and other character traits often have at least as much to do with success in sports, and in many other fields, as natural ability.

Unfortunately, this response will not suffice, for it is vulnerable to the original argument pressed at a new level. That is, coolness under pressure, dedication, courage, and other success-making characteristics also can be seen as the product of a natural lottery, the fruits of which we have done nothing to deserve. As Rawls puts it, "the assertion that a man deserves the superior character that enables him to make the effort to cultivate his abilities is equally problematic; for his character depends in large part upon fortunate family and social circumstances for which he can claim no credit."[17]

Carried to its logical extreme, this argument implies that the idea of personal desert is not a basic element of distributive justice. "It's mine because I deserve it" may function as a legitimate form of justification within a preexisting set of rules already independently judged to be fair or just but cannot function as a fundamental criterion of fairness or justice itself. There are no fundamental claims of desert, independent of rules and practices judged just on other grounds, for outcomes are determined by purely fortuitous factors ultimately beyond the control of the individual participants.

Does this mean, as some critics have suggested, that we should handicap talented individuals to make up for their natural assets? At its most absurd, this suggestion implies that attractive people be disfigured, intelligent ones be drugged, and strong individuals be weakened, so that we all come out even in the end. In sports, we might find "two identical people playing tennis . . . but neither could ever win. The game would never get beyond 40-40 or perhaps since neither was the least bit better than the other, the very first rally of the match would be interminable, or at least last until both players dropped from exhaustion, presumably at the same time." [18]

Fortunately, few, if any, thinkers have defended such an absurd proposal. In fact, Rawls himself did not recommend that we dispense with the idea of desert. Rather, even in Rawls's theory, people can deserve things by conforming to rules which are just on other grounds. Thus, if the rules for running the men's U.S. Open Golf Championship are fair and it is just for the winner to be paid a large reward, then in a sense the winner does deserve the reward. But the winner deserves the reward because (by independent principles of justice) the championship and accompanying distribution system are fair and just. They are not fair and just because they give the winner what he deserves, for, on the Rawlsian argument, there are no independently justified claims of desert to begin with.

What makes a set of rules fair and just? According to Rawls, the implications of the genetic-social lottery leads not to the handicap system, but to a much more plausible alternative. According to Rawls, we should think of principles of justice as the result of "an agreement to regard the distribution of natural talents as a common asset and to share in the benefits of this distribution whatever it turns out to be. Those who have been favored by nature, whoever they are, may gain from their good fortune only on terms that improve the situation of those who have lost out." [19]

This intuitive argument is reinforced in the Rawlsian system by a theoretical account of the proper way of reasoning about justice. In this view, if we are to reason from the perspective of justice, rather than merely consider our own interests, we must reason *as if* we were ignorant of our own personal characteristics, including our race, sex, and religious and value commitments as well as of our interests and social circumstances. Thus, we are forced by such a "veil of ignorance" to see things from a universal rather than a personal perspective that might be biased in favor of ourselves or the groups and communities with which we identify. The principles of justice, according to Rawls, are those principles that would be adopted as fundamental rules governing the basic structure of a society by impartial deliberators behind the veil of ignorance. Behind such a veil, the argument goes, it would be rational to choose to regard natural talents as common assets, to be used for the benefit of all. This is because the deliberators would be ignorant of just how talented or untalented they individually are and would want to protect themselves from turning out to be among the less talented in a purely meritocratic society.

In a Rawlsian view, then, inequalities in the distribution of the scarce benefits of sports may sometimes be justified, but only when the practices that generate such inequalities, such as professional sports within a free market system, operate in the long-run interests of the disadvantaged. Such a view surely is more defensible than either the idea of imposing handicaps on the advantaged or libertarianism, for it neither insists on rigidly imposed identical outcomes nor denies all positive obligations to others. In other words, Rawlsian justice can be regarded as plausible compromise between those who favor operation of the free market, regardless of what harms it produces, and those who insist that virtually *any* differences in outcome are unjust and unfair.

But should we conclude that there can be no justified claims of personal desert based on merit over and above the entitlements of Rawlsian justice? After all, possession of healthy bodily organs is just as much an undeserved benefit of the natural lottery as the ability to run fast or jump high. May individuals keep their healthy kidneys only if allowing them to do so ultimately favors the disadvantaged? Should we view healthy bodily organs as common assets to be used for the benefit of all, or do individuals have independent entitlements to them?

According to this line of criticism, the Rawlsian approach in effect nationalizes the individual—an approach hardly consistent with the idea of respect for persons that Rawls claimed is at the center of his theory. [20] However, this line of criticism may not be entirely fair to Rawls's theory. After all, Rawls did not favor seizing individuals and forcing them to use their assets for the common good, so he need not be committed to seizing their kidneys either. Rather, what Rawls proposed is allowing people to develop their talents as they choose. However, as their possession of talents is due to the luck of the lottery, society allows them to be *rewarded* for their skill only to the extent that the more disadvantaged also gain. [21]

However, while this reply may be successful, it does not get the Rawlsian theorist entirely off the hook. For one thing, Rawls seems to view a person's abilities and talents, along with character and motivation, as accidental features that the individual possesses fortuitously. But if you subtract character, talent, personality, and the like from the individual, what is left? There seems to be no person left over to whom respect is owed.[22] More important for our purposes, because people express themselves through their character, personality, and use of talents and skills, to fail to respond appropriately is a serious failure of respect for personhood. Thus, if Sue and Amy both choose to develop their abilities in tennis, but Sue works harder and is more committed and more talented, we arguably have failed to respond to her as a person if we do not recognize the merit of her performance as compared to that of Amy. Thus, one important function of the practice of recognizing claims of desert based on merit is that it allows the choices people make, the effort they expand, and the personal assets they choose to develop, to significantly influence outcomes. In other words, it provides them with a degree of control over their lives that otherwise would be lacking.

A system that regards individual assets and abilities as merely common property to be used to benefit the disadvantaged arguably fails to respect persons conceived of as doers or agents. It also may fail to respect them conceived of as responders, critics, and consumers of performances of others. This point is illustrated by the following example.

Imagine a small educational community of teachers and students who are joined by a new instructor, Professor Jones. He is a particularly interesting, acute, and stimulating individual. Soon, more and more students are attending his lectures and, as a result, fewer attend those of his colleagues. Other scholarly communities hear of Jones's abilities and try to induce him to join them. As a result, Jones has more opportunities than most other colleagues. Moreover, other teachers adopt some of Jones's new methods, such as allowing discussion rather than simply lecturing, in an attempt to improve their own teaching. As a result, the overall quality of instruction improves. In addition, Jones ends up with a better professional reputation and higher salary than most of the other faculty.[23]

What leads to this inequality of result is Jones's expression of his teaching ability in action *and* the responses of those exposed to his skill as an instructor. The point of the example would be the same if we substituted gymnastics for education and Mary Lou Retton for Jones. Inequalities of result may legitimately arise as a result of our different responses to the performances of others. Gymnastics has increased in popularity in the United States in part because athletes such as former Olympic star Mary Lou Retton captured the imagination of much of the public at a crucial time in the sport's development. If we were not free to respond appropriately by recognizing Retton's merits, our liberty as rational agents would be significantly curtailed, as would the area in which we could respond to each other as persons.[24]

For example, providing special financial incentives for better teachers to teach in inner city schools may lead to economic inequality among teachers but also may improve the quality of education for many children from lower income groups. But that is not the only—or necessarily the most important—reason why they sometimes are not unjust. Rather, inequalities also can be legitimatized when they arise through the free interactions of persons, at least when such interactions take place within fair background conditions of choice. Such inequalities are legitimate in part because they arise from and express our nature as persons. A system through which perceived merit is acknowledged and rewarded can reflect our free collective evaluation of what individuals do with their assets, assets to which they are not always merely contingently attached but which may express their individual nature as well. Those who benefit most from such an arrangement may well have special obligations to contribute to the betterment of the worst off, but it does not follow that the *only* reason for recognizing merit is benefit to the disadvantaged.

Rawls himself might not mean to dispute such a conclusion, although his emphasis on the point that natural abilities, including character and motivational traits, should be viewed as common assets may lend itself to the suggestion that the talented person should be valued as a means for improving the position of others. Rawls, however, may not really mean that talents and abilities are *properties* of the community in the sense that the community can dictate how they are used and developed. Rather, all he may want to insist upon is that those whose abilities are rewarded by the community have an obligation to the worst off, which they themselves would acknowledge from behind the veil of ignorance. Thus, a Rawlsian view, properly understood, still might point out that initial possession of a package of personal assets is fortuitous. It also would acknowledge, however, that we would fail to respect persons as autonomous agents if we did not respond appropriately to individual choices about how such packages of assets are developed and used.

In considering this point, we might ask whether we would want to protect ourselves not only against bad luck in the natural lottery, but also against the possibility of winding up with talents that cannot be valued or preferences we cannot express because no gains for the disadvantaged thereby are promoted. If we would want to include some protection of individual merit into our social contract, the Rawlsian theory may be extended to make some room for merit and desert in ways its original presentation did not seem to allow. This does not mean respect for merit is the only principle of social justice we should recognize or that it should take priority over provision of a reasonable safety net, but only that it is one element of social justice, one especially important for recognizing and expressing our character as persons.

An Alternate Defense of Desert

So far the critique of desert based on the natural lottery has been criticized on the grounds that it disrespects persons to view their talents, character, and personality as merely part of a common pool to be developed for the benefit of the disadvantaged. A second line of criticism well worth our attention was developed by George Sher in his article "Effort, Ability, and Personal Desert."[25]

First of all, Sher pointed out that even if people don't always exert equal effort in performing some tasks, such as doing a drill in basketball practice, it doesn't follow that they couldn't have tried harder than they did. Perhaps you tried harder than I did, not because you have an innately greater capacity to exert effort than I, but because doing well in basketball means more to you than it does to me. If Sher is correct, it may be wrong to assume that, due to the natural lottery, people differ in their innate capacity to exert effort. And if people don't differ in that capacity, it might be a suitable basis for making distinctions in personal desert. You deserved to be on the starting five because, although our abilities were roughly equal, you tried much harder to develop yours.

However, even if the capacity to exert effort does differ among individuals, Sher argued that equitable judgments about desert still may be possible. This will be so if the people relatively less talented in some areas are more talented in others. Thus, even if you have a greater capacity to exert effort in basketball than I do, I may have greater quickness, while Smith, who lacks your capacity to exert effort and my quickness, seems better at analyzing game situations and making the strategically proper response. All three of us, in different ways, have the overall capacity to do well in basketball, although none dominates the others in all areas of talent. Moreover, other individuals who are not well suited for basketball need not play basketball. There are other sports that reward subtly different combinations of abilities. Finally, people need not aim for success in sports at all but can focus their efforts in other areas.

Sher's argument suggests that judgments of merit are not inequitable, despite the natural lottery, so long as it is not unreasonable to expect individuals to use whatever combination of talents they have in a way that allows them to be competitive with others and as long as there are a sufficient number of practices, professions, and activities throughout society so that many different combinations of talents can achieve reasonable success in some of them. This is not to deny that certain barriers to achievement, such as poverty or discrimination, are inequitable and unjust. However, it does call into question the claim that the natural lottery by itself renders all judgments of desert based on merit arbitrary and unjust. Thus, while Sher's argument surely is not free from criticism, it, along with the consideration of respect for persons advanced earlier, suggests that the lottery argument itself is open to significant objection and does not necessarily rule out as illegitimate all claims to unequal shares of the scarce benefits of sports based on merit and personal desert.[26]

Inequality in Sports

Our discussion suggests that inequality of result, in sports or elsewhere, although sometimes grossly unjust, should not be equated a priori with unfairness or injustice. Indeed, unequal shares of the scarce benefits in sports may arise because skilled athletes create internal goods of sports, which we value and seek to share. As long as this occurs within fair background institutions, perhaps those satisfying the Rawlsian requirement of redistribution to the disadvantaged, it is hard to see what makes such inequalities unjust.

This conclusion does not imply that any inequality of outcome, however great, is morally legitimate so long as a reasonable safety net is in place. Arguably, large concentrations of wealth may undermine democratic values by allowing the rich to wield undue political influence or may lead to harmful social and class structures that undermine respect for those on the bottom. Our discussion has not examined which claims may or may not be justifiable. Our conclusion is more modest—namely, that inequalities of outcome in sports and elsewhere can sometimes be justified by the very value of respect for persons that gives equality its moral force in the first place.

Thus, it seems that sports policy in America should have two goals. First, our discussion suggests that a decent society should strive to provide adequate opportunities for exercise for all its citizens. In one view, citizens have a moral right to such opportunities. From this perspective, a society that can provide them but fails to do so without adequate reason treats its citizens unjustly. However, libertarian concerns about personal liberty do set reasonable limits on what we have an obligation to provide for others. Therefore, it is problematic whether people actually have extensive rights to such goods. Even if there are rights to minimal levels of recreational opportunities in sports, provision of relatively extensive sports facilities and other costly opportunities for participation in sports should be left to either the private market or the discretion of local communities.

Second, we have seen that in addition to the basic and the scarce goods of sports, there are internal goods that can be shared by the whole community. Our capacity to appreciate and respond appropriately to superior performances enriches our lives. Thus, our legitimate concern for greater participation by the many should not lead us to ignore the excellence and achievement of the unusually talented. The fine athletes who demonstrate excellence in sports, whether in the major leagues or the Little League, adhere to standards at which all competitors aim and which we all can appreciate. Our legitimate concerns with equality, then, should not lead us to equate identity of treatment with justice. Conversely, inequality of result need not be unjust, bad, or otherwise unfair. Rather, when it reflects our autonomy by arising from our choices and actions, it not only can conform to standards of justice and equity but also can express our commitment to excellence as well.

6

Sex Equality in Sports

In all cases, excepting those of the bear and the leopard, the female is less spirited than the male ... more shrinking, more difficult to rouse to action, and requires a smaller quantity of nutriment. ... The fact is, the nature of man is the most rounded off and complete.

—Aristotle,
History of Animals, Book IX

Games and recreation for all types of girls, by all means, which develop charm and social health, but athletic competition in basketball, track and field sports, and baseball? No!

—Frederick R. Rodgers,
School and Society, 1929

The passages quoted above express attitudes that have probably been dominant in most periods of Western civilization. The belief that women are naturally sedentary was reinforced by the customs of Aristotle's culture, which kept women largely confined to the home. Not only were women forbidden to compete in the Olympics in ancient Greece, but legend has it that any woman found in the immediate area of the competition would be thrown off the nearest cliff.

These attitudes sometimes have been challenged. However, the challengers sometimes shared more with proponents of the dominant outlook than they might have acknowledged even to themselves. For example, a Women's Division of the National Amateur Athletic Federation was formed in 1923 to stress "sports opportunities for all girls, protection from exploitation, enjoyment of sports, female leadership (and) medical examinations."[1]

In fact, the purpose of this "creed," as it was sometimes called, was to promote greater participation in sports for all women rather than promote intense competition for highly skilled female athletes. "Soon

123

female competitive athletics began to decrease. . . . In place of competition, play days and sports days were organized. This philosophy of athletics for women and girls continued into the early 1960s."[2]

As a result, those women and girls who really did want to participate in competition all too often were made to feel strange or unfeminine. Former tennis star Althea Gibson described what it was like to be a female athlete in high school in the south in the 1940s:

> The problem I had in Wilmington was the girls in school. . . . "Look at her throwin' that ball just like a man," they would say, and they looked at me just like I was a freak. . . . I felt as though they ought to see that I didn't do the things they did because I didn't know how to and that I showed off on the football field . . . to show there was something I was good at. [3]

Although the attitudes that troubled Gibson have not been eliminated, the once dominant inegalitarian attitude toward women in sports has been facing its greatest challenge in recent years. The growth of women's and girls' sports and the intensity and quality of their performances in the 1970s and 1980s is unprecedented. For example, in 1970-1971, 3.7 million boys and only 300,000 girls participated in interscholastic sports. By 1978-1979, 4.2 million boys and 2 million girls were participants in interscholastic athletics. A similar rate of increase in the participation of women in intercollegiate athletics took place during the same period.[4]

Sorting Out the Issues

Title IX

The changes described above were not easily achieved. *Sports Illustrated,* in a 1973 article, reported widespread indifference, even among educators, to women's athletics.[5] There is no doubt that prior to the recent increase in interest in women's athletics, and broader feminist concerns about sex equality, women's sports were separate and unequal. Only a tiny fraction of athletic budgets was devoted to the needs of women students, who were excluded from participation in most varsity and intramural programs.

Such inequalities were defended on the grounds that relevant differences between men and women justified the differences in treatment. Women were held to be less interested in participating than men, or less aggressive and hence less in need of the outlet of intense athletic competition.

Although, as we will see, sex differences may be relevant to the form sex equality takes in sports, they hardly justify the exclusion of women from sports or the relegation of women's sports to second class status. First, the recent rise of participation of girls and women in organized competitive sports is a most convincing refutation of the claim that they have little interest in taking part. Second, the claim that women are naturally less aggressive than men, even if it were true, is *irrelevant* to the right to participate and compete. After all, males who have less need to discharge aggression against other males are not excluded from participation.

In any case, whether or not competitive sports are instrumental in helping some of us discharge aggression (a controversial empirical claim at best), they are also of value in part because they are an important source of fascination, challenge, recreation, and fun. As we have seen, much of the intrinsic value, ethical importance, and interest of competitive sports lies in the framework they constitute for the pursuit of challenges set by opponents. Opponents respond to each other as persons within the rules of the sports contest. Males and females have an equal claim to participation. Members of both sexes may seek the challenges presented by competitive sports. Whether or not sports fulfill other social functions, such as allowing for the harmless discharge of aggressive impulses, their value does not lie primarily in such consequences. As persons, women are entitled to the same respect and concern as men in seeking excellence through the challenge of athletic competition.

What are the requirements of sex equality in athletic programs at the intercollegiate and interscholastic levels? Does sex equality simply require lack of discrimination? Should the coaches simply pick the best players to be on teams, regardless of sex? On the other hand, does sex equality require separate teams for women? If so, are such teams required in all sports or just those in which women are physiologically disadvantaged with respect to men? Are separate teams for physiologically disadvantaged men also required? Does sex equality require greater emphasis on competition in sports, such as gymnastics, where women may have physical advantages, or the introduction of new sports in which the sexes can compete equally?

It will be useful to begin our examination of these and related questions by considering the most important federal legislation addressing sex equality in sports. *Title IX* of the *Education Amendments of 1972* prohibits sex discrimination in federally assisted education programs.[6] The section of *Title IX* dealing with athletics states that "no person shall, on the basis of sex, be excluded from participation in, be denied the benefits of, be treated differently from another person or otherwise be discriminated against in any interscholastic, intercollegiate, club, or intramural athletic program offered by a recipient." (Section 86:41a) One plausible interpretation of this section requires that athletic programs not make *any* distinctions on the basis of sex. As long as no discrimination takes place, men and women have been treated by the same standards and so have no grounds to complain of inequity. On this view, sex equality in sports requires that we pay no attention to the sex of participants.

The problem with this, of course, is that if it were applied, there would be far fewer women than at present competing in interscholastic or intercollegiate varsity contests in such sports as basketball, soccer, lacrosse, track and field, tennis, and golf. Although many women athletes in such sports have more ability than most men, it does appear that males have important physiological advantages, for example in size and upper body strength, that make a crucial difference at top levels of competition.

To avoid the virtual exclusion of women from varsity competition in many sports, particularly so-called contact sports, *Title IX* departs from simple nondiscrimination by allowing institutions to sponsor separate teams for men and women. *Title IX* does not require that there be separate teams for each sex in each sport an institution offers but does stipulate that, through an appropriate combination of mixed and single-sex teams, the opportunities for each sex be equivalent.

As described above, *Title IX* seems to represent a combination of two approaches to sex equality. According to the first, sex equality is equated with blindness to sex. Thus, a coeducational college that pays no attention to the sex of applicants in deciding whom to admit has adopted the first approach. A second approach to sex equality is to acknowledge sex differences in order to insure that members of each sex get equivalent benefits. For example, a medical clinic that made sure its staff included some physicians specializing in treatment of special medical problems affecting men and some specializing in treatment of special medical problems affecting women has adopted the second approach.

The two approaches are, at best, not easily reconciled and, at worst, plainly inconsistent. The first requires us to ignore sex and to assign no special significance to it; the second requires that we recognize sex differences when they are relevant to our activities and practices. *Title IX* combines elements of each approach. The policy of instituting separate sports programs for each sex requires viewing sex as a relevant ground for making distinctions, but the requirement that no one be treated differently with regard to sex seems to require that sex not be viewed as a relevant ground for making distinctions.

Perhaps a policy combining these two approaches to sex equality might be consistent if it does so in a coherent manner. Thus, perhaps sex is relevant in sports where one sex has a physiological advantage over the other, but not in sports where such advantages do not exist, such as riflery. However, before turning to attempts to provide a synthesis of the two ideals, we would do well to examine the merits of each as a general ideal of sex equality. We can then determine whether each ideal is defensible or indefensible before applying it to sports and athletics.

Ideals of Sex Equality

Like virtue, honesty, and truth, sex equality has few contemporary opponents, at least in public. Even those who opposed the Equal Rights Amendment, including former President Ronald Reagan, claimed to support equal rights, properly understood, for men and women.

What is not so often noticed is that sex equality is open to diverse interpretations. Just as equal opportunity can be understood in a variety of ways—as requiring simple nondiscrimination, as requiring conditions of background fairness, as requiring equal life chances for representative persons from all major social groups, and so on—so too there are diverse and competing conceptions of sex equality. Thus, abstract support for a general ideal of sex equality from a wide variety of perspectives can obscure deep divisions on just how sex equality is to be understood, what it specifically implies in concrete contexts, and how it might best be achieved.

To those who identify sex equality with assimilation, a society has achieved sex equality when, as one writer put it, no more significance is attached to the sex of persons than is attached in our society to such features as eye color.[7] In this view, sex equality is equated with almost total blindness to sex. In the assimilationist or sex-blind society, at least in its most uncompromising form, one's sex would play no role in the distribution of civil rights or economic benefits and at most would play a minimal role in personal and social relations. This assimilationist model of sex equality strongly resembles the integrationist ideal of racial equality. In particular, it implies that "separate but equal" is as unacceptable in the realm of sex equality as it is in the context of race. The implication of this for sports is that separate teams for each sex is a violation of what sex equality ideally requires.

Perhaps the principal argument for the assimilationist ideal is that it is required by the value of personal autonomy. Although "autonomy" is far from the clearest notion employed by moral philosophers, it refers at a minimum to our capacity to choose our actions for ourselves and to determine the course of our own lives. It has to do with self-determination rather than determination by others.

Defenders of the assimilationist ideal argue that it is justified by the moral requirement of respect for the autonomy of women because autonomy requires the withering away of sex roles. As Richard Wasserstrom, a distinguished advocate of the assimilationist ideal, argued, "sex roles and all that accompany them, necessarily impose limits—restrictions on what one can do or become. As such, they are . . . at least *prima facie* wrong."[8] Perhaps what Wasserstrom had in mind here is that roles set up proper norms of behavior for those who fill them. Deviation from the norm exposes one to criticism from others. Conformity is enforced by social pressure. The effects of sex roles in sports was seen in a 1975 study, which reported that 90 percent of the respondents, selected from the general population, believed that participation in track and field would detract from a female's femininity, while only 2 percent thought participation in swimming, a more traditional sport for girls and women, would have the same effect.[9]

Of course, no society can exist without roles of any kind. But according to proponents of the assimilationist model of sex equality, sex roles are especially objectionable. Whether they arise from biological differences between men and women or socialization and learning, they are unchosen. As Wasserstrom maintained, "involuntarily imposed restraints have been imposed on some of the most central factors concerning the way one will shape and live one's life."[10]

The sex-blind conception of equality favored by the assimilationist does seem particularly appropriate to many significant areas of life in our society. For example, in the areas of basic civil rights and liberties, justice and equity surely are sex blind. Freedom of assembly, religion, or speech are rights of all persons equally, regardless of their sex. Similarly, in employment or distribution of important social benefits, the making of distinctions by sex normally seems arbitrary and unfair.[11]

But should sex equality be identified across the board with blindness to sex, as the assimilationist model requires? What, for example, are we to say of sexual attraction? If sex equality requires blindness to the sex of others, does it follow that people with relatively fixed sexual preferences, whether for members of the opposite sex or their own, are engaged in the social counterpart of invidious sex discrimination? This consequence of the assimilationist model is particularly hard to swallow.[12] Accordingly, we might want to consider ideals of sex equality other than assimilationism, for the identification of sex equality with sex blindness may not always capture our sense of what is just or reasonable in this area.

In particular, as we have seen earlier, equal treatment in the sense of identical treatment is not always a requirement of justice or fairness. Sometimes, equality is to be understood as requiring equal respect and concern, which in turn requires us to acknowledge the significance of relevant differences among persons. For example, equal respect for persons may require us to respect their choice to meet the challenge of athletic competition, thus leading us to evaluate their performance differently, according to how well they meet the challenge set by the opponent.

A second ideal of sex equality, which recognizes the significance of difference, might be called the pluralistic model. As Wasserstrom pointed out, the pluralistic conception of equality is best illustrated by the tradition of religious tolerance in the United States. According to this tradition, religious equality does not require that we accord to religious differences only the significance presently attached to eye color in our society. Rather, a defensible conception of religious equality requires not that we regard religious differences as insignificant but rather stipulates that no religion be placed in a position of dominance over others.[13]

Unlike assimilationism, pluralism does not reject the ideal of "separate but equal" out of hand. Thus, it might allow separate but equal athletic programs for women. Although the pluralist rejects rigid sex roles that place men in a position of dominance over women, the pluralist is open to the suggestion that some important sex differences may exist and that they be taken into account in a fair and equitable manner in public policy.

Can the pluralist respond satisfactorily to the charge of the assimilationist that any tolerance of sex roles violates personal autonomy by forcing women (and men) into the straightjacket of fixed social expectations? Is pluralism or assimilationism the more defensible model of sex equality? Which approach has the most acceptable implications for sex equality in sports? We will consider these questions in the next section.

Sex Equality in Athletic Competition

Sex Differences and Sports

As we have seen, much of the controversy over sex equality in sports concerns whether men's and women's athletic programs are being treated equally in our schools, colleges, and universities. Is the women's program getting its fair share of the budget? Does the women's basketball team get the same kind of publicity as the men's team? Are there equivalent opportunities for men and women to play intramural sports? What does it mean for opportunities to be equivalent?

Such questions presuppose that separate sports programs for men and women are requirements of sex equality in sport or are at least permissible ways of implementing such equality. But, as we have seen, there are different and competing conceptions of sex equality, not all of which would endorse separate athletic programs for men and women. Which of the ideals we have considered, assimilationism or pluralism, is more defensible in the realm of sports?

The problem with assimilationism in sports is that sex blindness requires us to ignore what seem to be relevant sex-related differences in the average athletic ability of men and women. On the average, women are not as big, strong, or as fast as men, although there is some evidence that over long distances, females may show as much or more stamina than males. It does seem clear that in the popular contact sports, such as football, lacrosse, and basketball, as well as in baseball, soccer, tennis, and golf, the greater size, speed, and strength of men gives them a significant physiological advantage over women. In short, if athletic competition were conducted on a completely sex-blind basis, women would be virtually excluded from competition at the highest levels in some of the most challenging and popular sports.

Before we consider possible responses to this argument, we need to be clear about its scope. For one thing, the argument seems most fully applicable to sports played at high levels of skill and intensity. Thus, even if the argument does justify separate teams for males and females in intercollegiate or interscholastic competition, it may not do so in a less intense recreational league or intramural program. Moreover, in sports where one sex did not have significant physiological advantages over the other, such as riflery or horseback riding, sex-blind competition may well be desirable or even required.

Accordingly, it is largely an empirical issue as to which sports the argument about physiological differences applies.[14] But is the argument acceptable even in sports played at high levels of competition and in which there are significant physiological differences between the sexes? We will consider three objections to the defense of pluralism based on physiological sex differences. The first is based on appeal to assimilationism. The second objection maintains that separate men's and women's programs are unfair to men. The third objection maintains that separate sports programs provide women with only the illusion of equality rather than the reality.

Evaluating Pluralism in Sports

To an advocate of the assimilationist ideal of sex equality, sexual pluralism in sports may seem morally pernicious. This is because, according to the assimilationist, pluralism may only express and reinforce the traditional system of sex roles that are held to restrict women's options and limit their autonomy.

However, such a rejoinder seems implausible for a variety of reasons. For one thing, the whole point of having separate athletic programs for women is to expand the options available to them. Without pluralistic acknowledgment of sex differences in sports, women would be virtually absent from the higher levels of competition in most major sports. Moreover, the opportunities that pluralism opens up for women are frequently in sports such as basketball and lacrosse, which until recently have been regarded primarily as for males.[15] A proponent of pluralism in athletics, then, can argue that separate athletic programs for men and women in those sports where performance is affected by physiological sex differences not only increase opportunities for women but also help break down stereotypes about what sports are appropriate for women.

A proponent of assimilationism might respond that if the ideal of sex blindness was implemented throughout society, it would not matter that few, if any, women played at the higher levels of athletic competition. This is because in the assimilationist society, when an individual's sex would be regarded as no more important than eye color is regarded in our society, it would not be important that virtually all the top athletes were male. At least, it would not be regarded as any more important than the widely acknowledged fact in our society that virtually no individuals under five feet ten inches in height have a chance to play professional basketball.

However, this rejoinder is open to two strong objections. The first is that because we are not yet in the assimilationist society, it would be unfair to apply the assimilationist ideal only to sports, an area where it would particularly disadvantage women. It is one thing to say pluralism in sports is unnecessary in the assimilationist society but quite another to say it is unnecessary in ours.

This distinction between the ideal and the actual raises a fundamental point that ought not to be passed over too quickly. Sometimes philosophers believe they have done their job when they present us with a defensible *ideal* conception of justice, equality, liberty, or some other value. They then view the problems of implementation as involving only practical choices of efficient means for attaining the ideal. But this ignores the issue of whether and by what route it is *morally permissible* to get to that ideal from where we are now. Attainment of an ideal is morally permissible for us if we can get to that ideal from where we are now without doing something morally impermissible along the way.[16]

For example, suppose a defensible ideal of equal opportunity required that we abolish the family, perhaps because different family circumstances lead to unequal environments. It doesn't follow from that conclusion that individuals presently part of families can just ignore their duties to other family members on the grounds that in an ideal society the family might not exist. Indeed, if there were no way to implement the ideal without seriously violating duties to members of presently existing families, that ideal may be morally unattainable for us. That is, even if we could in fact create a society without families, and even if such a society might be ideally just, it may be morally impermissible for us to create such a society because we cannot do so without committing prohibitive injustices along the way.

A similar point may apply to the assimilationist ideal of sexual equality. Even if assimilationism is superior to pluralism as an ideal, which is controversial, it seems morally impermissible to introduce assimilationism in sports, where it would disadvantage women, before it is implemented elsewhere in society.

But is assimilationism superior to pluralism as a comprehensive ideal of sex equality? The second objection is that assimilationism itself may not be fair, just, or equitable. The assimilationist feels we must be sex blind because sex roles restrict the autonomy of women. Because violation of the norms implicit in such roles leads to social criticism, strong pressures are exerted on females to conform to society's ideal of femininity.

However, sports stand as a counterexample to the thesis that recognition of sex differences always involves coercive sex roles. On the contrary, the recognition of sex differences in sports frees women from traditional restrictions and makes it possible for them to engage in highly competitive forms of athletics in a variety of major, traditionally male, sports. In sports, it seems to be assimilationism rather than pluralism that limits options and opportunities for women.

Similarly, if there are other significant physiological or psychological sex differences between men and women, equality might involve equal respect for such differences rather than denial of their importance. Socializing men and women to ignore such differences or to inhibit gender-linked forms of behavior may be just as subversive of autonomy as the socializing of women to conform to traditional sex roles. Although a conception of sex equality required by justice surely rules out a rigid system of sex roles, it is doubtful if sex equality requires us to forget about one another's sex either.[17]

Unfair to Males?

So far our argument suggests that the ideal of sex equality as blindness to sex (assimilationism) does not provide adequate grounds for rejecting separate men's and women's athletic programs, at least in those sports where physiological sex differences significantly affect performance. Rather, the importance of providing equal opportunities in sports for both men and women is a reason for abandoning, or at least limiting, the application of the assimilationist ideal.

However, if the reason for having separate athletic programs for each sex is physiological, why separate athletes by sex at all, rather than according to physiology? Doesn't consistency require that different teams or levels of competition be provided for persons of different physiological endowments, *regardless of sex*? As one writer on the subject, Jane English, has suggested:

> if we have a girl's football team in our school, is it unfair to prohibit a 120-pound boy who cannot make the boy's team from trying out for the girl's team? . . . Our 120-pound boy is being penalized for the average characteristics of a major social group to which he belongs, rather than being treated on the basis of his individual characteristics.[18]

In reply, it can be argued that women form a major social group, the members of which tend to identify with the success and failure of each other. As English has suggested, "If women do not attain roughly equal fame and fortune in sports, it leads both men and women to think of women as naturally inferior. Thus, it is not a right of women tennis stars to the scarce benefits but rather a right of all women to self-respect that justifies their demand for equal press coverage and prize money."[19]

What English seems to be suggesting here is that there is a relevant basis for distinguishing between the claims of the 120-pound male and the 120-pound female. Failure to have women's sports programs undermines the self-respect of women as a class. Failure to have a team for smaller men does not undermine the self-respect of males as a class.

Unfortunately, this suggestion faces at least two difficulties. First, it is unclear that the self-respect of women as a group is as closely tied to equal access to the scarce benefits of sports as English suggests. Is it plausible to hold, for example, that the self-respect of the typical woman suffers, say, because there is no professional basketball league for women comparable to the National Basketball Association? Equal opportunity throughout society may be a prerequisite for self-respect. However, equal opportunity in some specific area, such as sports and athletics, probably is not.[20]

A second and more fundamental difficulty concerns English's emphasis on groups rather than individuals. Why is concern for women as a group more important than fairness to all individuals, regardless of sex?

In other areas, supporters of women's rights often argue that women ought to be treated as individuals rather than categorized by sex. For example, until recently, insurance companies have paid women lower monthly annuity payments than men on the grounds that the average woman lives longer than the average man. On this view, the payoff will be equal for males and females as groups only if monthly payments for men and women are unequal, to compensate for the greater longevity of women. However, many people objected that this treatment discriminated against woman. Individual women, who might not live longer than individual men, received lower annuity payments than men each month because of their sex. Their complaint was accepted by the courts. But isn't the complaint of English's hypothetical 120-pound male football player relevantly similar? His claim is that special teams are created for females because they cannot compete in football against larger males, but that he is in the very same situation.

Perhaps we should have teams both for females and for smaller males. But aside from the fact that budgets often will not allow for such a plethora of teams, this response fails to explain why there should be a women's team at all. Why not just have a team, selection for which is sex-blind, for players of different sizes and degrees of strength?

One kind of response might be that given the degree of past discrimination against women in sports and the virtual exclusion of women from competitive athletics, women need special encouragement now to catch up with male athletes. In view of past handicaps facing women in sports, separate athletic programs may be justified as a transitional step towards assimilationism in sports.

This response, which in effect views women's sports as a kind of affirmative action program, although not without force, is not entirely satisfactory either. If, as seems plausible, physiological differences between the sexes exist and significantly affect performance in many major sports, the future goal of assimilationism in such sports may be unattainable. If women on the average are not as tall, fast, or strong as men, they will face serious handicaps in competing with men at the top levels of such sports as basketball, volleyball, tennis, football, golf, soccer, and track. Thus, the defense of women's sports programs as a kind of affirmative action designed to help women athletes catch up to their male counterparts may be unrealistic. It does not tell us what is fair or equitable if sex-blind competition in sports would severely disadvantage women.

Should we conclude that pluralism, with its emphasis on group differences, applies to sports, or should we maintain that individuals and not groups are the proper subject of evaluation, thereby accepting assimilationism, at least as our ultimate goal in sports? If the former, how can we reconcile our view with the idea, advanced elsewhere by supporters of women's rights, that viewing women as members of groups rather than as individuals is to stereotype them unfairly?

I see no easy choice here. However, our analysis of sports suggests that women would be severely disadvantaged by assimilationism in competitive athletics. In all existing cultures, one's sex is recognized as an important basis of social identity. It seems arbitrary to implement sex blindness in an area, such as competitive athletics, where its implementation would exclude women from participation. One's sex, unlike one's size or strength, is an important basis of self-identification. We think of ourselves as men or women, distinguish male and female friends, and often identify with achievements of individuals of the same sex. This itself may be what assimilationists would regard as a sexist practice; however, it is difficult to see why the making of such distinctions is necessarily invidious or discriminatory. If the distinction between the sexes is seen as basic and fundamental, and if its recognition in a given area is not invidious, why isn't it acceptable to be pluralists there?

Accordingly, the existence of separate athletic programs for each sex, whether or not we also have programs for individuals of different degrees of size and strength, seems justified because of the basic importance assigned to the difference between sexes in human life. We do recognize sex differences and regard them as important. As long as this does not involve invidious discrimination, this seems acceptable, especially in areas where recognition of differences creates opportunities for women that otherwise would not exist. Of course, if we are to treat similar cases similarly, we may want to acknowledge that group differences should be recognized in other areas, perhaps even in the dispute about annuity payments, but only where such application is fair and is not invidious.[21] Pluralism, after all, is a model supporting recognition of the equal worth of differences, not subordination of one group by another.

Our discussion so far suggests that the pluralist model of sex equality not only is appropriate for athletics but may have force in other areas of our society as well. But is it really so acceptable, even in the realm of sports? Pluralism has been defended as necessary for equal athletic opportunity for women. But some critics argue that contrary to appearances, pluralism does not provide equality but only the illusion of equality. Are they right?

Unfair to Females?

Does pluralism in sports really work to the advantage of women? A critic might respond that if men really are better in certain sports, the women's teams in those sports necessarily will be thought of as inferior. Rather than liberate women, such teams will stigmatize women. As one writer maintains, "The number and prestige of sports in which men are naturally superior help perpetuate an image of general female inferiority which we have moral reason to undermine."[22] This perception of inferiority, the critic contends, accounts for the generally lower attendance at contests between women's teams and generally lower public recognition of the achievements of top women athletes than of top male athletes.

However, as we have already pointed out, if competitive sports were organized according to the assimilationist model, females would be almost absent at the top levels of competition. Is that preferable to pluralism? Is it fairer?

More important, we need to scrutinize the perception that women's sports are inferior versions of male sports. Perhaps much of the public does perceive such sports as inferior, but is that perception justified?

The claim that in the traditional major sports women's competition is inferior to that of men at similar levels of competition could mean one or more of the following:

1. Women's programs receive less financial and coaching support than men's programs.
2. Contests between women or women's teams are less interesting and less exciting than are contests between men or men's teams.
3. Men's teams will always beat women's teams in a particular sport if both play at roughly the same level of competition, e.g., intercollegiate athletics.

What are the implications for our discussion of sex equality of these different interpretations of the claim that women's sports are inferior? If claim (1) is true, and women's programs receive less financial and coaching support than men's programs, this shows only that pluralism has not been fully implemented, not that it should be abandoned. The obvious remedy is to provide equivalent support for the women's program, not eliminate it.

Claim (3), however, is likely to be true. It is hardly likely, for example, that even a top women's intercollegiate basketball team will be able to beat an average male intercollegiate team. In fact, if (3) were not true, there would be no need for separate women's sports teams in the first place. What does (3) imply about pluralism in sports?

Many would argue that claim (3) justifies (2). It is precisely because men's teams can beat women's teams at similar levels of competition that women's sports allegedly are inferior and uninteresting. However, although much of the sporting public may accept such an inference and, unfortunately, stay away from women's contests as a result, the inference is in fact fallacious. Simply because the men's team would beat the women's team, it doesn't follow that the men's contest is more exciting, more interesting, or of greater competitive intensity. It would be just as fallacious to argue that simply because the worst professional basketball team could beat the best high school team, a contest between two mediocre professional teams will be more exciting, more interesting, and more competitively intense than a game between two top high school teams.

If what is of major interest in a competitive sports contest is the challenge each competitor or team poses to the other, and the skill, intensity, and character with which the participants meet the challenge, there is no reason why women's contests should be less exciting or less interesting than men's contests. This has long been known in Iowa, where girls' high school basketball is a state mania, or at colleges like the University of Texas or Louisiana Tech where the championship women's teams have huge followings. It surely is accepted by tennis fans as top women stars such as Steffi Graf, and now the new young sensation Jennifer Capriati, get as much attention as their male counterparts.

Indeed, in sports such as tennis and golf, and perhaps others as well, one can plausibly argue that the women's game differs from the men's in ways that make it at least as good if not better as a spectator sport. In tennis, the power of male players' serves limits the extent of volleying, but the women's game is characterized more by clever use of ground strokes. Similarly, in golf, women must have superb timing and coordination to compensate for their lack of strength in comparison to males. Why shouldn't it be just as exciting and interesting to watch the timing and tempo of a top female player, such as Nancy Lopez or Patty Sheehan, as to watch the force applied by Craig Stadler? In women's basketball, the dunk or jam is virtually absent, and one-on-one moves may be somewhat less spectacular than in the men's game, but the intelligent use of screens to get open shots, movement without the ball, and brilliant individual play are all there. It is simply a matter of appreciating different aspects of the game as well as the competitive intensity and character of the women playing it.

If women's sports can be as exciting and interesting as men's sports, in part because they are equally competitive and in part because subtly different qualities are being tested, it is hard to see why pluralism in sports necessarily stigmatizes women. Full appreciation of these sports may require better education of the general public, but it is hard to see why women should be denied the opportunity to compete provided by pluralism simply because many fans are fascinated, perhaps unjustifiably so, by the power game played by males in many sports.

Upon reflection, then, we might find that the charge that women's sports are inferior, and hence that separate sports programs for men and women are inherently unequal, itself rests upon too narrow a conception of what qualities in sports are worth appreciating. If such a suggestion has force, it is not that women's sports are inferior, but rather that more of us need to make the effort to appreciate the diverse qualities that are exhibited in athletic competition.

Such considerations may have some appeal even to those feminists who have been suspicious of the notion of "separate but equal" as a model of sex equality. However, they might go on to suggest that if women's performances in what are now thought of as major sports reveals qualities and abilities somewhat different from those of men, why not place more emphasis on those sports in which "female" abilities or qualities are especially advantageous?

The suggestion here is that we redefine our catalog of major sports. The intuitive idea here is that equal opportunity, even on the pluralist model, requires more than equal recognition of or appreciation for women's athletics. It also requires equal emphasis on sports in which women can be the top athletes, and not merely the top "women athletes." Thus, Betsy Postow, a philosopher who has written on sex equality in sports, has recommended that we "increase the number and prestige of sports in which women have a natural statistical superiority to men or at least are not naturally inferior."[23] Jane English has given a concrete example of what Postow may have had in mind: "Perhaps the most extreme example of a sport favoring women's natural skills is the balance beam. Here, small size and flexibility and low center of gravity combine to give women the kind of natural hegemony that men enjoy in football."[24] In other words, these writers have suggested that our traditional catalog of major sports has a built-in bias towards athletic activities favoring men. The way to remedy this bias, we are told, is not simply to introduce athletic programs that institutionalize female inferiority. Rather, we should radically revise our conception of which sports are most worthy of support and attention.

As we have seen, however, the charge that pluralism in sports merely institutionalizes the inferiority of women is at best highly controversial. However, the suggestion that we should learn to appreciate, and if necessary develop, sports that reward the physiological assets of women, just as we now tend to appreciate those that reward the physiological assets of men, does have merit. Properly understood, it does not require the abolition of women's programs in basketball, volleyball, soccer, tennis, and other traditional sports, but the addition and increased support of other sports, such as gymnastics, in which women are physiologically advantaged (or at least physiologically equal).

This suggestion is supported by considerations of fairness and equity, but two competing considerations have to be kept in mind. First, individuals may continue to prefer traditional or currently more popular sports, even after they are introduced to alternatives. The general public may continue to prefer watching and playing basketball and football to watching or participating in gymnastics and high diving. This may be as true for the majority of female athletes as much as anybody else, especially since traditional sports seem open to a wider variety of age groups and body types than gymnastics. To require or compel individuals to attend or participate in certain kinds of sports against their will would be a serious violation of individual liberty. It is one thing, for example, to require that schools introduce students in physical education classes to a wide variety of sports and athletic activities, a significant number of which are not biased in favor of male physiology. It is quite another to insist that female athletes compete in such activities, even if they are more interested in playing basketball, soccer, lacrosse, tennis, or golf. It is possible, of course, that a broad program of public education could change individual preferences. However, such a program, if morally permissible, must appeal to people as autonomous moral agents and not dictate in advance which sports people "ought" to find more interesting or of greater worth.

Second, the goal of providing what might be called "female dominant sports" as a balance for traditional "male dominant" sports is not in accord with the assimilationist ideal of sex equality. Rather, the goal is to assign weight to physiological advantages of females, which requires being sex conscious rather than sex blind. Once again, it looks as if sex equality in sports requires implementation of a pluralist rather than an assimilationist approach, although different sorts of pluralists may disagree internally about just which sex-conscious approach is best. However, in order to insure that we have been fair to assimilationism, let us reassess the arguments for identifying sex equality with blindness to sex.

Does Sex Equality Require Forgetting Sex?

The conception of sex equality as blindness to sex is most plausible in the realm of civil and political rights and in the economic marketplace. The right to vote, the right to freedom of speech, and the right to be free of discrimination in the marketplace should not be dependent upon one's sex.[25]

But however plausible the assimilationist model may be in the sphere of civil, political, and economic rights, it seems highly implausible in the *social* sphere. As we have seen, it implies that there is something morally questionable in having a fixed attraction for members of a particular sex.[26] Anyone with such a relatively fixed attraction is not sex blind in the social arena as the assimilationist model requires. But, as critics of the assimilationist model would argue, it is morally permissible, and in fact desirable, for people to take their partner's sex into consideration when choosing a mate.

Moreover, while sexual attraction may seem like an isolated exception to assimilationism, it may well lead to further breaches of the assimilationist ideal elsewhere. We already have seen that considerations of equity in sports provide a second set of considerations counting against assimilationism as a comprehensive model of sex equality. Bernard Boxill has also pointed out that differences in voice between males and females call for different roles in certain kinds of musical performances.[27] Carol Gilligan and others have argued that the moral development of women differs in significant respect from that of men. Women, Gilligan suggests, tend to attach a greater significance to such values as caring and to particular contextual solutions to moral problems, than men, who tend to attach a greater significance to impartiality and justice.[28] Thus, sex differences may be significant in a wide variety of areas of profound human significance. Equality may require their recognition rather than suppression.

It might be replied, however, that such alleged sex differences are the result of socialization into sex roles. It is socialization or conditioning that is held to violate human freedom and autonomy.

At least two sorts of difficulties face such a retort to the pluralist. First, it is at best unclear that all behavioral and psychological differences between men and women are *entirely* the result of socialization. Sex differences *may* have a biological component. This does not imply either that "biology is destiny" or that environment is not also a crucial determinant of behavior. Even if genes influence the development of psychological sex differences, they clearly do so only in interaction with environmental variables. Moreover, environmental causes need not be any more or any less open to change than genetic ones, and in some cases may be far more difficult to alter. In any case, this is hardly the place to pursue the complex issue of whether genes or the environment are predominant factors affecting human development, except to note that whether or not all psychological sex differences are due solely to socialization is at present an unsettled and controversial issue.

However, *if* there is a genetic component involved, behavioral and psychological sex differences are not entirely the result of socialization but may emerge, to various extents, in the course of normal development. That is, the differences may not be entirely imposed from the outside. If so, efforts to socialize children to be entirely blind to the significance of sex or to prevent all sex differences from emerging, may be a kind of "reverse socialization" or conditioning, which can undermine freedom and autonomy in the same way that many feminists claim present forms of socialization do.

Suppose, on the other hand, that there is *no* significant biological component to account for the emergence of behavioral and psychological sex differences. It doesn't follow that recognition of sex differences is unjust, inequitable, or unfair. Of course, a rigid system of stereotypical sex roles does restrict human freedom and autonomy. But pluralism is not committed to such a system. Rather, it argues that *if* men and women tend to exhibit somewhat different forms of behavior and make somewhat different choices over the course of their lives, this is unjust only if it produces a further difference in the *concern* and *respect* shown to men and women.

According to this argument, what justice requires is not identical outcomes but recognition of the equal worth of all persons. All persons as persons are entitled to equal concern and respect. Thus, if more women than men, under conditions of fair choice, decide to spend a significant period of time raising children or to work in professions involving care for others, pluralism requires that such choices should be accorded due reward and respect. Or if women and men exhibit subtly different but equally valuable qualities when doing similar work, pluralism requires that the contributions of females be weighed equally with those of males. In other words, if pluralism is correct, the mere existence of sex differences need not imply injustice. Rather, pluralism requires equal respect for difference.

Thus, although assimilationism may be the favored conception of sex equality in many areas, such as civil rights, it is doubtful if it is acceptable across the board, in all areas of human concern. As our discussion of sports suggests, the assignment of significance to sex is not always a form of sexism.

We have not been shown, then, that separate athletic programs for men and women in those sports where one sex is at a physiological disadvantage are morally suspect or illegitimate. Unlike the doctrine of "separate but equal" in the context of racial segregation, separate athletic programs do not stigmatize one group or the other, are not imposed against the will of either sex, and actually enhance the freedom and opportunity of the previously disadvantaged group. Thus, sports seem to provide a model of a defensible pluralistic approach to sex equality. In sports and perhaps in other areas as well, sex equality does not require blindness to sex.

Legislating Equality

What are the implications of the preceding discussion for policy? In particular, what concrete requirements should legislation designed to promote sex equality, such as *Title IX*, actually require?

Equal Funding or Equitable Funding

One proposal that should be considered is that equality of opportunity, when applied to institutionalized athletic programs such as those in schools and colleges, requires *identical* financial support. If, at a given institution, different amounts of money are spent on men's and women's sports, then the requirement of equal opportunity has been violated.

It is easy to understand why many supporters of women's sports might be tempted to view equal expenditures as a proper criterion of equal opportunity. For far too long, women's sports have received only an infinitesimal fraction of the budget of many institutional athletic budgets. James Michener, writing about the period before promulgation of *Title IX*, reported that

> one day I saw the budget of . . . a state institution (a university), supported by tax funds, with a student body divided fifty-fifty between men and women. The athletic department had $3,900,000 to spend, and of this, women received exactly $31,000, a little less than eight-tenths of one percent. On the face of it, this was outrageous.[29]

However, one should not jump too quickly from the outrageousness of the policy described by Michener to the conclusion that *identical* funding should be provided for men's and women's sports programs. Consider an example from another area. Suppose that half the children in a particular school want to develop their musical abilities and half want to learn computer science. The school buys a number of musical instruments adequate for instruction and provides for sufficient computers and faculty to allow the formation of a computer science program. However, because computers cost more than musical instruments, the school spent several times more money on the students in the computer program than on the musicians. Even so, the opportunities are equal for both groups. All the children have an equal chance to pursue their interests, whichever interest they happen to have.

The same point applies even if among the musical group two-thirds of the children prefer to play the guitar and the remaining third prefer to play the piano. Suppose that one piano, which is enough to accommodate the second group, costs as much as five guitars, which are needed to accommodate the first group. If so, more money will be spent on one-third of the children than on two-thirds of them, but once again it is far from clear that anyone has been treated unfairly or denied equal opportunity. On the contrary, both guitar and piano players have an equal chance to develop their talents on their favorite instrument.

These examples suggest that "equal expenditures" and "equal opportunities" are two distinct notions. Moreover, the examples have clear analogies in the world of sports. For example, football, which is played predominantly by men, requires more expensive equipment than virtually any varsity sport played by women. Thus, our examples suggest that an institution may legitimately spend more on the men's athletic program than the women's when the difference in expenditure is due to differences in cost of equipment.

A second factor that may justify differences in expenditures between men's and women's athletic programs are different rates of participation by men and women. Clearly, if more men than women participate in an athletic program, more money will be spent on the former than the latter. This may be ethically acceptable, so long as the institution provides equal chances and encouragement for men and women to participate, but the sexes respond in different ways.

Accordingly, although the degree of inequality cited by Michener clearly is unjustified, sex equality in organized institutional athletic programs need not require identical funding for men's and women's sports. Even if the men's and women's athletic programs receive different amounts of financial support from the same institution, it does not *follow* that there is an injustice involved. A variety of factors may show the difference to be justified. Thus, investigation may be needed to determine whether the difference in funding has an acceptable or unacceptable explanation, but the inequality in expenditures by itself is not evidence of discrimination.

The Formula of Per Capita Equality

Should we shift from a requirement of equal overall expenditures for men's and women's athletic programs to one of equal expenditures per participant? Proponents of the latter suggestion acknowledge that differences in the total budget of men's and women's athletic programs might be different, perhaps because of different rates of participation by men and women, but argue that it is unfair that more be spent on individual men than on individual women. In their view, if State U spends an average of $300 on each male athlete, it should spend an average of $300 on each female athlete as well.

This suggestion is plausible. Normally, if one is comparing similar sports offered by the same college or university, one would expect equal per capita expenditures on each athlete. Thus, one would expect that as much is spent on each member of the women's basketball team as on the men's basketball team.

Even here, however, some differences may be acceptable. Suppose referee's fees are higher for the men's sport, which may be more difficult to officiate because of the greater speed at which it is played? Suppose the coach of the women's team is older and more experienced than the coach of the men's team, and as a result draws a higher salary?

Other purported justifications for difference may be more controversial. Suppose the men's team has national stature but the women's team plays a largely regional schedule? Should a college or university be allowed to make one of its teams, often a men's team, a "showcase" for the institution? Does the revenue and attention the team attracts justify the extra expenditures allotted to it?

Although care needs to be exercised in this area, perhaps institutions ought to be allowed to support such showcase teams, but only if the following conditions are satisfied. First, the institution must be making an honest effort to make at least some of the women's teams into showcases as well.[30] Second, a significant proportion of the revenues generated by the showcase teams must be used to support the teams receiving the lesser support, or alternately be used to support disadvantaged students who need financial aid, or some similar broad purpose.[31]

When one turns from comparisons among similar sports to expenditures across an entire athletic budget, the formula of equal per capita expenditures faces even more serious difficulties. Because some men's sports, such as football, cost far more than women's sports, more will be spent, on the average, on each male athlete than on each female athlete simply because of the subsequent imbalance created by the more expensive male sports.

One might object that rather than simply accept such imbalances as given, either the more expensive male sports should be eliminated, or extra opportunities for women should be added to make up the difference. The first alternative seems too harsh, however. It seems unfair to deny a football player the opportunity to play his sport just because it is more expensive than sports played by women. If football is too expensive to support, or too violent, perhaps it should be dropped from the athletic budget. But it seems quite another thing to eliminate it just because more is spent per capita on football players than on female athletes. After all, we don't think it unfair that the institution spends more on the piano players than the guitar players in our previous example because each is being given the same opportunity to play a favorite musical instrument. Similarly, aren't the football player and field hockey player being given the same opportunity to play their favorite sport?

Perhaps football and other expensive male sports should not be eliminated but rather more opportunities to compete should be provided for women than for men. Thus, an intercollegiate or interscholastic athletic program might offer competition in a greater number of women's than men's sports, at least if the more expensive men's sports continue to be offered. This suggestion has merit and will be considered in the next section for it seems to emphasize *equivalent* opportunities for females, rather than identical per capita expenditures.

In any case, the goal of equal per capita expenditures per athlete does seem required by considerations of equal opportunity. As the case of the piano and guitar player illustrates, we can achieve equal opportunity even when per capita expenses differ. As we will see, we may want to offer more sports for females than males, so as to provide equivalent opportunities for members of each sex but we do not seem morally required to do so just to insure that equal amounts of money are spent on each individual athlete.

Our discussion suggests, then, that neither the formula of equal total expenditures or equal per capita expenditures is a defensible criterion of sex equality in organized athletic programs. Perhaps what we should require of such programs, then, is that they provide equivalent opportunities for members of each sex. Although equivalent opportunities need not be strictly identical, they must be equally valuable.

Equivalent Opportunity

But what makes opportunities equivalent? There is no easy answer to this question. Once the shift is made away from quantitative criteria that can be measured in dollars and cents, greater weight must be put on qualitative judgments, which, although they may not be "subjective," may well involve complex value judgments that are inherently controversial. A full examination of the issues that arise in evaluating whether opportunities are equivalent is not possible here. Factors that would clearly be relevant, however, include the availability and quality of coaching, availability of facilities for practice, and equal good faith efforts to encourage participation by members of each sex, and to promote women's sports as well as major men's sports.

As our previous discussion indicates, equivalent *opportunity* for men and women should not be confused with equal *results*. At many schools and universities, women's teams may not generate the same sort of fan support or attention from the media as men's teams. Sometimes, this may be due to inequitable behavior by the institution, which, of course, should be corrected. However, the games fans choose to attend or the publicity the media decide to devote to particular teams and sports often will be beyond the control of the school or university. Individuals may make questionable choices but still may have a right to make them nevertheless. On the other hand, superior performance and a supportive institution can generate large, enthusiastic crowds and appearances on national television, as attested, for example, by the recent successes of the women's basketball teams of such institutions as the University of Texas and Louisiana Tech.

Are there instances where the support provided for men's and women's programs should be inequivalent? One kind of case might involve nationally recognized men's intercollegiate teams in such major sports as basketball and football. These sports are alleged to generate huge amounts of revenues and support for their home universities—income that supposedly supports men's teams in sports that do not produce revenue and much of the women's athletic programs besides. Thus, CBS purchased the rights to televise the NCAA Men's Basketball Championship for three years for a reported price of one billion dollars, a sum to be distributed among member institutions. In cases where the men's team can generate significant income and support, is it legitimate to provide them with such extras as national scheduling, a greater number of coaches, advantageous practice times, and extensive support in the area of public relations?

In considering this issue, it should be noted that, in many cases, men's football and basketball often not only fail to produce revenue, they frequently operate deep in the red. Thus, in 1976–1977, for example, about "one half of the colleges with Division I football lost money on that sport, and almost all Division II and III football programs lost money."[32] Although the major men's teams of a number of major colleges and universities do bring in enormous income, due in part to what seems to be ever-increasing television contracts, the argument for special treatment of men's programs in major sports, based on their capacity to generate income, applies to fewer institutions than is often thought.

In fact, the emphasis on intercollegiate athletics as a source of revenue can lead to inequitable treatment of women's athletic programs. In the spring of 1990, the University of Oklahoma announced it was ending its women's basketball program, in part because of lack of support from the university community and in part because it was expensive to run.

Because the timing of the announcement was horrendous, coinciding with the women's NCAA basketball championship televised nationally by ESPN, and because of protests by coaches of women's teams, Oklahoma's decision was criticized vigorously in the national media. Was the criticism justified?

The university defended itself by claiming the money saved by cancelling the basketball program would go to support other, more popular women's sports. Moreover, Oklahoma officials pointed out that one fourth of the women's total athletic budget was spent on basketball, even though the women's basketball team only drew an average of slightly over two hundred fans to each game.

Although Oklahoma argued that its decision was best for the overall benefit of the women's athletic program, a good case can be made that women's sports were being judged by a standard that may have been inappropriately applied, namely, their capacity to generate revenues. In fact, Oklahoma spent on women's intercollegiate athletics only about a tenth of the amount spent on men's intercollegiate athletics, a difference which, on the face of it, does not seem entirely justifiable by the kinds of factors discussed above. More important, basketball, a highly visible sport, played throughout the nation at the interscholastic and intercollegiate levels, had important symbolic value for women's athletics. For a major university to eliminate its women's program, especially as men's sports that were not producing revenue went untouched, seemed a denial of commitment to women's athletics. Finally, it was charged that Oklahoma had not made a major effort to publicize and support its women's athletic program in basketball.

However, the issue is not simply whether Oklahoma could have generated more fan support and more revenue for its women's basketball program, as have universities with highly visible women's basketball programs, such as the University of Texas. Also at issue is whether a women's sport should be cut primarily because it is not as visible or as financially successful as revenue-producing men's sports, in a university where women's sports in general receive only about a tenth as much financial support from the university as men's sports. We will discuss this issue further in our examination of intercollegiate athletics. In any case, the University of Oklahoma did restore its women's basketball program, in the face of the protests its decision to eliminate the program had generated.[33]

Nevertheless, in those cases where men's programs do generate large income, it can be argued that some differences in the treatment of revenue-producing sports might be justified. Thus, although the University of Oklahoma may have been unjustified in eliminating women's basketball, it may have been justifiable to develop more of a national schedule for the men's team because of the expected return such an investment might bring.

However, even though the argument for special treatment may have some force in such contexts, it should be implemented only when certain other conditions also are satisfied. These conditions should be based upon justifiable requirements designed to insure that the assignment of special status to men's teams in major sports does not block the emergence of women's athletics or deny them the chance to achieve "showcase" status of their own. If we did not accept some such conditions on grounds of equity, we would be conceding that the utility produced by major sports justifies us in overriding the claims of each person to equal respect and equal consideration. The result of such a view is that the individual is reduced to a mere resource for use by others. If we want to respect individuals and their rights, we cannot allow a concern for efficiency alone to simply override concern for persons and their entitlements.

What moral limitations might apply to institutions where large revenue-producing sports warrant special consideration? It is difficult to formulate an exhaustive list, but perhaps the two following guidelines can serve as a basis for discussion.

1. The revenues generated, over and above those covering expenses, must either go into the general university budget for the benefit of the entire university community or must be distributed within the athletic program so that the women's sports program receives the greatest benefit.
2. The university must be making significant efforts to insure that some women's sports have a reasonable opportunity to achieve the status of the showcase men's sports.

These criteria ensure that broad segments of the university community can benefit from the revenues generated by the men's program, with emphasis of providing greater funding of the lesser funded sports programs, so they could be accepted by all members of the university from a position of impartial choice. Accordingly, they are at least arguably fair and equitable.[34]

So far we have been considering what the standard of equivalent treatment for men's and women's athletics implies for *funding*. However, problems with equivalency arise in other areas as well. Are the coaches in the men's and women's program similarly qualified? Are practice times allotted equitably? Are facilities shared or are women's teams relegated to inferior fields or gyms?

In such cases, there probably will be no precise or exhaustive formula for determining what counts as equivalent support. The trick is to strike a balance between blind adherence to a frequently inequitable status quo and too rigid a commitment to inflexible requirements of absolutely identical treatment. For better or worse, the attainment of equity is likely to rest far more on the sound judgment of men and women of good will than on quantitative formulas or rigid principles applied in ignorance of the particular context at hand. Accordingly, even though the formula of equivalent support and respect is undoubtedly vague and raises many problems that cannot be dealt with adequately here, it nevertheless seems far more acceptable than the more quantitatively oriented egalitarian approaches that we have considered.

Conclusion

This chapter has argued for two main conclusions. First, it has maintained that sex equality is not always to be equated with blindness to sex. In particular, the ideal of sex equality as sexual assimilation (sex blindness) seems inappropriate to the realm of sports. Second, it has been argued that the general emphasis of *Title IX* on equivalent opportunities for each sex in sports is more justifiable than strict requirements of equal total or equal per capita expenditures on men's and women's athletics in institutional contexts. The operative principle should be equal concern and respect for all participants, and this may sometimes justify differences in actual treatment, including differences in expenditures between men's and women's athletic programs.

Our discussion also has implications for our view of sex equality beyond athletics. In particular, it suggests that equal respect and concern are compatible with recognition of difference. Recognition of difference, conversely, does not necessarily require relations of subordination and dominance. In sports, and perhaps elsewhere as well, sex equality does not require forgetting sex.

7

Do Intercollegiate Athletics Belong on Campus?

The NCAA college basketball tournament is a showcase for intercollegiate athletics. The games usually are not only well played but also often are thrilling contests decided only in the last few minutes of play. A case in point is the 1982 final game between Georgetown and the University of North Carolina, which was decided on a last-minute jump shot by then-freshman sensation Michael Jordan. The game was well contested and hard fought and the two universities had fine academic reputations. In addition, the competing coaches, John Thompson of Georgetown and Dean Smith of North Carolina, were known both for their knowledge of the game and also for their concern for the academic success and well-being of their players.

Thus, it may have appeared to many spectators as well as to the national television audience that intercollegiate athletics never had been in better shape. Unfortunately, if viewers did form such an impression, further reflection on recruiting scandals and academic deficiencies of athletes in many major college athletic programs, as well as on much that was to come in the 1980s, would have dispelled that impression.

Big-time intercollegiate athletics continues to enjoy great popularity and continues to be highly profitable for many institutions as well. Sale of rights to televise the NCAA men's basketball tournament were sold recently to the Columbia Broadcasting System (CBS) for over a billion dollars. Yet intercollegiate athletics continues to be plagued with major problems, particularly where the major intercollegiate athletic powers are involved. Many observers consider these problems so serious as to call the whole practice of intercollegiate athletics itself into serious moral question.

Thus, only a few months after North Carolina's victory over

Georgetown, another national basketball power, the University of San Francisco (USF), which in the past had been represented by such great players as Bill Russell and K. C. Jones, announced that it had dropped intercollegiate basketball in order to preserve its "integrity and reputation." According to the Rev. John Lo Shiavo, then president of USF, "There are people for whom under NCAA rules the University is responsible, who . . . are determined to break the rules presumably because they are convinced that the university cannot stay within the rules and maintain an effective competitive program."[1]

The particular violations that broke the back of the intercollegiate basketball program at USF involved payments by alumni to a USF athlete and other payments by another alumnus to cover high school tuition for an athlete the university was trying to recruit. However, these violations are no more serious than many other recent infractions in intercollegiate sports.

In the past fifteen years, we have seen universities put on probation by the NCAA for a variety of recruiting transgressions, including submission of forged transcripts for players who otherwise might not have gained admission or remained eligible for competition. Respected figures, such as Notre Dame basketball coach Digger Phelps, have charged that covert payments to star college athletes, as well as other forms of cheating, are common.

A particularly shocking example of abuse of rules is provided by former Clemson basketball coach Tates Locke in the book *Caught in the Net*.[2] As Locke describes the situation at Clemson during his tenure there, there was tremendous pressure on him to win. Clemson is a member of the highly competitive Atlantic Coast Conference, which includes such college basketball powers as North Carolina, North Carolina State, and Duke. A number of these institutions not only have fine academic reputations but have locations that made it easier for them to recruit black athletes from the inner cities than it was for Locke in the somewhat more rural Clemson area.

It appeared to Locke that Clemson could not win as long as it abided by the recruiting rules laid down by the NCAA. As he acknowledges in *Caught in the Net*, Locke at the very least failed to prevent (and possibly turned a blind eye to) under-the-table payments to players by boosters. He also may have condoned deception in order to lure recruits to Clemson. Thus, he reports that the daughter of an assistant coach took college entrance examinations for academically deficient recruits. Moreover, in order to attract black athletes to Clemson, which was virtually all white, blacks from Columbia, South Carolina, were paid to pretend to be student members of a fictitious black fraternity on weekends when black athletic recruits visited the campus. A false picture of extensive on-campus social life for blacks was created on what was in truth a virtually lily-white campus.

Other problems have plagued college athletics as well. These range from low graduation rates for male athletes in major sports at many Division I institutions, to falsification of academic records or distortion of the academic process, to resignation under pressure of university presidents, such as the president of the University of Kentucky, who internally investigated suspect athletic programs, to the kind of not only embarrassing but also dangerous misbehavior and sometimes criminal activity of academically marginal athletes in some big-time intercollegiate programs. University of Oklahoma football players in the late 1980s served jail sentences for such crimes as rape, shooting a teammate, and sale of illegal drugs. Although there are many fine athletes and coaches in major college sports, in too many cases a concern for winning, and the status and income that go with it, seem to have taken priority over the academic mission of the university. In his announcement of the termination of the USF's basketball program, the Rev. John Lo Shiavo surely raised a fundamental ethical question about college sports when he asked

> How can we contribute to the building of a decent law-abiding society in this country if educational institutions are willing to suffer their principles to be prostituted and involve young people in that prostitution for any purpose and much less for the purpose of winning some games and developing an ill-gotten recognition and income?[3]

Moreover, the moral questions that can be raised about intercollegiate athletics go well beyond an examination of violations of NCAA rules. We can ask questions about the rules themselves. For example, should colleges and universities be allowed to give athletic scholarships at all? Does the NCAA permit teams to play too many games to the academic detriment of the athletes?

At an even more fundamental level, we can question whether intercollegiate sports even belong on campus in the first place. After all, shouldn't colleges be educational institutions rather than minor leagues for professional sports? Is the academic mission of the university compatible with a commitment to intercollegiate athletics? Is commitment to excellence in athletics in conflict with commitment to academic excellence?

This chapter is an examination of the value, if any, of intercollegiate athletics. Its central question is what place an athletic program should have on a college or university campus. In investigating this question, we shall be concerned not only with the proper role of athletics on campus but with the very nature and mission of the university itself.

The Role of Sports in the University

Why should a university support an intercollegiate athletic program? After all, many distinguished institutions, including the University of Chicago, Emory, and the California Institute of Technology, have well-deserved reputations for academic excellence yet at various times in their history have not supported a full intercollegiate athletic program or, in some cases, have not had any such program at all.

In evaluating the role of intercollegiate athletics in the academy, it will be useful to distinguish three separate questions:

1. Is it wrong for colleges and universities to have an intercollegiate athletic program?
2. Is it desirable for colleges and universities to have an intercollegiate athletic program?
3. If colleges and universities should have an intercollegiate athletic program, what kind of program is most desirable?

It may be, for example, that it is not wrong for colleges and universities to support intercollegiate athletics programs, but such programs are undesirable because the money spent on them could be better spent elsewhere. Perhaps all sorts of intercollegiate athletic programs are not equally desirable. For example, intercollegiate athletic programs may be desirable if run along the lines of Ivy League or Division III programs but not if run in a more expansive manner.

Is there any reason for thinking that intercollegiate athletics programs are wrong? Should intercollegiate sports be prohibited? The question here is a broad one for many sorts of programs, ranging from those of Division III schools (such institutions do not offer athletic scholarships, compete regionally rather than nationally, and emphasize athletics less than schools in Divisions I and II) right up to the athletic giants such as UCLA and Notre Dame.

Perhaps it is best to begin by considering an idealized but important model of what the university should be. By gradually modifying the model through the introduction of athletics, we can see the resulting benefits and costs.

The University as a Refuge of Scholarship

Why have an institution such as the college or university at all? What would be lacking in an educational system that devoted the elementary and high school years to imparting basic skills in reading, writing, and mathematics? After high school, students either would seek employment or go on to specialized professional training. Is there any special function that a college education serves that such a system would fail to satisfy?

Traditionally, the role of education in the liberal arts has been thought to fill an important gap that is ignored by merely professional training and that is not fully approachable by those still mastering basic skills. Education in the liberal arts exposes students to "the best that has been thought and said" in their own and other cultures. By reflecting critically and analytically on the works the best minds have produced throughout human history, students should become better able to acquire a broad perspective on the human situation, learn to critically analyze difficult problems, and appreciate excellence in the arts, humanities, and sciences.

Similar rhetoric can be found in the catalogs of most colleges and universities, for behind the language lies an institution which, though evolving, traces its heritage from ancient Greece, through the medieval universities of Europe, to the modern colleges and universities of our own time. The primary or most important function of these institutions, it can be argued, is to transmit the best of human intellectual achievement, to subject different viewpoints to critical analysis, and to add to human knowledge through research.

Although today's huge multiversities perform many functions, including provision of professional training in such fields as medicine, business, education, nursing, and law, it can be argued that the most important function of the university still is to transmit, examine, and extend the realm of human knowledge. This function often places the university, or at least some of its members, in an adversarial relationship with the rest of society, because the university's function commits it to the often critical examination of popular ideas of a given time and culture. If that function were not performed, many bad ideas would not be subjected to criticism, and even good ideas would be less appreciated or understood as their advocates would never have to modify or defend them in the face of objection.[4] In other words, if our ideas are false, the error can be discovered through critical discussion, and even if our ideas are warranted, their justification is better understood if they meet the test of critical inquiry.

Accordingly, although the model of the university as a refuge of scholarship and critical inquiry does not describe the multifaceted colleges and universities of today, let us consider it as a normative claim about what the principal function of the university should be. Can a case be made for the inclusion of an intercollegiate sports program in the university conceived not as a business or as a training ground for tomorrow's professionals but as a center of scholarship, humanistic education, and learning? Can intercollegiate athletics serve an educational function in the university?

Athletics as Education

It does seem morally permissible for colleges and universities to decide not to support a program of intercollegiate athletic competition. Even though faculty and students may not be prevented from engaging in recreational athletic competition at the informal or intramural level, for such a prohibition would violate their rights to liberty of action, teaching and scholarship can proceed without the presence of athletic departments, football weekends, games with traditional crosstown rivals, or even NCAA national championships. In fact, in some European countries, colleges and universities do not support intercollegiate teams. Athletic competition, often conducted at a relatively high level, is supported independently by a network of local and regional clubs and athletic associations. It is not morally required, then, that colleges and universities support intercollegiate athletic competition.

However, even if intercollegiate sports are not morally necessary, they may be educationally desirable, at least if conducted within certain bounds. Let us consider whether they add anything of *educational* value to the university, conceived of as refuge of teaching, scholarship, and learning.

Many educators would argue that college education and intercollegiate athletics are in conflict. Even if we ignore the abuses in many major intercollegiate athletic programs in the United States, there seems to be a basic contradiction between the aims of education and the aims of athletics. Thus, the time students spend on the athletic fields is time spent away from their studies. Moreover, many of the values associated with athletics, such as obedience to the orders of coaches, seem at odds with the kind of inquiring and questioning mind professors attempt to develop in the classroom. Finally, some critics see athletics as a mindless activity in which only physical skills are developed, while education is concerned with sharpening the mental skills of students. Thus, in the minds of many college and university faculty, athletics are at best a necessary evil, perhaps useful in allowing students to let off steam, but in basic conflict with the educational values they are trying to foster.

Is this alleged contradiction between education and athletics real? In fact, the place of athletics in the university traditionally has been defended on *educational* grounds. This seems entirely appropriate. If it could be shown that athletics, particularly intercollegiate athletic competition, has significant educational value, a strong case can be made that colleges and universities should support such activities.

Two kinds of arguments for the educational value of athletics need to be distinguished, because each relies on different premises and hence is open to different sorts of objections. The first goes back to the ancient

Greeks and views athletics as *intrinsically* educational. The second, which can be traced at least as far back as the British public schools of the nineteenth century and is captured in the novel *Tom Brown's School Days*, stresses the extrinsic value of sports as a character builder. These different approaches to sports are aptly characterized by the late A. Bartlett Giamatti, former resident of Yale and commissioner of major league baseball:

> The Greeks saw physical training and games as a form of knowledge, meant to toughen the body in order to temper the soul, activities pure in themselves, immediate, obedient to the rules so that winning would be sweeter still. The English ideals, on the other hand, aim beyond the field to the battle ground of life, and they emphasize fellowship, sacrifice, a sense that how one plays is an emblem of how one will later behave; they teach that victory is ultimately less important than the common experience of struggling in common.[5]

Let us examine each of these approaches in turn, beginning with the consequentialist emphasis on character building regarded by Giamatti as central to the English approach.[6] The principal argument presupposed by such an approach might be stated as follows:

1. Participation in competitive athletics contributes to the formation of certain traits of character, such as courage, integrity, dedication, and coolness under pressure.
2. The formation of these traits is desirable and should be promoted.
3. Therefore, participation in athletics is desirable and should be promoted.

Stated in this way, however, the consequentialist argument is open to a number of objections. The first is that, as we have already seen in Chapter 2, even if there is a high correlation between athletic success and possession of certain desirable character traits, it is far from clear that participation in athletics is the cause of such character development. Instead, individuals who already possess the desired character traits may tend to be attracted to competitive athletics and tend to do well in them. Rather than developing character through participation in sports, those with certain character traits already formed may tend to be successful athletes.

However, although this sort of objection does show that Premise 1 above is controversial, it does not conclusively undermine it. The consequentialist can reply, not unreasonably, that even if we cannot prove that participation in sports influences character, it is plausible to think there are some significant effects, even though the causal process may be complex. Similarly, those humanists who criticize athletics cannot prove that humanistic education promotes certain educational and moral virtues—perhaps those who already possess humanistic virtues are those most drawn to seek such education—but it is plausible to think there is some positive effect of humanistic education on character. At least, if it is not plausible to draw the connection in the case of sports, is it any more plausible in the case of academics? We need to beware of applying a double standard of proof here.

Moreover, even if participation in competitive athletics does not by itself cause the development of positive character traits, it may reinforce or help promote their development. Thus, youngsters who tend to be disciplined may have that tendency reinforced more by participation on an athletic team than by hanging out on the corner. Finally, athletic contests can illustrate or exemplify values for participants and spectators alike. Michael Jordan's coolness and grace under pressure or Florence Griffith-Joyner's determination in her Olympic victories illustrate important values for the whole community and provide examples of behavior we all may try to emulate, not only in sports, but in any difficult situation.

Accordingly, the consequentialist argument can be reformulated as follows.

1a. Participation in athletics either causes the formation of certain desirable character traits, *or* reinforces or in some way contributes to their development, *or* illustrates their significance in human life.
2a. These effects of participation in athletics are desirable.
3a. Therefore, participation in athletics is desirable.

Critics might still attack the argument by reminding us that we must consider all the effects of participation in athletics. Sometimes participation may have bad effects. It may teach and illustrate a win-at-all-costs attitude. Perhaps the adulation we heap on young athletes has bad effects on their character. They may come to think the world revolves around them because of their athletic success and fail to perform in the classroom or show loyalty to friends or teammates, or fail to develop concern for larger social issues.

However, this sort of objection is not decisive, even if the points made by the critic are often true, because the consequentialist argument, properly understood, is not simply a descriptive thesis about the actual effects of participation in sports under all conditions. Rather, Premise (1a) should be understood as making a claim about the likely effect of participation in sports under proper and appropriate guidelines. The consequentialist might point out with considerable force that just as we would not demean the value of a liberal arts education because students who are improperly taught, or who try to learn under adverse conditions, fail to benefit from it, so too we should not demean the value of participation in sports simply because it does not produce desirable effects under adverse or inappropriate conditions, such as the presence of unethical coaches or overemphasis on athletic success.

Perhaps the most serious problem with the consequentialist argument is not the truth of the premises, which, although debatable, are not implausible when properly understood, but its relevance to the university. For even if we accept (1a) and (1b), construed as assertions about properly administered athletic programs, they say nothing about the involvement of athletics with higher education.

Why should the university administer often highly expensive intercollegiate athletic programs? If its primary function is to transmit, examine, and extend the best that has been thought and said, perhaps it should stick to that task, which it does best. Participation in sports may be valuable but it can be pursued informally within the university, or more seriously in clubs, through regional leagues and athletic associations, or through other organizations outside colleges and universities. Moreover, who is to say what kind of character the university should promote? It may be the job of the university, perhaps through philosophy departments, to examine the question of which kind of character is best, but it is not the function or right of colleges or universities to impose that kind of character on others.

One way of answering these objections is to make a case for the *educational value* of participation in athletics, particularly intercollegiate athletics. In fact, such a case can be made along two lines of argument.

First, if the values that participation in sport, properly conducted, promotes are so broadly based as to be presuppositions of virtually any sort of productive activity, particularly including scholarship and learning, they can be defended as important components in the educational process. Such virtues as courage, dedication, willingness to face and overcome one's weakness, and appreciation of excellence are values not only promoted by participation in sports but also are among the very values presupposed by tough-minded critical inquiry or, indeed, any other activity that calls for the best within us. If so, the kind of commitment required by an intensive intercollegiate athletic program can be defended as a component of the educational process, for it provides a context in which athletes test themselves in what we have called a mutual quest for excellence.

However, even if we remain sceptical about the consequences for character of participation in sports, a second argument for the inclusion of intercollegiate athletics is perhaps more compelling. That is, the experiences of the competing athletes in a good sports contest are themselves educational, even discounting any future effects of development of virtuous character by the participants. Let us consider this argument carefully for if it is sound, good sports programs, properly administered, should have an honored place in the academic community because they are an integral part of the educational process.

In particular, if we consider the model of athletic competition as a mutual quest for excellence through challenge, it has several features that make it a desirable supplement to a liberal arts education. On this model, athletic competition can be thought of as a test through which competitors commit their minds and bodies to the pursuit of excellence. To meet such a test, they must learn to analyze and overcome weakness, to work hard to improve, to understand their own strengths and weaknesses, and to react intelligently and skillfully to situations that arise in the contest. In the sports contest, they must use judgment, make decisions that are open to reflective criticism (often known as second-guessing), apply standards of assessment, critically analyze play, and are often called upon to exhibit various virtues such as perseverance and coolness under pressure. In the course of a season, athletes can learn and grow by understanding their physical and psychological weaknesses and trying to improve.

Clearly, many of these same traits are also required for successful study in the humanities and sciences. Moreover, an important part of education is learning to know and understand oneself, and that kind of self-knowledge is one of the most valuable kinds of knowledge that can emerge from participation in sports. In calling for the best that is within each participant, a good athletic program can provide educational experiences that are unusually intense and unusually valuable, and that reinforce and help develop many of the same traits that promote learning elsewhere. But even leaving aside such consequences, the good sports contest arguably is a crucible in which learning of an important kind takes place, and which involves kinds of discipline, understanding, and analysis that are related to learning in other parts of the curriculum.

Critics might object that even if these points are correct, they do not show that intercollegiate athletics is a necessary part of an educational curriculum. After all, if the same values are directly promoted, taught, and exemplified in the classroom, the additional indirect reinforcement provided by athletics is at best marginal and at worst distracts students from more academic pursuits where the most important aspects of education are dealt with.

However, this sort of critical rejoinder is not decisive. As philosopher

Paul Weiss has pointed out, students, particularly undergraduates, are novices in the academic disciplines they study. At best, the more advanced undergraduates may become something like apprentices in some areas, by assisting professors in research, but they rarely have the chance to be at the cutting edge of achievement in a discipline until later in their careers. Athletics, along with the performing arts, are perhaps the only areas in most colleges and universities where students can have the experience of achieving and publically demonstrating excellence in achievement—excellence not just as apprentice learners but in performances that rank among the best at a high level of comparative judgment.[7]

In addition, and perhaps more important, appreciation of achievement in athletics is widespread, far more so than understanding of achievement in mathematics, physics, philosophy, or other specialized disciplines. Because of this, athletics can and should serve as a kind of common denominator allowing people from vastly different backgrounds, cultures, social classes, and academic interests to experience together the lessons of striving to meet challenges. These experiences can be not only educationally valuable to the participants but also can inspire, teach, and inform other members of the wider university community who also enjoy the competition. Thus, because of the intensity and high level of the competition, intercollegiate athletics can serve as a common medium through which large and diverse segments of the academic community can demonstrate and appreciate excellence of performance and the struggle to meet challenge.

Finally, because athletics is accessible to and attracts the interest of wide segments of the population, it can be a unifying force in an intellectual community often split along ideological, ethnic, religious, socioeconomic, and disciplinary lines. Although this function is perhaps distinct from its primary educational functions, intercollegiate athletics can help create bonds that allow communication to persist when it might otherwise break down because of differences within the university.

Our discussion suggests, then, that although intercollegiate athletics are not, strictly speaking, part of an education in the way the classroom experience is, they can and should add a desirable educational component to the university. Of course, our account has been highly intellectual and is not meant to deny that intercollegiate athletics can provide other benefits to the academic community as well. These benefits include opportunities for relaxation, opportunities to make new friends and meet different kinds of people, and generation of a sense of community and loyalty on campus. However, while these other benefits are significant, it is important to consider the educational benefits of athletics as well if we are to determine their proper role in the university. For example, one might argue that if athletics have educational value, coaches should be evaluated primarily as teachers rather than according to their record of wins and losses or their ability to generate funds for the university.

Perhaps the most defensible view of the proper role of intercollegiate athletics on campus is to compare them, not to mass entertainment or to devices for raising funds, but to note their similarity *in some respects* to academic honors programs. That is, they can provide special opportunities for testing, growth, and development of self-knowledge for unusually talented and dedicated individuals as well as special opportunities to appreciate and enjoy excellence for the rest of us.

Intercollegiate athletics, then, can be defended as an educationally valuable element of the academic community. Such a defense is normative, not descriptive, in that it justifies a position athletics ought to hold in academia, rather than describing the actual operation of "big-time" intercollegiate athletic programs. But an account does not lack value because it is partially prescriptive rather than entirely descriptive. Rather, it can be used as the basis of criticism of many actual practices precisely because it tells us what ought to be rather than what actually is the case.

Academic Attitudes and Athletic Success

The educational defense of intercollegiate athletics applies largely to the kinds of athletic programs found in the Division III schools of the NCAA, including the small liberal arts colleges, as well as to the Ivy League, and to institutions with similar philosophies. These colleges and universities view participants as students first and athletes second. Financial aid is given only for need and no athletic scholarships are awarded. Athletic ability is surely taken into account in making admissions decisions, even at the most academically selective schools, on the grounds that athletes make special contributions to the well-being of the university community, as do others with special talents and abilities. However, although exceptions occur, ability to contribute athletically normally does not make up for serious academic deficiency, and the athletes at these institutions tend to be typical of the student body in educational attainment. Recruiting is much less intense than at the major athletic powers, seasons are shorter, and the academic progress of the student is regarded as of fundamental importance. Although a number of major intercollegiate athletic powers are academically distinguished, the pressures on and time commitments required of even their athletes raise questions about whether the requirements of the educational model can be satisfied outside the more modest framework of the Division III and Ivy League philosophies of sport.

Even at the more modest level, many faculty feel uncomfortable with their college's athletic success. At academically distinguished Swarthmore College, located outside Philadelphia, football players on the excellent 1982 team became so angered by a negative review of athletics on campus that they refused to wear the college letters on their helmets. Faculty critics, their suspicions apparently having been aroused by the team's 7-0 record, implied that its members were unrepresentative of the student body—a polite way of saying that the school's admissions standards had been significantly lowered to recruit good football players. When it turned out that the football players' graduation rate at Swarthmore had been higher than that for the school as a whole, much of the furor died down, although a faculty member was heard to say on national television that Swarthmore's reputation for academic excellence might be tarnished by its athletic success.[8]

On the contrary, our discussion suggests that excellence in athletics, when properly achieved, should be an object of appreciation and enjoyment for the whole university community. The positive effects of an outstanding basketball program on a university campus are captured in an article by Oregon State Professor of English Michael Oriad.

> My colleagues and I recognize the most important functions of the university to be teaching, research, and service. . . . But on Friday or Saturday night from December through March, we cannot conceive of a finer place to be than in Gill Coliseum watching what the locals have termed the Orange Express. . . . These games are the major social events of our winter months, and our enthusiasm for the team is compounded of many elements. Some of us have had players in class and usually have favorable reports of the experience. . . . Most of us never appreciated the art of passing until we saw how O. S. U. executes it. . . . It is a particular kind of excellence that our basketball team exhibits and that most appeals to us. Ralph Miller speaks the truth when he calls himself not a coach but a teacher, and we teachers in other disciplines appreciate what his pupils have learned to do.[9]

Problems of "Big-Time" Intercollegiate Sports

Clearly, the ideal of intercollegiate athletics as a model of a quest for excellence in the face of challenge is at best only partially adhered to even by those schools whose athletic program most resemble it. When we turn to practices in major intercollegiate athletic programs, the resemblance may be minimal at best. In view of the abuses that have been detected within many such programs, ranging from recruiting violations to failure to educate athletes, some of whom may not have had the educational background that would even permit them to benefit from a college education, we need to ask whether big-time college athletics can be justified at all. Many college and university athletic programs are run honestly, and student-athletes in such institutions do get an education and develop athletically as well, but the reported abuses are sufficiently serious and the incentives for abuse sufficiently great to justify our concern.

The Corruption of Intercollegiate Sports

In many of the athletically prominent colleges and universities of our land, sports have become big business. Television revenues and the visibility and support accompanying success in the major "visibility sports," such as men's football and basketball, seem to many to undermine the educational ideal of sports. In order to gain visibility, and the revenues and support that go with it, a program must be successful. But "success" in this context means "winning," and so the temptation is to do what is necessary. to win. For example, coaches who teach their athletes effectively and who recruit only academically qualified players may not be as valuable to an institution interested in athletic success as a coach who wins, who can handle the media, and whose scruples about recruiting are less strict. Corners get cut. Other schools feel they too must cut even more corners, just to be competitive, and soon real abuses are far too common.

Violations of NCAA rules and misbehavior of athletes who many believe are only marginally qualified as students, such as the series of criminal charges brought against Oklahoma football players during the late 1980s, get much of the publicity. However, perhaps the most significant form of abuse is deeper. In particular, if the purpose of participation becomes winning for the sake of external goods, such as visibility and financial support, won't players come to be viewed as mere means to that end rather than as students to be educated? Indeed, education can be viewed as an obstacle athletic programs must overcome in order to keep their players eligible. The result may be large numbers of players who receive an inadequate education and perhaps never graduate. Former star Minnesota Viking lineman Alan Page has described a meeting of eight defensive linemen to go over the team's playbook:

> We had each spent four years in colleges with decent reputations . . . and
> I remember that two of us could read the playbook, two others had

some trouble with it but managed, and four of my teammates couldn't read it at all. . . . The problem seems to be that these athletes—and there are many more like them, blacks and whites—were never expected to learn to read and write. They floated through up to this point because they were talented athletes.[10]

The highly publicized case of former Creighton University athlete Kevin Ross is an illustration. A highly recruited basketball player, Kevin was something of a disappointment on the court for Creighton. What was far worse, however, was that Kevin never learned to read or write or do simple arithmetic. Many of his courses were in such areas as ceramics and theory of basketball, and his fundamental academic deficiencies were never dealt with during his days as a student. To its credit, Creighton later acknowledged Kevin's academic deficiencies and helped him to acquire fundamental skills in reading, writing, and arithmetic by sending him to a prep school for *elementary* school students.

It took a good deal of courage and determination on Kevin Ross's part to go through such an experience, but one still has to ask basic questions about the incident and what it suggests. What kind of educational system allows athletes to float through because of their skills on the playing field in virtual disregard of their academic progress? And for every university which tries to rectify its mistakes, how many don't care?[11]

Thus, perhaps the morally most damaging charge brought against major intercollegiate athletics is that it exploits the participating athlete. Such athletes are ostensibly offered scholarships to play their sport in return for an education, but in too many cases, the athlete is expected to give everything on the field, sometimes to the huge financial benefit of the university, while little or no time or effort is expanded on insuring parallel success in the classroom.

For example, football at major universities, and often at smaller schools as well, is virtually a year-round sport. Practice starts in late summer. The season can extend into December, and even further if postseason competition in the major bowls is involved. The season itself may be followed by an off-season "informal" weight training program, which goes through winter, which may, in turn, be followed by spring practice.

As we will see, the colleges and universities constituting the NCAA, headed by a commission of college and university presidents especially designed for the purpose, have tried with some success to introduce reforms. Before considering attempts to alleviate the problems we have touched on, however, the problems themselves need further examination.

The Problems of the Black Athlete

The problems discussed above, especially those involving the exploitation of athletes, may apply particularly to the black athlete. Although blacks constitute about 12 percent of the population of the United States, they constitute well over a third of college football and basketball players, about 40 percent of professional football players, and about two-thirds of professional basketball players. Disproportionate representation is even greater in the major intercollegiate programs, and at the very top levels of major professional sports, where all-star teams often are dominated by black players.

What explains the disproportionate representation of black athletes in certain sports? Theories of innate or genetic physiological racial differences have been used to explain this phenomenon. However, writers such as Harry Edwards have advanced plausible grounds for questioning the hypothesis of innate differences. Edwards argued that sociological and demographic knowledge indicates that inbreeding between whites and blacks in America has been extensive, not to speak of the influences of inbreeding with various other so-called racial groupings. Therefore, to assert that Afro-Americans are superior athletes due to the genetic makeup of the original slaves would be as naive as the assertion that the determining factor in the demonstrated excellence of white pole vaulters from California over pole vaulters from other states is the physical stamina of the whites who settled in California.[12]

A very plausible explanation for the unusual representation of blacks in many sports is environmental. If blacks perceive many doors as closed to them because of discrimination, sports may seem the best escape route from poverty and the ghetto. The effects of discrimination may also lead to there being a dearth of nonathletic role models in the black community, a gap filled by successful black athletes. Or such alternate role models may exist but may be less appreciated than is warranted because of the attention focused on such black athletic superstars as Michael Jordan or Bo Jackson. As a result, success in athletics may come to be more highly valued in the black than in the white community. Thus, blacks become disproportionately involved in athletics, especially such sports as basketball, track, football, and baseball, which normally do not require large investments in equipment and for which inexpensive nondiscriminatory facilities are widely available in urban areas.

The following quotations from interviews with black baseball players tend to support the environmental hypothesis:

> It has been an avenue for me out of the ghetto. Hadn't I played baseball,
> I probably would have finished school but I doubt seriously I would be

doing exactly what I wanted to do. Blacks just don't get an opportunity
to do what they always want to do.

Very definitely, I escaped through sports. For poor blacks there aren't
many alternative roads. Sports got me into college and with college I
could have alternatives. . . . I've worked hard at baseball to get away
from the way of life I led growing up.

Yes. . . . It's helped a lot of blacks. There ain't too many other things you
can do. There are other things, but you don't have the finances to do
it.[13]

If it is true that sports are more often viewed as the path of choice to
upward mobility in the black community than the white, we might
worry whether black athletes are more vulnerable to athletic exploitation
than whites. For example, as many black youngsters might tend to see
sports as the major and perhaps only avenue to success open to them,
they may be more prone to neglect their studies than others. The hope
of obtaining an athletic scholarship and of perhaps playing professional
sports may interfere with developing the educational tools that make for
success in a variety of other areas.

As a matter of fact, although athletic scholarships are available for
many athletes, including underprivileged blacks and whites, the odds of
obtaining them are not high. The odds of achieving a career in pro sports
not only are even lower, they are astonishingly small.

At the present time there are fewer than 900 blacks making their living
in the three major professional sports. If we add to that number the
black professional athletes from other sports along with black coaches,
trainers, and minor league baseball players, it is doubtful that it would
be increased much beyond 1500. Since there are over 24 million blacks
in the United States, this means that professional sport provides opportunities for 1 out of every 18,000.[14]

Unfortunately, it appears that black youngsters tend to overestimate
their chances of playing college and professional sports more than whites
do, and so may be led disproportionately to assign a higher priority to
athletic than academic success. A Louis Harris Poll released in 1990
reported that 55 percent of black high school athletes expected to play
ball in college and 43 percent said they could make it in professional
sports. Only 39 percent of the whites thought they could get to play in
college while just 16 percent thought they could compete at the professional level. In reality, only about 3 percent of high school athletes make

it in college sports and only 1 in 10,000 go on to compete at the professional level.[15]

For those who neglect educational opportunities, athletic talent may be far more likely to lead down a dead-end street than to the pot of gold at the end of the rainbow seemingly provided by professional sports.

The Case Against Major Intercollegiate Athletics

To review, the criticisms of "big-time" intercollegiate athletics arise from the change of emphasis from athletics as an educationally valuable activity supplementing the normal academic curriculum to athletics as a source or revenue, support, and high visibility. These benefits—revenue, support, and visibility—depend upon winning which, in turn, depends largely on recruiting the best athletes. The pressure to win can become so intense that coaches and athletes as well as university administrations (often under pressure from influential alumni boosters) make decisions which reflect athletic priorities rather than educational ones. The players are more and more treated as means to athletic success rather than as students who should be educated. At their worst, the pressures lead to recruiting and other violations, to misbehavior and even criminal activity by athletes who perhaps are not educationally prepared for college, and to other abuses that have too often dominated the sports pages of our daily newspapers.

In addition, the kind of disrespect for the educational mission of the university, along with violations of NCAA rules and misbehavior by athletes themselves, undermines overall respect for the university. If the ideal of the university is that of an institution concerned for preservation and discovery of truth and the recognition of human excellence, isn't that ideal compromised by sacrificing the education of athletes for athletic victories, and even more so by outright cheating? Even though it is true that the modern university has become what has been called a social service station, fulfilling a variety of social needs, its most important function still is to formulate, test, teach, and evaluate achievement in the arts, sciences, humanities, and professions. How can the university claim to represent such fundamental values when it subverts them in its own practice?

Of course, even at the level of major intercollegiate sports, not every school cheats or exploits its athletes. Many, probably most, coaches, even in the high visibility men's sports, are concerned about their players as persons and students as well as athletes. In fact, some studies indicate that even at the Division I level, where athletic scholarships are given and recruiting often is intense, "varsity football and basketball players enter college with relatively poor high school records and test scores . . . yet graduate from college at only a slightly lower rate" than other students.[16] Moreover, such athletes sometimes may take less demanding curricula than other students but they often do as well or better in the employment market afterwards, whether they are black or white.[17] Academic performance in athletes in such less visible sports as swimming, soccer, tennis, and golf often are superior.

In addition, athletes themselves also have responsibilities to seek a good education, which they themselves do not always carry out. Not every case of an athlete failing to get an education is the fault of the institution rather than of the individual.

Nevertheless, there clearly are significant pressures in major intercollegiate athletic programs, which often lead at worst to blatant violation of NCAA rules and, even at best, to tendencies to short-change athletes academically in order to achieve competitive success. Even favorable studies, which suggest that many athletes in such highly visible college sports as football and men's basketball often do well after college, acknowledge that athletes disproprotionately enroll in educationally less demanding courses.[18]

Reasonable people may doubt, then, whether intercollegiate sports should be played at the level of national competition and intensity found in the major football and basketball conferences of our nation. Many would argue that the only reputable intercollegiate athletic programs are those resembling the Division III or Ivy League levels where no athletic scholarships are given, athletes are expected to be students, and competition normally is regional rather than national in scope. Perhaps this kind of intercollegiate competition is the only kind compatible with respect for the athlete as a person, with respect for the educational value of athletic competition, and with respect for the integrity of the university itself.

Reforming Intercollegiate Athletics

However, before we accept the conclusion that major intercollegiate athletics at the national level are *inherently* unethical, important counterarguments need to be considered. In particular, proponents of major intercollegiate athletics maintain that provision of entertainment for the campus community and for regional and national audiences is not inherently wrong, especially when it results in financial and other kinds of support for the university. After all, it can be said with considerable justice that many critics of intercollegiate athletics would not complain if the university's drama or dance companies or the choir received national recognition by providing a huge television audience with many evenings of enjoyment. If it is permissible for the university to be a social service station in other areas, why shouldn't it provide entertainment to society, in return for rewards, in athletics as well?

Can major athletic programs be justified in terms of the good consequences of their operation? This appeal to consequences is utilitarian in form. It appeals to the greatest good of society as a whole. Utilitarian arguments, although arguably they are not the only kind of moral considerations that we should weigh, are not irrelevant to moral evaluation. After all, we surely ought to consider whether major athletic programs promote more good than harm when morally evaluating them.

But if defenders of major intercollegiate athletic programs are to appeal to utility, they must consider *all* the relevant consequences, bad as well as good. Bad consequences, including harm to athletes and to the reputation and operation of the university, need to be minimized or eliminated for they are disutilities.

Moreover, as we have seen, utility itself does not normally override other sorts of ethical considerations involving fairness and individual rights. On the contrary, rights function as constraints on the direct pursuit of utility. Without the protection provided by individual rights, individuals could be unduly sacrificed for minimal gains in the good of society as a whole. Because one of the charges against major intercollegiate athletic programs is that they too often exploit athletes, violating their rights, utilitarian arguments alone will not carry the day.

Both utilitarian and rights-related approaches, then, suggest that major intercollegiate athletic programs are morally required to operate within strict ethical restraints. If such programs could conform to the required restraints, they would be ethically defensible. But what restraints should be in place? Can educational values and respect for persons be preserved in intercollegiate athletics without losing the quality of excellence and the levels of intensity and enthusiasm characterizing the NCAA basketball championships or Big Ten football?

Should College Athletes Be Professionals?

One proposal, defended by Senator Bill Bradley, himself a former college and professional basketball star, is that college athletes playing major sports in "big-time" intercollegiate programs be professionals.[19] According to one version of such a proposal, the athletes would be paid to play and need not be students. Such individuals could attend classes and obtain a degree if they fulfilled the normal requirements for admission to the academic program, but they would not be required to do so.

Rather they would be employees of the college or university for which they played.

This proposal would have several advantages. First, it would be honest. Illegal payments to athletes would not be necessary since the athletes would be openly paid a fair salary. Second, the fiction that all players are "student athletes" would not have to be maintained. Athletes not academically qualified to attend classes as well as those not interested in doing so would not be expected to perform academically. Third, athletes would not be exploited. They would share in the profits produced by their play, and their pay would be set by the market. Finally, such athletes could have access to education and enroll in classes and earn a degree if they wished to do so, but only by meeting the same academic standards of admissibility and performance as other students. Accordingly, athletic excellence and the academic integrity of the university would both be preserved by the proposal that college athletics be professionalized.

However, although such a proposal has virtues, it may be a case of throwing out the baby with the bathwater. If it were adopted, what we would have is not intercollegiate athletics but just another professional minor league. Critics might object that "just another professional minor league" is what we have now, but perceptions, and sometimes the reality, differ. In spite of the abuses, many, perhaps most, athletes in major intercollegiate programs are working towards degrees and are students at the schools for which they play. The enthusiasm of the crowds and the spectacle of college sports makes it distinctively different from professional sports, and part of this difference undoubtedly arises from the belief that college teams in some sense represent their institution. Students, alumni, and other members of the university community generate enthusiasm because of their loyalty to their institution and because of what they believe is the similar relationship of the players to the school. It is an open question whether the distinctive character of college sports would survive professionalization.

Of course, critics could object that the perceptions of the fans often are distorted and that college athletes in high visibility sports in major programs really are (poorly paid) professionals. However, the issue is whether we should further encourage this development, openly and honestly, or try to take college athletes in the direction of the educational model presented earlier. The latter policy has the advantage of both preserving the distinctive character of college athletics and preserving the educational values that a good intercollegiate athletics program can promote.

In addition, another serious problem faces the proposal that major intercollegiate athletics should be professionalized. Once the university

consciously enters professional sports with the primary goal being officially to make a profit, isn't there even greater danger than at present to
the educational priorities of the institution? Will favorite players be
traded or let go if their salary demands are too high? Will games be
scheduled off campus whenever possible to insure high attendance by
those most able to pay high prices for tickets? Will students be treated as
second-class spectators, with even more limited access to tickets than
currently provided at some profit-hungry institutions, because they can
afford to pay only relatively little for them? Will making a profit on high
visibility sports be regarded as so important that the educational lessons
to be learned from good competition are lost? Won't winning be the
bottom line, regardless of how it is achieved? At best, it is unclear if
professionalization will help most intercollegiate athletes significanly.

Moreover, will professionalization really avoid the exploitation of
athletes? Will universities be able to pay athletes large salaries without
diverting funds from education? If salaries are less than market value,
won't athletes still be underpaid but have even less chance of getting an
education than at present? Won't colleges sometimes end up firing
athletes who become too old to perform at top levels but who haven't
been paid the huge funds available to big leaguers and who have never
even been encouraged to develop academically?

Some of these trends exist already at the level of major intercollegiate
sports, but professionalization may only accelerate them. Before we
decide if that is the best alternative, others ought to be considered as
well.

The Academic Reform Movement

In the late 1980s and early 1990s, widespread disgust with the state of
major intercollegiate athletics led to a reform movement within the
governing body of college athletics, the NCAA. Headed by a commission
led by selected presidents of NCAA institutions, a series of reforms were
proposed, debated, and sometimes implemented. The goal of these
reforms was to reaffirm the priority of educational values in intercollegiate sports. Although proposals arising from this reform movement
undoubtedly will continue to be proposed and debated throughout the
1990s, the basic idea of reasserting the primacy of educational values
over profits and won-lost records deserves examination as an alternative
to professionalization. In order to evaluate the idea of reform, let us
consider a series of steps, some of which have been considered by the
NCAA and some of which have been proposed by those who maintain
that the reforms considered by the NCAA are inadequate.

Should Athletic Scholarships Be Eliminated?

One proposal, not officially proposed by the President's Commission of the NCAA but nevertheless well worth examination, goes to an opposite extreme from the recommendation to professionalize college sports. According to this proposal, all institutions should conform to rules like those presently in place in Division III or in such Division I conferences as the Ivy League. In particular, in this view, there should be no special financial aid for athletes. Prospective athletes would then pick their college or university according to how it could best fulfill their educational needs rather than on the basis of what special athletic scholarship they would receive. Financial aid would be awarded only on the basis of need, not athletic ability. Moreover, while admissions officers might give some special weight to candidate's athletic talents, similar weight would be given to the nonathletic talents of other applicants, such as ability in music or drama. Colleges and universities would look for true student athletes, not just athletes who attend only because it costs them nothing to do so while receiving a chance to get exposure in front of professional scouts. In other words, big-time college sports would be significantly deemphasized in order to fit the educational model defended earlier in this chapter.

This is a very attractive proposal. It would avoid the objection that major intercollegiate sports exploit athletes because only athletes who are concerned with the education an institution can provide would enroll. Moreover, athletic programs would be run as part of the institution's educational program rather than as revenue producers. For example, coaches might be given faculty status and be judged primarily as teachers rather than according to their record of wins and loses. Generating income and support would not be the primary purpose of the program's existence. Athletes would be admitted on the same basis as other students, so much of the motivation for the recruiting abuses that have plagued major college athletics would have been removed.

Nevertheless, although this proposal might express the ideal framework for structuring intercollegiate athletics, it has a number of serious defects. For one thing, it is impractical in the sense that it is extremely unlikely ever to be adopted. Given the huge amounts of money and support generated by the most successful athletic programs as well as entrenched support by alumni and fans for their favorite teams, a radical deemphasis of intercollegiate sports probably could not be achieved.

Of course, the policy of deemphasis still might be morally justifiable even if is difficult or impossible to implement. But even though there is much to be said for the moral justifiability of this approach, there also are moral objections to it. According to these objections, some deemphasis on athletics is justified, but radical deemphasis, including elimination of athletic scholarships, is not.

In particular, it is far from clear that the award of athletic scholarships or the use of athletic programs to generate revenue and support is inherently immoral. Athletic scholarships can be used to attract top talent to particular programs and make competition exciting. They also provide the opportunity for talented athletes, many of whom come from disadvantaged backgrounds, to use their athletic talent to acquire an education that would otherwise be beyond their grasp. Moreover, the income and support generated by success in high visibility sports benefits others within the university community. In addition to tangible benefits, such as money, athletics can enhance the visibility of the university, create cohesion within the university community, and create enjoyment for the region and sometimes the entire nation as well. What is immoral in this view is not major intercollegiate competition itself, but specific abuses resulting in exploitation of athletes and violation of academic ethics. Reforms should aim at cleaning up big-time intercollegiate athletics, not eliminating them.

How are these positions to be evaluated? Each seems to rest in large part on empirical or factual assumptions that are difficult to confirm. The proponents of deemphasis doubt whether incremental reforms actually can curb the kind of abuses arising when large amounts of money and status are at stake. Proponents of incremental reform are more optimistic. They believe that specific changes short of major deemphasis, some of which will be discussed below, actually can work. At present, it probably is unclear which of these factual assumptions is true.

However, in addition to consequentialist arguments about the effect of reform, there is another sort of argument for the view that award of athletic scholarships is immoral. Why, a critic might ask, should an athlete receive financial aid to attend a college or university when an educationally better qualified student is turned away? Why should limited openings in a college class be filled by those whose primary talent is athletics, instead of by those who could do best in the classroom? Even worse, why should a disadvantaged but not athletically talented student be denied financial aid, and hence denied an opportunity to receive an education, in favor of an athlete who may not even need the money and who may be uninterested in obtaining an education?

These are good questions but they are not unanswerable. We have already seen that a good athletic program can provide educational and other benefits for both participants and spectators alike. Although it is widely agreed that athletes who are not educationally qualified should not be admitted, athletes can be given some special consideration in admission because of the overall goods they provide for the whole community. Similarly, if there are other kinds of students who can provide similar benefits for the university as a whole, they should receive special scholarships as well. Perhaps rather than eliminate athletic scholarships, we should create special sorts of financial aid to lure students with other kinds of special talents to the university. (We probably would do so if they could generate the same kind of income attainable through athletics!)

These rejoinders may be defensible. In particular, *if* the benefits provided by high visibility sports in major college athletic programs are shared so as to benefit other members of the university community, such programs, including the award of athletic scholarships, may be morally permissible if the kinds of incremental reforms of the sort proposed by the NCAA actually are effective. In addition, it is important to consider proposals for reform for, even if they are not ideal, they may constitute a second-best solution to the problems of intercollegiate athletics that ought to be implemented if the ideal solution proves unattainable. Let us consider the idea of reform further.

Incremental Reforms

The incremental changes designed to restore the academic integrity of major intercollegiate athletics include revenue sharing, reducing the length of the competitive season for many sports and amount of practice and travel time that can be devoted to them, and tightening the academic requirements that athletes must satisfy in order to be eligible to play.

Of these, one of the most important is revenue sharing because it removes one of the main incentives for recruiting violations and other forms of cheating in order to insure a successful competitive record. Although different legislative proposals differ, the general idea is that the funds generated by contracts with the media for broadcasting major events as well as for appearances of teams in such events as the NCAA men's basketball championship be shared among the members of a large pool of colleges and universities. Hence, winning would not generate immense financial rewards. Rather, all the institutions in the relevant group would share the revenues regardless of whether their teams were successful or not. As shares would be roughly similar regardless of competitive success, the financial incentive to cheat would be significantly diminished. Unfortunately, controversy probably will continue to exist over whether the NCAA should distribute revenues from the media equally among, say, all Division I schools, which would be the most effective way of reducing incentives to cheat (because successful and unsuccessful athletic programs would get the same shares) or instead allow awards to differ according to factors that might favor larger more active programs, such as the number of athletic scholarships offered by an institution.

Nevertheless, revenue sharing seems a step in the right direction. The same can be said about reducing the length of seasons and time that can be allotted to practice, although many coaches and athletes point out that players, most of whom are highly motivated to achieve excellence, will often practice on their own even if they are excused from formal practices. Moreover, it may be inappropriate to apply a single limit on the number of hours per week that may be devoted to practice and competition across the board to all sports. Not only do demands of such sports as swimming and golf, for example, differ from those of, say, football, but participants in such sports often may be more successful academically than the average student in their institution. Olympic swimmer Janet Evans, who carried a 4.0 (or A) grade-point average at Stanford, is said to have left school because she felt she could not adequately prepare for world class competition under the new NCAA rule, adopted at its 1991 convention, limiting required practices to twenty hours each week.

In spite of perhaps justified claims that some proposed reforms are not appropriately applied to all sports, one only wonders whether the general range of proposals that the NCAA eventually might adopt will go far enough, particularly when proposed restrictions may reduce the revenues produced by major sports. For example, if faced with the choice between scheduling a men's basketball game on a weekday night when it can be televised or scheduling it on a weekend when programming competition might preclude television coverage, as well as the status, income, and visibility that goes with it, what decision will officials make? Shortening the season by a week of so might make less difference to a student-athlete's ability to succeed academically than reducing the total number of games played, or limiting the total field of the NCAA basketball tournament, or the amount of class days that may be missed because of athletics, but the latter sorts of changes may decrease income. In fact, decreasing the length of the season without other changes may make it more difficult to keep up academically because more games simply will be crowded into less time to play them.

Another proposal with considerable merit is to make first-year college students ineligible for varsity competition. Because the educational and social demands of college are so different from what many students have experienced, they often need a period of adjustment to college life. To expect them to meet the educational demands of their new institution, adjust socially, and compete on the varsity level may be asking too much, particularly of the marginal student athlete. Such individuals might do better educationally yet still compete athletically if they played on special freshmen teams with limited schedules.

Such a restriction on eligibility might not be entirely fair to the freshman athletes who are strong students (perhaps exceptions could be made for them) and might be more justifiable for some sports than others. Thus, football, where varsity practices and sometimes games take place even before classes begin, might be a prime target for such restriction but spring sports, which take place after all athletes have had a chance to adjust to college life, might not. Such a restriction may be ineffective in any case, since first-year athletes undoubtedly will participate on freshman teams, although such teams might play only a modest local schedule in order to allow participants to adjust academically and socially to the demands of college life.

Be that as it may, the most controversial proposals have involved restrictions on eligibility for first-year students who have not met what the NCAA regards as minimal academic standards before enrolling at a college or university. These restrictions seem to many to be discriminatory and even racist, while to others they seem necessary to prevent the exploitation of educationally disadvantaged students, black or white.

Entrance Requirements, the SAT, and Proposition 48

It hardly is surprising that those who have advocated reform of major intercollegiate athletics have fought for uniform minimum academic entrance requirements for entering athletes. If all students have to meet minimum entrance requirements, we can be reasonably sure that all are able and prepared to do college work. Athletes could not be admitted for their athletic ability alone if it was clear they were unable or unprepared to make satisfactory educational progress at the college level.

However, several issues arise concerning the nature of the requirements that should be imposed. Should they be the same for all schools or vary according to the nature of each institution? Should they involve minimum course requirements, such as three years of English in high school, a minimum grade-point average, or minimum performance on some standardized test such as the Scholastic Aptitude Test (SAT), or some combination of all of these?

Several reasons seem to count in favor of including performance on standardized tests among the criteria for eligibility. Such tests can be used to establish a minimum standard of competence that applies nationally. Courses, even in the same subject and the same level, can vary in content and difficulty from region to region and even from school to school. Similarly, grading standards in one school can be very different from those in another. Finally, it seems desirable to have a common national standard of eligibility. There is a loss of flexibility if colleges and universities are not allowed to individualize their eligibility requirements. Arguably, however, there is a minimum standard of competence below which it is unlikely college level work can be done at all. After all, nothing prevents individual institutions from setting *higher* standards of eligibility than the national one, but the existence of a national standard does prevent schools from instituting eligibility requirements that might be too low in order to recruit athletes with little chance of becoming academically successful.

In January 1983, the NCAA, responding to pressures for tougher academic standards for eligibility, adopted a highly controversial set of entrance requirements. In addition to requiring that potential student athletes had completed a core curriculum, an additional rule was adopted. According to this rule, called Proposition 48, only freshmen having a *combined* score of 700 on the verbal and mathematical sections of the SAT or a score of 15 out of a possible 36 on the American College Test (ACT) would be eligible to compete in college athletics. Proposition 48 would allow colleges to admit athletes who fell below the standard established by Proposition 48, and even award them athletic scholarships, but such "Prop 48" students would not be eligible to compete in intercollegiate athletics as first-year students. Although the requirements established by Proposition 48 were minimal, its passage caused heated controversy and led to cries of racial discrimination directed against the NCAA.[20]

The claim of discrimination arises from the difference in average scores of blacks and whites on standardized tests. According to the College Board, the mean score of all whites taking the SAT in 1981 was 442 on the verbal and 483 on the mathematical section. For blacks the comparable figures were 322 and 362.[21] Although there has been some narrowing of the gap since then, it still remains substantial.

Arguing against the rule, officials at predominantly black colleges pointed out that a disproportionate number of their students, athletes or not, would fail to pass the 700 cut-off on the SAT. Officials of the black colleges argued that their students acquired the needed skills during their tenure as college students, were often motivated by the chance to play a sport, and should not be denied that opportunity as long as they were making satisfactory academic progress at their own institution. More generally, Proposition 48 would disproportionately disadvantage blacks because their average test scores were lower than those of whites. Moreover, many educators argued that standardized tests such as the SAT are not as good predictors of academic success as grades for blacks. Tests such as the SAT are alleged to discriminate against blacks and poor whites and hence constitute an inappropriate and even racially discriminatory standard for eligibility.[22]

Moreover, Proposition 48 can be criticized as giving the academically more selective colleges an unfair competitive advantage in athletics. For example, a selective institution such as Duke, whose students have high average test scores, might be able to allow freshmen athletes whose scores are significantly lower than the average for the school to play. A less selective school might have to declare ineligible freshmen whose scores are about average for the institution. Thus, a school where the average SAT score for freshmen is very low might not be able to allow students whose scores were *above average* for their class to compete, even if it does a better job than many selective schools in imparting academic skills to athletes.[23]

The situation became even more heated in 1988–1989, when Proposition 42, an addition to Proposition 48, was considered by the NCAA. Proposition 42 prevented the award of athletic scholarships to students who failed the Proposition 48 requirements.

To many critics, this was the last straw. Not only would black athletes be disproportionately disqualified from participating in athletics as freshmen, now they could not even be given the financial aid that would enable them to attend college and acquire academic skills in the first place. Charges of unfairness, discrimination, and even racism, again were raised against the new regulation, the NCAA, and by inference against the member institutions of the NCAA that supported the new legislation. Georgetown University basketball coach John Thompson was so outraged that he walked out of a nationally televised game with Boston College to protest the new legislation.

Both Proposition 48 and 42 are indeed controversial. But do they unfairly discriminate against blacks? Are they expressions of racism? Proponents of these requirements, including a number of prominent black educators, argue that the propositions are justified. Are they correct?

It does seem true that both Proposition 48 and Proposition 42 disproportionately disadvantage black athletes. But is this enough to make the propositions discriminatory, in the sense of making unfair or unjust distinctions? Arguably, a rule is not discriminatory just because it has a disproportionate impact on a racial or ethnic group, even one that has been particularly victimized by past discrimination. Thus, we would not want to say that a rule requiring applicants to medical or law school to be college graduates is unjustly or unfairly discriminatory even though a higher proportion of whites than blacks are college graduates.

In order to prove discrimination, at least one of several other factors would have to be present as well. Among such factors might be the intent to harm the disadvantaged group. More controversially, a rule might be discriminatory, even if promulgated on apparently race-neutral grounds, if such grounds were unrelated to any important purpose, if the acceptance of the apparently neutral justification was actually motivated by perhaps unconscious or unintentional prejudice or bias, or if the rule, however neutral, violated some moral right of those disadvantaged by it. If *none* of these factors applied, how could the claim that a rule was unfairly or unjustly discriminatory be defended?

In fact, a number of educators, including some prominent and hardly conservative African-American scholars, have argued that the standards set by Proposition 48 are *too low*. If, as suggested above, socioeconomic factors predispose black youngsters to overemphasize athletics at the expense of acquiring basic academic skills, the setting of a standard by legislation like Proposition 48 may create an incentive for reversing priorities. As sociologist of sport Harry Edwards has argued,

> Rule 48 communicates to young athletes . . . that we expect them to de-
> velop academically as well as athletically. . . . Further, were I not to sup-
> port Rule 48, I would risk communicating to black youth in particular
> that I, as a nationally known black educator, do not believe they have
> the capacity to achieve a 700 score on the SAT . . . when they have a
> significant chance of scoring 460 by a purely random marking of the
> test. Finally, I support the NCAA's action because I believe that . . . the
> black community must insist that black children be taught and that they
> learn whatever subject matter is necessary to excel on diagnostic and all
> other skills tests.[24]

Professor Edwards's position here hardly seems unreasonable, let alone racist or discriminatory. If his point is correct, there is a justification for Proposition 48 that does not seem to reflect either prejudice or bias, but which expresses concern for the welfare of black youngsters rather than disregard of their rights.

What about the charge that standardized tests such as the SAT are culturally biased against blacks and other ethnic minorities? There are legitimate grounds for concern here. For example, in the past, IQ tests were used in unscientific ways to suggest that Jews and other immigrants were not as intelligent as other Americans.[25] Today, concern exists over whether some group differences in test scores reflect cultural bias written into the tests as much as ability. If whites are more likely than blacks to come from backgrounds where the answers are available, it is not surprising that they score higher.

Are standardized tests such as the SAT biased in any pejorative sense? A complete discussion of the issue would take us too far afield, but there are at least some grounds for being sceptical. The black-white gap on the

SAT in mathematics is as significant as the gap in English, yet it is hard to argue that mathematics is culture bound. Likewise, the issue is complicated by socioeconomic considerations. The economically worse off tend to do worse on the SAT than the more affluent. Because a higher percentage of blacks than whites are economically disadvantaged, socio-economic differences may explain more of the black/white gap on SAT scores than racial or cultural differences.

Suppose, however, that the tests are culturally biased. Does it follow that an eligibility requirement of a minimum score on standardized tests should not be applied to blacks and whites alike? Although any position here is likely to elicit disagreement among thoughtful people of good will, there are good grounds for doubting whether such a conclusion follows. After all, if the tests examine for skills that are important for everyone in our culture to have, blacks no less than whites need to acquire them. Racial minorities, like everyone else, need these skills to succeed in the broader culture. In particular, if Proposition 48 is used to exclude those who fail to satisfy the minimum standard from participation in athletics, rather than from higher education, it may well be permissible. After all, Proposition 48 does not restrict the award of athletic scholarships but only limits the chance to actually participate in intercollegiate athletics as a first-year student. (However, if the tests are culturally biased, then, even if scores reflect grasp of knowledge valuable in the broader culture, perhaps the tests should not be given as much weight in evaluating credentials of minority applicants as in evaluating credentials of whites.)

Proposition 42 is more dubious than Proposition 48 because it prohibits the award of athletic scholarships themselves. It stipulates that athletes who fail the standard set by Proposition 48 cannot be financially supported by athletic scholarships. One can understand Coach John Thompson's concern that Proposition 42, in effect, excludes many blacks from the chance of even acquiring a higher education.

But, contrary to Coach Thompson's view, Proposition 42 does not prohibit institutions from admitting students who fail the Proposition 48 standard and providing them aid based on need. Alternatively, it does not prohibit the university from offering athletic scholarships to more academically well-qualified (but not as athletically well-qualified) applicants, many of whom might also be members of minority groups. Thus, although Proposition 42, at first glance, might look exclusionary in a perhaps biased manner, a fuller evaluation might yield a quite different conclusion. Be that as it may, although Proposition 48 seems now to be widely accepted, Proposition 42 remains in a kind of legislative and moral limbo.

In any case, it is doubtful that Proposition 48 itself can be dismissed as unjustly discriminatory and, in fact, seems to be a permissible way of dealing with eligibility for first-year college athletes. Perhaps, however, the idea of eligibility requirements as well as requirements for provision of athletic scholarships could be handled in a different manner that might avoid much of the controversy over standardized tests and gave more weight to the diversity of institutions on the American educational scene.

That is, why not relativize the test score required for eligibility to the school at which the athlete competes? Higher education in America is extraordinarily diverse. The average scores on standardized tests of students at Duke, Stanford, and Michigan, for example, are significantly higher than those for most other institutions. Why, then, should we prevent first-year students from competing at an institution with low average SATs, if their scores are nearly average for their institution, while allowing students with higher absolute scores to play, say, at Duke, when their scores are significantly lower than average for their school?

If these questions suggest that a more flexible alternative to Proposition 48 is desirable, perhaps eligibility requirements should be relativized to each school. For example, why not stipulate that freshmen are eligible for intercollegiate athletics only if (in addition to meeting whatever other requirements concerning high school curriculum and grade-point average already in effect) their scores on the SAT or ACT are in the top two-thirds of the entering class of their own institution?[26]

Alternately, the NCAA might consider prohibiting all first-year students from participating in intercollegiate competition on the varsity level. This proposal would have the advantage of allowing everyone to have a year to adjust academically and socially to college, without the pressures of varsity competition. Freshmen football players, for example, would not have to arrive on campus before other new students and would be able to meet all kinds of students rather than have their first college associations be primarily with other football players. This may well be unfair to those academically well-qualified freshmen student athletes. However, limited athletic competition could be allowed on the freshmen and junior varsity level but first-year students would be given time to adjust academically before being expected to perform at the athletically most demanding level.[27]

Accordingly, while a good case can be made that proposals such as Proposition 48, which use standardized test scores to limit freshmen eligibility, are acceptable, other policies may be even more acceptable. In particular, both the proposal that eligibility requirements be relativized to institutions and the prohibition on competition on the varsity level for first-year students, at least in major Division I athletic programs, seem warranted and deserve full consideration.

Insuring Academic Progress

Overall, although it is far from clear that participation in athletics adversely affects academic performance, many major college athletic programs fail to exhibit sufficient concern for the academic progress of their students. In the worst cases, contempt is shown for the academic process itself. Thus, one former athlete of an earlier generation reported that his university

> recruited top football players regardless of their academic ability, and the athletic department's biggest jobs were to get football players admitted and then to keep them eligible. I remember the citizenship course which all . . . freshmen were required to take. I knew most of the other players hadn't been going to class or done any studying and I couldn't figure out how they were going to pass. . . . Then, just before midterms, we had a . . . meeting with one of the tutors hired by the athletic department. . . . He told us cryptically that if we copied down what he said, we would do all right on the exam. He wasn't joking: when I took the exam I discovered he had given us the answers to the test questions.[28]

We can hope that such blatant abuses largely are a thing of the past, but it is clear that if colleges and universities are not to exploit players, they have a positive obligation to provide genuine opportunities for athletes to receive a worthwhile college education. Passage of requirements such as Proposition 48 is not enough. For one thing, Proposition 48 applies only to first-year students and leaves open whether additional requirements concerning academic progress of athletes throughout their undergraduate years also should be implemented.

Many suggestions for promoting academic development of athletes in major college and university athletic programs have been made. Perhaps the following are most attractive:

1. Graduation rates for varsity athletes in each school's intercollegiate athletic program (or by sport within the overall program) not vary significantly from the graduation rate for the student body as a whole.
2. Course selection for athletes be in the hands of academic advisers, not the Athletic Department.
3. Course selection by athletes not differ significantly from that of other students unless a good educational reason can be given for the difference, e.g. athletes take more education courses or coursesin physical therapy than other students because they are more interested in becoming teachers or therapists than others.

Regardless of what specific reforms are adopted, the moral requirement is clear. The administration and faculties of colleges and universities that engage in major intercollegiate sports have a moral obligation to insure their players are not treated as mere means for attaining victory on the playing field and for gaining the external rewards that come with winning. Only an infinitesimal percentage of such athletes will ever play at the professional level. The university can avoid exploiting such players by providing genuine opportunities for their educational growth and monitoring the educational development of athletes to insure that their obligations as athletes do not interfere with their growth as students. Although many intercollegiate athletic programs, even those of some of the major sports powers, may already satisfy these criteria, it is the substantial number of those not satisfying them that contribute to the present blight on intercollegiate sport.

Personal Responsibility and Institutional Blame

Our discussion has emphasized the responsibilities of colleges and universities towards their athletes. This emphasis has been justified since many athletes are not yet mature enough to handle the academic and educational pressures they face. However, individual athletes also have a responsibility, equal to that of other students, to get an education. After all, these athletes are taking up spaces that could be given to other students. In addition, they, like other students, will face responsibilities as citizens and will need an education to help them meet their obligations reasonably and intelligently.

Just because an athlete fails educationally, it does not follow that it is always the fault of the institution, athletic program, or coach. It may be the fault of the individual athlete. In fact, to always view athletes, especially those from disadvantaged backgrounds or who are members of minority groups, as victims of institutions is to deny their personhood and ability to control their own lives. As John Thompson has asked, "Why can't we ask the student athletes who graduate without having learned to read what they were doing when they should have been cracking the books?"[29] By not acknowledging the responsibilities of student athletes for their own actions, well-meaning reformers may be disrespecting as persons the very individuals they are trying to help. Unprepared young athletes should not be expected to overcome actual obstacles to educational achievement placed in their way by big-time athletic programs but neither should they be exempted from responsibility for not taking advantage of opportunities genuinely made available.

Thus, educational institutions have an obligation not to exploit athletes and to provide genuine educational opportunities for them. Correlatively, athletes have a responsibility to take advantage of such opportunities if they are provided in an environment where reasonable and informed choice of goals can be expected.

Conclusion

The ideal role for intercollegiate athletics in the university, it has been argued, is educational. At their best, intercollegiate athletics allow for development, reinforcement, and expression of desirable states of character—the virtues. In fact, the virtues promoted by athletic competition, such as dedication, concern for knowledge of self and others, and courage, are also important educational virtues. Perhaps most important, participation in the test provided by an athletic contest, as well as in the preparation for it, is itself educational in that it provides an almost unique opportunity for obtaining knowledge of oneself and others. In addition, intercollegiate sports provide an example to the rest of the community of men and women pursuing and exhibiting excellence.

At its best, the university is a place where standards of excellence are formulated, applied, and debated in the arts, sciences, and humanities. Competitive intercollegiate sports provide a clear institutional framework where the value of standards of excellence in meeting challenges is demonstrated and reinforced.

Finally, intercollegiate sports help make a university a community by providing fun, recreation, and a common sphere of interest for a substantial number of its members. In fact, on campuses that often are split along ideological and intellectual lines, sports can provide a common framework allowing for lines of communication to remain open to individuals of significantly distinct ideological, intellectual, ethnic, religious and socioeconomic backgrounds.

Of course, the large multiversities of today are more than simple refuges for scholarship and teaching. In addition, they provide professional certification and training, can be the cultural centers for an entire region, and the research conducted within their halls can be of vast significance commercially and in its global effects on the world in which we live. Athletics can be and often is conceived of as an important source of revenue, visibility, and support for such institutions. Its teams can be identified with by masses of individuals, many of whom have no formal connection with the institution, who as a result come to share at least some of its goals. In short, intercollegiate sports can promote many of the purposes of the university and can be defended on consequentialist as well as educational grounds.

However, pursuit of the consequentialist goals is open to strong objection if ethical constraints are violated along the way. In particular, college athletes should not be exploited and the university should not violate its own ideals of intellectual honesty and integrity in the pursuit of victory and of the external rewards that go with it. Even if the modern multiversity is more than a refuge for scholarship, it still plays a unique role in our society. If it does not provide an arena for the examination of intellectual, artistic, and scientific standards of excellence, who will? This task is essential, not only for its utilitarian benefits, but also because without such standards, we could not function fully as free and autonomous agents. Instead, we would be far more vulnerable to victimization by ignorance, prejudice, and insularity than if protected by the kind of free critical inquiry the university supports.

Surely it is indefensible for the very institution charged with examining standards of truth and excellence to cheat in order to win ball games or to use athletes to achieve fame and fortune while ignoring its educational obligations to them.

According to a widely repeated anecdote, a midwestern university president, while trying to raise funds for his institution before a state legislature, is said to have asserted, "We need money to build a university our football team can be proud of." On the contrary, the institutions involved in major intercollegiate sports will have much to be proud of only when their teams are part of the educational community that constitutes the heart of the university.

8

Sports and Social Values

In previous chapters, we have examined the ethics of competition in sport as well as ethical issues, such as those involving use of performance-enhancing drugs, that arise within competition itself. In addition, we have looked at questions involving the relationship of sports to issues of equality, participation, and education. It is fitting that we conclude our examination by briefly considering some of the implications of the ethical values that should apply in sports for society in a broader social context.

In particular, we should ask if sports can and should play a significant role in broader spheres of moral development, especially in education and in the conduct of our personal lives. Because claims for the moral import of sports have often been exaggerated and because of many abuses within the actual practice of competitive sports, many people regard sports as a symptom of our moral decline rather than a positive moral influence. But perhaps such a negative view has been overstated. Do sports have an important role to play in our moral lives after all or are sports of no special moral significance?

Values, Morality, and Sports

The Reductionist Thesis

How are values in sports related to values in the larger society? According to one influential thesis, which we can call reductionism, values in sports are reflections and perhaps reinforcers of values in the broader society. This view is "reductionist" in that it attempts to explain all values in sports as expressions of dominant social values, thereby reducing the values in sports to those of the wider society. This kind of reductionism asserts, for example, that if a society is intensely competitive and stresses advancement of individuals over that of the group, sports will reflect and perhaps reinforce adherence to those values. If, in another society, competition is frowned upon, and loyalty to the group is held to be more important than individual advancement, there will be less emphasis on the importance of winning and more on teamwork than in the first society. Moreover, some reductionists might add, the emphasis on such values in sports may reflect back on the prevailing social values and reinforce commitment to them in the broader culture.

Reductionism can be an explanatory theory if its claim is that the nature of values in sports is fully explained by the existence of values in society. In addition, it can also be understood as a normative theory if it holds that the worth or justification of values in sports is no different from the worth or justification of more fundamental social values.

We already encountered an example of reductionism in sports in our discussion in Chapter 3 of Hoch's critique of football. Hoch, a critic of American society, sees it as too militaristic, capitalistic, and egoistic. In his view, football reflects and reinforces these values, which he regards as prevalent in our society.

Some forms of Marxism also tend to be reductionist not only in their view of values in sports but also about values generally. At least some kinds of Marxists tend to view all social institutions as reflecting the values of the economic structure of society. An emphasis on individual moral rights, according to this kind of Marxist analysis, is not part of a universal, objective morality, but is characteristic of capitalistic, competitive societies in which individuals compete with one another for success in the market. Individuals "stand on their rights" against others precisely because the free market puts them in cutthroat competition with each other in the first place. Thus, claims about equal individual rights might well be unintelligible in a feudal society, where the hierarchical structure emphasizes the morality of one's station and its duties, or in tightly knit communities where the individual, rather than being viewed as a separate autonomous unit, is in part defined by his or her place in the communal structure.

However, the reductionist position faces some very serious objections if it is extended to cover all ideas and values. If ideas, moral codes, and social practices are mere reflections of underlying and more fundamental economic relations, isn't that true of the reductionist thesis itself? If so, and if reductionism is used to debunk the universalist claims of other positions to objectivity and truth, the reductionist thesis cannot claim to be an objective truth applying in all times and places but can itself be dismissed as a parochial belief fostered by a particular economic system.[1]

Of course, reductionism, or Marxism itself, need not be based on so crude a form of economic determinism. Moreover, such a criticism does not apply to reductionist analyses of values in sports because such analyses do not claim that all values are mere reflections of a more fundamental underlying basis. Rather, their claim is only that values *in sports* are expressions of dominant social values; it is not about all values everywhere.

Perhaps the major objection to reductionist analyses of the values in sports is that sports often seem to express values that go counter to prevailing moral beliefs. An interesting example is given by Drew Hyland, a former Princeton basketball star and now a philosopher. Hyland has suggested that the emphasis on the merits and skills of the basketball players on local playground basketball courts can help to overcome racial prejudice and suspicions. When the only way to retain one's place on a crowded neighborhood court is to put together a winning team, whether other persons are good players will tend to count far more than their race, religion, or even sex. "In this situation, the pres-ervation of . . . racism has a clear price, the likelihood that you will lose and have to sit."[2]

Our own discussion throughout this book also indicates that there might be values internal to sports that are not mere reflections of a prevailing social order. For example, in a society that disvalues excellence and challenge, the values expressed in good sports contests, conceived of as mutual quests for excellence through challenge, would conflict with rather than reflect dominant social values. If so, sports might be an important source of moral values and even have a signifi-cant role to play in moral education, a point which, as Hyland has reminded us, was suggested by the French philosopher Albert Camus, who once remarked that the only context in which he really learned ethics was sports.[3]

The Inner Morality of Sport

Consider the case of a person who claims to be a serious athlete committed to competitive success but who, in spite of having time to practice, virtually never does so. In addition, this person shows no desire to learn about his weaknesses in his sport or to analyze different strategies that might be used successfully against opponents. Surely, in the absence of any special explanation, this person's behavior would undermine his claim to be a dedicated athlete.

This case suggests that there are some values, such as discipline and dedication, which are central to competitive sports, in the sense that any individual or team concerned with competitive success would have strong reason to act upon them. Thus, in a society in which little emphasis was placed on achievement or hard work, those committed to competitive success in sports would be endorsing and acting upon values that conflicted with the prevailing values of their culture. In fact, if such athletes become sufficiently influential or if the example they set is emulated, the values they act upon as athletes may change and even replace the prevailing value system.

Other values also seem closely connected with a desire to compete in sports and athletics. Consider concern for playing by the rules. Although some athletes may be tempted to cheat and may even do so on particular occasions, no athlete normally can endorse disrespect for the rules as a universal value to be held by all athletes in a competition.[4] For if cheating becomes a universal practice, there is no athletic competition in the first place. The very idea of such a competition is that of an activity governed by the appropriate constitutive rules, which at least partially define the game.

Concern for excellence and recognition of standards of excellent performance are other values that are intimately connected to competitive sports. Even if a competitor's main concern is winning rather than achieving excellence, such an athlete must intend to play better than the opposition. This presupposes a conception of better and worse play, and hence a conception of standards for evaluating performance in the sport. In a culture that is sceptical of all standards or holds all standards to be merely indefensible and arbitrary subjective preferences of the holder, or equally arbitrary reflections of class, economic status, race, or gender, the concern for standards in competitive sports may represent an important counter to the prevailing view.[5]

In fact, some values may be so intimately connected with sports that they are internal to it. As noted in Chapter 4, goods are internal to a practice or activity just when they logically cannot be understood or enjoyed independently of that practice or activity itself. For example, the value of being a skilled playmaker cannot even be understood without some understanding of the constitutive rules of basketball and appreciation of the strategies and nuances of the game. In a society where such external goods as fame and fortune are highly valued by the majority, athletes who value securing the internal goods of sports may exemplify a way of life that conflicts with and that might tend to undermine or call into question the norms of the majority.

To cite one last example: although there are different and competing conceptions of which ethical principles should apply to competitive sports, an ethics of competition can stand apart from and even conflict with moral principles that are widely accepted in other domains. Thus, the ethic of competitive sports as a mutual quest for excellence conflicts both with the view that competitive values are bad, wrong, or always to be abjured, and the view that defeating others should be the only fundamental goal of the competitive athlete.

These illustrations strongly suggest not only that the reductionist thesis is seriously flawed but also that the practice of competitive sports and athletics is value laden in a number in a number of important ways. Some values, such as concern for excellence, discipline, and dedication, are traits that all competitive athletes have strong reason to commend and act upon themselves. Others, such as respect for the rules, are values that any competitive athlete has good reason to maintain; they should be part of the universal set of norms upon which all athletes should act. Still other values, such as the particular excellences of particular sports, are internal goals that all serious players of the sport normally seek to exemplify and that reflect standards for evaluating the play of oneself and others. Finally, different conceptions of the ethic of competition, such as the model of the mutual quest for excellence, constitute moral standards purporting to be morally justified.

These different normative features constitute what might be called the inner morality of sports. They may be more or less in harmony with the ethic of some cultures, or subgroups within cultures, but they can conflict with the moral codes of others and may themselves promote change in existing moralities. Although there may be different conceptions or interpretations of the content of the inner morality of sports, perhaps even different and conflicting inner *moralities* of sports, such a moral code or codes seem capable of profoundly influencing both social and individual moral development.

Accordingly, our discussion suggests that the reductionist thesis—that the values exemplified, expressed, or reinforced within the world of sports are mere reflections of the values of the broader social context—is mistaken. Sports may well be value laden, but at least some of those values are grounded in the domain of sports and can conflict radically with values found elsewhere in the social order.

If participants in athletic competition can act upon an inner morality (or moralities) of sports, which can be expressed or illustrated by their actions on the field, we can ask what its broad social role might be. Should it (or they) apply, at most, only within the world of sports or should they be influential elsewhere in our lives? Such a question raises too many issues to consider here. However, one issue which is worth our special attention because of the long association it is purported to hold between competition in sports and character building is the role sports might play in moral education.

Sports and Moral Education

Because moral values play a large role in sport, it is not surprising that sports often are thought of as an area where values can and should be taught and transmitted to the next generation. In fact, we have seen in Chapter 2 that a traditional defense of athletic competition is in terms of its allegedly good effects on the building of character. In Chapter 7, it was argued that intercollegiate and interscholastic sports can have educational value when conducted properly.

Many people see a decline in values in our society. Random violence seems to be increasing. Drugs, gangs, and urban decay create risks for youngsters that seem to be higher than those with which children of the previous generation had to contend. With the rise in the divorce rate and the decline of the nuclear family, many children seem to many to be receiving less attention at home than in previous generations. The schools increasingly are asked to take on many functions, such as sex education, which used to be left, however wisely or unwisely, to the home, church, or synagogue. It is natural to ask, then, whether the schools should provide moral education and direction. Should sports have a role in moral education? If so, what should that role be?

Should schools be involved in teaching values? If so, whose values should be taught? Should there be formal courses in moral instruction? What, if anything, gives public schools, and through them the state, the right to decide upon an "official" morality to be taught to our children?

These questions suggest two important difficulties with the idea that schools should be responsible for moral education. The first might be called the problem of *partisanship* and the second the problem of *indoctrination*. According to the first, the public schools have no business teaching values, at least in a pluralist democratic society, because there is no one set of values that all agree should be taught. The schools, and through them the state, have no business deciding on a particular partisan set of values and making them the official ideology of the land. Imagine how you would feel, for example, if you were a political and social conservative (or liberal) and the schools taught liberal (or conservative) values as the correct morality. Moreover, even if we could agree on a set of values that should be taught, which many people regard as unlikely as best, we would be in the position of indoctrinating many of our students. Since many students are not yet sufficiently mature to rationally evaluate complex moral systems, we would in effect be imposing a value system upon them (quite possibly the wrong system in the eyes of many) without their autonomous consent.

Perhaps because of these difficulties, existing programs of moral education have emphasized either teaching students to clarify their own values, whatever they may be, or have focused on teaching procedures of moral reasoning, such as role reversal and hypothetical contractualism as tests of impartiality, rather than on endorsement of substantive moral principles. Such views attempt to avoid the charges of partisanship and indoctrination by restricting themselves to the form rather than the content of moral thought and by encouraging development of autonomy. However, even these approaches have been severely criticized on various grounds, including the charge that they themselves express a hidden agenda of an abstract but highly partisan morality. Thus, advocates of such approaches have been accused, in the case of values clarification, of teaching a disguised moral relativism ("It doesn't matter what values you hold as long as you can clearly articulate them and authentically accept them") or, in the case of concern for the form of moral reasoning, of presupposing a "male-oriented" universalist ethic of impartiality (as opposed, for example, to communitarian ethic or "female-oriented" ethic of caring).[6]

Whether or not these criticisms are justified, our discussion of the inner morality of sports suggests that informal moral education is going on in the schools all the time. For example, coaches of athletic teams normally do stress such values as dedication, discipline, teamwork, concern for excellence, and respect for the rules. Indeed, it is hard to see how they could avoid teaching such values, since some values are presupposed by the attempt to succeed in competitive sports. Coaches may also teach related values associated with their conception of the ethics of competition, including a conception of sportsmanship, fair play, and the principles required by conceiving of sports as a mutual quest for excellence by the participants.

Classroom teachers also are involved in informal moral education. Related to the inner morality of sport, one can argue that there is an inner morality of scholarship, which minimally requires civility in the classroom, respect for evidence, willingness to consider the views of others, and respect for them as fellow participants in critical inquiry. Such values as dedication, discipline, and respect for the rules of evidence apply not just in sports but more importantly to intellectual inquiry as well. Thus, elementary school teachers who insist on civility and nonviolent behavior in the classroom help their pupils to learn to discuss their differences in an attempt to find a justifiable reconciliation rather than simply allow them to beat up opponents.

Not only do teachers and coaches often stress such values, it seems entirely appropriate that they do so. An emphasis in the classroom on concern for evidence and willingness to listen to other points of view clearly is not neutral in the sense of being totally value free; rather, it seems to be presupposed by the educational process itself. Similarly, an emphasis on the playing field on teamwork, discipline, striving for excellence, and respect for the rules, seems to be presupposed by the process of competition in sports and athletics. Accordingly, such values may be neutral in a sense other than that of value freedom; that is, it is reasonable to suppose that such values would be agreed upon by all concerned with the practices at issue (education and competition in sports). The inner morality of sports (and of scholarship) are neutral rather than partisan, in that they concern values that all committed to the activities in question have good reason to support.

If this last point is justifiable, the inner morality of sports seems to avoid the charge of partisanship directed against the idea of moral education in the public schools. But is it really free of ideological bias? Aren't we trying to have it both ways here? On one hand, the claim is that there is an inner morality of sports that is independent of and can even conflict with prevailing social values. On the other hand, it is claimed that such values are nonpartisan and, in some sense, neutral. Are these claims mutually compatible?

Thus, critics of competitive sports agree there is an ideology of athletics but reject it as overly competitive, egoistic, and conservative. We have seen in Chapter 3 that critics identify adherence to the rules with blind subservience to the existing order, regardless of its moral standing. The critics are correct if what they are pointing out is that sports can be used to transmit messages about values that are extrinsic to athletic competition. For example, a conservative coach can call for blind loyalty to the team, regardless of the behavior of the players, and equate that with the sentiment of "my country right or wrong."

However, although such values as discipline and respect for the rules might be central to an inner morality of sports, it can be argued that blind loyalty is not. The difference is that the former values but not the latter are presupposed by the practice of competitive sports. Discipline, unlike blind loyalty to a team, is a value *anyone* interested in competing well in sports has reason to pursue regardless of his or her ideological commitments. Similarly, respect for the rules cannot be equated with blind loyalty to the status quo. Rather, respect for the rules is a way of recognizing the equal moral standing of others by abiding by the public conditions for competition that every competitor is entitled to believe will apply. Respect for the equal moral standing of others is not value free because it is incompatible with viewing the interests of others as of less moral significance than one's own, but it does seem to be presupposed by the idea of fair and meaningful competition.

Similarly, the classroom teacher who insists that students discuss differences rationally rather than force their opinions on others through violence, is rejecting some values, such as intimidation as a means of settling disagreements. However, rationality and willingness to respect others as participants in the discussion is central to education and inquiry in a way that intimidation is not. Thus, we can argue plausibly that in applying both the inner morality of sports and of scholarship, the schools are not imposing a partisan "official" ideology upon pupils but are teaching values that are presupposed by activities properly included in the educational curriculum.

What about the charge of indoctrination? Many coaches and teachers do not explicitly discuss the core moralities they are acting upon but simply impose them on students, many of whom are themselves too young or immature to make competent and autonomous decisions about morality. Teacher who insists that the bigger children in their elementary school classes do not beat up smaller ones are not offering a philosophical defense of civility but rather are simply commanding their pupils to be civil. Similarly, by simply disciplining young athletes who loaf in practice, coaches are not engaging in Socratic dialogue about the value of commitment and dedication but rather are insisting that their players act in a disciplined and committed way. If this isn't indoctrination, what is? In particular, what gives athletic coaches the right to impose such values on players?

Here, we need to ask if what is going on is indoctrination in any pejorative sense of that term. In particular, as some writers have suggested, perhaps not all values can be autonomously adopted. Rather, some may be presupposed by the practice of autonomous reflection itself.[7] For example, before one can autonomously evaluate the justifiability of conflicting points of view, one must acquire the disposition to evaluate evidence and consider arguments, rather than merely going along with one's friends or popular opinion. The acquisition of such a disposition cannot itself be the result of critical inquiry and autonomous reflection because one must already have the disposition in order to engage in critical inquiry and autonomous reflection. Training that helps immature and not yet competent individuals develop such traits is not a harmful kind of indoctrination, which subordinates critical thinking, but instead is part of a social process that develops critical and autonomous persons.

Similarly, the inner morality of sports, insofar as it forms part of a defensible practice of moral education, is not a system of values placing athletes in intellectual blinders. Rather, values such as commitment, discipline, respect for the standing of others, and appreciation of excellence also are presuppositions of moral and rational development. It is reasonable to think such values also are presupposed by rational inquiry in a wide variety of areas.

If this position can successfully withstand critical examination, what are its implications for educational policy? In particular, they suggest that moral education of a limited sort is properly the function of our schools and that organized athletics can and should be part of it. Moral education of the kind at issue is limited to promotion of those dispositions of mind and of character that can reasonably be regarded as prerequisites of the capacity to engage in autonomous critical inquiry with others.   Just which values are to be cultivated will often be controversial, but a strong case can be made for those core values constituting the heart of what we have called the inner morality of both scholarship and sports.

If this approach is defensible, it provides an important reason why athletic programs should be considered a significant part of the curriculum of public education and not just a "frill" to be done away with as soon as school taxes get too high. By reinforcing values taught in the classroom, athletic competition in which people from diverse backgrounds and perspectives engage in a common quest for excellence can help promote and illustrate values to that all committed to fostering development of autonomy and reason in both public and private life have reason to support.

Sports and Moral Responsibility

If sports can play an important moral role in society, does it follow that individuals involved in sports have special moral responsibilities to the rest of us? Consider, for example, the tragic case of Pete Rose. Rose, formerly a star baseball player for the Cincinnati Reds, became known as "Charlie Hustle" because, through hard work and effort, he was able to turn what many regarded as less than extraordinary athletic ability into a distinguished major-league career. Rose ended his career having recorded more base hits than anyone else who ever had played the game. His place in the Baseball Hall of Fame seemed assured. To many, Rose was not only a star player but also was a symbol of what dedication and commitment to excellence could accomplish, not only on the athletic field, but elsewhere in life as well.

Following an investigation of charges alleging that Rose, then manager of the Reds, had gambled extensively on baseball games, Rose was banned from baseball for life in 1989. Not only was Rose claimed to be a compulsive gambler, he was convicted of felonies involving tax evasion, presumably committed to support his gambling habit, and served a jail sentence in 1990 as a result. In addition, Rose is precluded from election to the Hall of Fame while he is under a lifetime ban from the game in which he excelled and, in the eyes of many, dishonored.

Did Pete Rose, as a star athlete and presumably a hero and role model to many youngsters, have a special obligation to behave ethically because of his participation in sports? Do athletes in general have special responsibilities to be good role models for the rest of us, particularly for the children in our community who look up to them as heroes? On the contrary, are athletes simply ordinary people with special skills, who have the same legal and moral responsibilities as anyone else but have no special obligation to be models for the rest of society?

Should Athletes Be Moral Role Models?

What does it *mean* to claim that athletes have special moral obligations to the rest of us to behave ethically? Although it is not always clear what proponents of such a view might be claiming, one thing that they might mean is that there are extra reasons, over and above those that apply to all of us, for athletes to behave ethically. A second thing they might mean is that if an athlete behaves unethically, it is somehow more seriously wrong, perhaps because it is more harmful, than if someone else commits the same unethical act. These might not be the only interpretations of what is meant, but we can work with them in exploring the scope of the moral responsibilities of athletes.

Why should we believe that athletes have any special moral responsibilities? Athletes, it might be argued, are just people who have particular skills but in other respects are the same as the rest of us. All of us have obligations not to wrong others. Why should the possession of a special talent, such as athletic skill, carry with it an additional moral obligation to be a moral exemplar for others? Athletes may indeed have special moral obligations within competition to, say, follow the rules and play hard so as to provide a challenge for opponents, but it is quite another thing to say they have a special responsibility to be ethical generally. Surely, from the premise that certain individuals have unusual athletic talents, it doesn't *logically follow* that they have special moral obligations outside of competition as well.

However, isn't it sometimes the case that we do think possession of a special talent at least provides a *reason*, if not always a conclusive one, for assuming a moral obligation? For example, if one has unusual musical ability, doesn't the possession of such talent provide a reason for thinking one ought to use it to bring pleasure to others? Again, if one is highly skilled at medical diagnosis, doesn't one have a reason to use that talent by becoming a physician rather than by choosing some profession in which one will do far less good for others?

Athletes, it can be argued, occupy a special place in our society. They often are regarded as heroes by children and young people, in particular, and to many disadvantaged youth, particularly minorities, many star athletes may illustrate that escape from deprivation is through success in competitive sports. Because athletes are revered by a large portion of the population, including many impressionable young people, they in fact are regarded as models to be emulated. Hence, they have both a special reason to behave morally—the unusually great influence they can have on others—and they can do more harm through their influence on others than the ordinary person when they behave immorally. Thus, athletes who are users of addictive drugs, for example, may, however unintentionally, convey the message that it is "cool" to take drugs and induce their fans to become "copycat" users as well.

This sort of argument, however, is open to many objections. In particular, perhaps instead of expecting athletes to live up to the perhaps unreasonable expectations of many of their fans, the fans themselves ought to become more realistic. Indeed, as we have seen, the hero worship of athletes can be harmful, especially when it leads youngsters to try to develop their athletic rather than academic skills in the grossly unrealistic hope of becoming professional athletes. In any case, why should fans, particularly youngsters, regard athletes rather than physicians, nurses, teachers, and scientists, as their heroes? On the other hand, why should athletes have any more responsibilities to be moral exemplars than other kinds of entertainers, such as movie or rock stars, who often not only fail to be desirable role models for young people but also are not usually assigned any special moral blame for their derelictions?

These points surely are worth our consideration. But are they decisive? It can be argued that sports not only do but should play a central place in our society because of their concern with excellence and because appreciation of sports does not require the kind of special training or background often needed to appreciate excellence in such fields as medicine, science, mathematics, and even the fine arts.[8] If so, sports is a practice which, by its very nature, is both accessible to large and diverse portions of the population yet expresses and illustrates a concern for excellence. Moreover, given the attention paid to sports by the media, and the love many children have for sports, it is doubtful if they suddenly will become "realistic." It is far more likely that they will continue to have special regard for national sports figures as well as athletes in their schools.

What has this to do with the moral obligations of athletes off the field? Arguably, because of the special connection between competitive sports and the quest for excellence and because of the broad accessibility of sports, it is not unreasonable for many segments of the population, particularly children and young people, to hold athletes in high regard and seek to emulate them. In fact, top athletes often profit from this emulation and are often represented to the public as having exhibited special virtues on the field. For example, Pete Rose was known for his dedication and hustle, Magic Johnson is loved for his enthusiasm for the joy of competition, tennis star Billy Jean King is remembered for her grit, and golfer Jack Nicklaus is known not only for his victories on the course but also his integrity and concern for high competitive standards in golf. Indeed, our own discussion of an inner morality of sports, and of the function of sports in expressing values, suggests there is an unusually intimate relationship between participation in athletics and ethics.

If so, and if it is therefore not unreasonable for the general public, particularly youngsters, to regard top athletes as heroic figures, and given that many top athletes accept and welcome the benefits of their position resulting from the way they are regarded, then perhaps it is not unreasonable to conclude that they have special reasons for at least avoiding the kind of immoral behavior that impressionable young people are likely to emulate, e.g. drug and alcohol abuse, various kinds of cheating, and law breaking. Clearly, if athletes are regarded as role models in part because of the values expressed through their play, they can do unusual harm if their misbehavior leads their fans either to emulate their misdeeds or become sceptical of the original values for which the athletes were thought to stand.

Perhaps a more important reason for thinking athletes have special moral obligations rests not upon controversial empirical claims about their effect as role models but on the special place values have in sports. If there is an inner morality of sport, in which such values as dedication, concern for excellence, and fair play are central, then athletes express such values through their play and benefit from adherence to these norms by other competitors. Without such commitment, we couldn't have the good sports contest and the basic, scarce, and internal benefits it provides. To express and benefit from adherence to such values in a central area of one's life and then undermine them elsewhere seems wrong in the same way it is wrong for a university to claim to value intellectual integrity and expect its students and faculty to conform to this value, yet violate intellectual integrity itself by tolerating admission of athletes who are academically unqualified.[9]

Such considerations need fuller support than has been presented here, and in any case are intended as invitations to reflection rather than decisive arguments. Perhaps, however, they are enough to show that the claim that athletes have special moral responsibilities is worth taking seriously. The point is not that athletes should be saints, but that they have special reason not to violate minimal standards of good behavior, particularly in areas where their example is likely to be highly influential, or act so as to undermine or discredit values central to the inner morality of sports. While we could take the opposite tack, and argue that athletes should not be our heroes, and should be respected only for their physical skills, the role of athletes in illustrating and expressing important values through their play suggests that their role in sports tends to thrust them into the moral spotlight in a way carrying some obligation with it.

Perhaps, then, we need to reflect not simply on the fun and beauty that can be provided by good sports but on the values embedded in the practice of athletic competition. What specific implications this might have for our actual practices, especially within educational institutions, needs further consideration, but at least two possibilities are worth mentioning. First, our discussion suggests that coaches in educational institutions ought to be evaluated more as teachers than according to their won-and-lost record. If appropriate standards of competitive sports have implications for life outside the playing field as well as on it, we need to find and reward instructors who can teach us to play according to a plausible version of an inner morality of sports rather than foster an amoral indifference to ethics in the pursuit of victory. For example, coaches in colleges and universities might be accorded faculty status and be judged for retention and promotion by the faculty, as are other educators in the academic community.[10] Second, perhaps we should expect athletes in our schools not simply to satisfy minimal standards of behavior and academic progress but expect them to be good citizens and good students as well. Although such specific suggestions may or may not have merit, an emphasis on the inner morality of sports and the lessons it can teach may have a role to play in moral education and, more broadly, in our moral life.

Sports and Fundamental Values

The principal theme running through this book is that sports raise a host of significant ethical issues. At their best, sports can constitute a stimulating challenge to mind and body alike; at their worst, they can be a joyless endeavor where losing is equated with personal failing and winning becomes just a means to egoistic self-posturing over others.

However, our discussion suggests that sports properly conducted provide values of enduring human significance. Through sports, we can learn to overcome adversity and appreciate excellence. We can learn to value activities for their own sake, apart from any intrinsic reward they provide, and learn to appreciate the contribution of others, even when we are on opposing sides. Through sports we can develop and express moral virtues and vices and demonstrate the importance of such values as dedication, integrity, fairness, and courage.

In particular, sports presuppose the importance of standards; standards of excellent play and standards for appropriate conduct as well. Whether or not we accept some version of the ethic of the mutual quest for excellence, some moral standard is needed in order to distinguish sports as they should be conducted from degradations of the sporting ethic. Such standards can be arrived at and examined only through the kind of critical reflection that is characteristic of philosophic inquiry.

Moreover, if there are justified standards that really do distinguish excellent from poor play as well as ethical from unethical behavior in sports, they provide reason for questioning the claim of many theorists that all standards are merely subjective and arbitrary references, simply reflecting our race, gender, socioeconomic status, religion, or cultural upbringing. Although what we learn surely arises from the particular social and historical perspective in which we find ourselves, whether our beliefs are or are not justified is another question. Our discussion about sports suggests that the search for justified standards is not necessarily fruitless. Our particular positions at a given time may always be fallible, and subject to criticism, but the claim that there are justified standards of excellence in play and in the ethics of playing morally, indicates that the search for justifiable standards need not always be in vain.

We could do worse, then, than conclude with the remarks of Socrates in Plato's *Republic*, whose remarks about music and gymnastics may apply to creative activity and to sports generally when he asserts that "there are two arts which I would say some god gave to mankind, music and gymnastics for . . . the love of knowledge in them—not for the soul and body incidentally, but for their harmonious adjustment."[11]

Notes

Chapter 1

1. Reported by George Vecsey, "A Nation of Sports Fans," *New York Times*, March 16, 1983, p. B11.

2. I owe this story to Professor Ed Pincoffs of the University of Texas, who assures me it is true.

3. For example, the claim that all knowledge must be scientific in nature does not itself seem to be a claim that can be defended through scientific inquiry but rather seems to be a claim *about* science made from some other perspective.

4. Allen Bloom, *The Closing of the American Mind* (New York: Simon and Schuster, 1987), p. 25.

5. Relativism about truth, at least in its crude forms, may well be incoherent because it seems to assert as correct or true in some "absolute" or universal sense that truth is relative. For application of this kind of argument to various forms of relativism, see Roger Trigg, *Reason and Commitment* (New York: Cambridge University Press, 1973).

6. At this point, there may be a temptation to reply that, of course, disagreement in science doesn't show the impossibility of a rational resolution of a scientific dispute but disagreement in ethics does show the impossibility of resolution of an ethical dispute. However, the whole point of the relativist argument in ethics is to establish that ethics is different from science with respect to its rationality. Clearly, the relativist cannot simply assume as true the very point that was supposed to be established by argument.

7. There are other difficulties with ethical relativism as well. For example, it is not clear how to distinguish between cultures or tell which culture's morals apply at a given time. Thus, if one is deciding whether or not to take steroids to enhance performance in sports, does ethical relativism prescribe taking the dominant view of one's country, of one's religious group, of one's peers in the sport, all of which might differ from one another? Are these different groups for moral purposes or are they just subunits of a dominant culture, e.g., Western culture? How are we to tell? For a fuller discussion of the issues raised by various forms of relativism, see Paul W. Taylor, *Principles of Ethics: An Introduction* (Belmont, Calif.: Wadsworth, 1975), pp. 13-30.

8. Aristotle, *Nichomachean Ethics*, Book 1, Chap. 2, Section 25, trans. W. D. Ross in Richard McKeon, ed., *The Basic Works of Aristotle* (New York: Random House, 1941), p. 936.

9. See particularly R. M. Hare, *Freedom and Reason* (New York: Oxford University Press, 1965).

10. John Rawls, *A Theory of Justice* (Cambridge: Harvard University Press, 1971).

Chapter 2

1. What Lombardi is claimed to have actually said is: "Winning isn't everything, but wanting to win is." Scott Morris, ed., *The Book of Strange Facts and Useless Information* (New York: Dolphin, 1979).

2. The statement by Rice is from *John Bartlett's Familiar Quotations* (Boston: Little, Brown, and Co., 1951), p. 901, and the remark by Evashevski is from *Sports Illustrated*, Sept. 23, 1957, p. 119. For discussion, see James Keating, "Winning in Sports and Athletics," *Thought*, Vol. 38, No. 149 (1963), pp. 201-210.

3. Judy Cooperstein, as quoted by Gerald Eskanazi, "Judy Cooperstein Still Has the Tempo," *New York Times*, July 2, 1981, p. B12.

4. I owe the distinction between the internal goal of a sport, as defined by the rules, and the goal or motive of those who play the sport to Bernard Suits's distinction between the lusory goal of a sport and the goal people have in playing it. The lusory goal, winning, can only be described in internal terms of the game being played, as when we describe winning in baseball as scoring more runs than the opponent within a specifiable set of innings. Suits also describes the prelusory goal of a sport as a goal describable independently of the rules. Thus, the lusory goal of golf would be scoring less strokes, as defined by the rules, than anyone else in the tournament; the prelusory goal might be getting the ball into the hole; and the personal goal of players might range from a desire for exercise to a love of competition. See Bernard Suits, "The Elements of Sport," in William J. Morgan and Klaus V. Meier, eds., *Philosophical Inquiry in Sport* (Champaign, Ill.: Human Kinetics Publishers, Inc., 1988), pp. 39-48 and especially Suits's delightful book , *The Grasshopper: Games, Life, and Utopia* (Toronto: University of Toronto Press, 1978). This book is one of the most important statements of the formalist view of sports, according to which the notion of sports is best conceived of or defined in terms of its constitutive rules, rather than its social role or the informal conventions involved in its play.

5. See Suits, *The Grasshopper*, for an extended and often amusing development of a view that has such implications. For a critique of the claim that cheaters necessarily fail to play the game, see Craig K. Lehman, "Can Cheaters Play the Game?" *Journal of the Philosophy of Sport*, Vol. 8 (1981), pp. 41-46, reprinted in Morgan and Meier, *Philosophic Inquiry*, pp. 283-287.

6. Quoted by John Loy and Gerald S. Kenyon, *Sport, Culture, and Society* (New York: Macmillan, 1969), pp. 9-10.

7. Utilitarians disagree over whether we ought to evaluate the consequences of specific actions (act utilitarianism) or of social practices or of general observance of rules (rule utilitarianism). Moreover, there are different versions of act and rule utilitarianism as well. Some philosophers believe that the two approaches can give different moral evaluations of the same act, as when the act

utilitarian favors a specific act, such as breaking a promise, in cases where it might be socially useful to do so, and the rule utilitarian condemns the act because it violates a rule, such as "keep your promises," that would be socially useful if everyone followed it. Other philosophers believe that any plausible rule will have so many legitimate exceptions built in that the distinction between the two kinds of utilitarianism will collapse. In any case, the distinction will not affect the argument in the text unless otherwise specified. For a useful introduction to utilitarianism, see James Rachels, *The Elements of Moral Philosophy* (New York: Random House, 1986), pp. 79-103.

8. Bruce C. Ogilvie and Thomas Tutko, "Sports: If You Want to Build Character, Try Something Else," *Psychology Today*, Oct. 1971, pp. 61-62.

9. *Ibid.*, pp. 61.

10. Walter E. Schafer, "Some Sources and Consequences of Interscholastic Athletics," in Gerald Kenyon, ed., *The Sociology of Sport* (Chicago: Athletic Institute, 1969), p. 35, quoted by Harry E. Edwards, *Sociology of Sport* (Homeward, Ill.: The Dorsey Press, 1973), p. 324.

11. See Edwards, *Sociology of Sport*, p. 323.

12. For further discussion of issues concerning moral education, see the discussion of moral education in Chapter 8.

13. The idea of an "expressive" theory of punishment is suggested by Joel Feinberg in "The Expressive Function of Punishment" in his *Doing and Deserving* (Princeton: Princeton University Press, 1970), pp. 95-118. Feinberg himself does not discuss the expressive function of sports. The idea of an expressive function of sports is explored by David Fairchild in his article, "Prolegomena to an Expressive Function of Sport," *Journal of the Philosophy of Sport*, Vol. 14 (1987), pp. 21-33.

14. John Schaar, "Equality of Opportunity and Beyond," in J. Roland Pennock and John W. Chapman, eds., *Equality*, Nomos 9 (New York: Atherton Press, 1967), p. 237.

15. Michael Fielding, "Against Competition," *Proceedings of the Philosophy of Education Society of Great Britain*, Vol. 10 (1976), pp. 140-141.

16. Richard Harding Davis, "Thorne's Famous Run," in Grantland Rice and Harford Powel, eds., *The Omnibus of Sport* (New York: Harper and Brothers, 1932), quoted by Edward J. Delattre, "Some Reflections on Success and Failure in Competitive Athletics," *Journal of the Philosophy of Sport*, Vol. 2 (1975), pp. 134-135.

17. Delattre, "Some Reflections," pp. 134-135.

18. Delattre, "Some Reflections," p. 134.

19. Delattre, "Some Reflections," p. 135. Similar themes are developed by Paul Weiss in his book *Sport: A Philosophic Inquiry* (Carbondale and Edwardsville, Ill.: Southern Illinois University Press, 1969), one of the pioneering works in recent philosophic study of sports.

20. A. Bartlett Giamatti, *Take Time for Paradise: Americans and Their Games* (New York: Simon and Shuster, 1989), pp. 35-36.

21. Robert Nozick, *Anarchy, State, and Utopia* (New York: Basic Books, 1974), p. 240.

22. Can't we just see if our current performance improves relative to our

past performance? Thus, if I shot a 90 in golf last month and an 89 today, haven't I showed improvement? Perhaps so, but whether that improvement is significant or worth noting depends on comparisons with an appropriate reference group. If players of similar athletic ability and training normally improve from 90 to 82 in one month, I may have no justification for regarding my "improvement" as worth noting or of significance at all.

23. Ronald Dworkin, *Taking Rights Seriously* (Cambridge: Harvard University Press, 1977), p. 227.

24. *Ibid.*, p. 272.

25. Or that it is morally unjustified in some other fundamental way.

26. Dworkin, *Taking Rights Seriously*, p. 272.

27. For a fuller argument that inequalities based on merit can sometimes be defended by appeal to the value of respect for persons, see Robert L. Simon, "An Indirect Defense of the Merit Principle," *Philosophical Forum*, Vol. 10, No. 2-4, (1978-1979), pp. 224-241.

28. Based on my memory of a postgame interview with University of North Carolina running back Kelvin Bryant in 1981.

29. Dworkin, *Taking Rights Seriously*, p. 272. This does not imply that such inequalities always are fair and equitable, but rather that (a) they are not shown to be unfair or inequitable simply by pointing out that they arise from competitive sports, and (b) there is a presumption in their favor, based on the right to treatment as an equal (or respect for persons), for regarding them as fair and equitable.

30. William J. Bennett, "In Defense of Sports," *Commentary*, Vol. 61, No. 2 (1976), p. 70.

31. *Ibid.*, p. 70.

Chapter 3

1. As used here, "sportsmanship" will designate a virtue that can be equally exemplified by males and females of all races and ethnic or socioeconomic backgrounds.

2. James W. Keating, "Sportsmanship as a Moral Category," *Ethics*, Vol. 75 (1964), pp. 25-35, reprinted in Morgan and Meier, *Philosophic Inquiry*, p. 244. All page references to this article will refer to *Philosophic Inquiry*.

3. Morgan and Meier, *Philosophic Inquiry*, p. 244.

4. *Ibid.*, p. 245.

5. *Ibid.*

6. *Ibid.*, p. 247.

7. *Ibid.*, pp. 247-249.

8. Bernard Gert, *Morality: A New Justification for the Moral Rules* (New York: Oxford University Press, 1988), pp. 129-133.

9. The idea of a hypothetical social contract can be useful in explaining the obligations of competitors in sports by identifying such obligations with what rational contractors would consent to under fair conditions of choice. However, the obligation here arises from the reasonableness and fairness of the conditions

under which choice is made, not from the dubious claim that people who may never have consciously thought of the terms of the contract actually have signed it.

10. Here I adopt part of Gert's definition, but leave out his requirement that the rules contain no explicit penalty for the act so as to not beg questions that arise later. My analysis of the wrongness of cheating draws on and is indebted to Gert's discussion, but I do not believe he would subscribe to all aspects of my approach. In particular, the emphasis on exploitation of other competitors is my own. See Gert, *Morality*, p.130ff.

11. My discussion here is indebted to Randolph M. Feezel's discussion in his article "Sportsmanship," *Journal of the Philosophy of Sport*, Vol. 13 (1986), pp. 1-13, reprinted in Morgan and Meier, *Philosophic Inquiry*, particularly pp. 254-256, where Feezel makes similar points.

12. Note that the issue here was not the judgment of the referees in applying a rule. Bad calls can be regarded plausibly as part of the game, in that participants play with the expectation that referees will use their own judgment in deciding whether the rule was violated. However, the Colorado-Missouri game did not involve a judgment call, such as whether pass interference was committed by a defender, but failure to apply a rule at all because of confusion about the number of downs that already had been used up.

13. Ken Johnson, "The Forfeit," *Dartmouth Alumni Magazine*, Oct. 1990, p. 16.

14. This does not imply that teams that actually have taken advantage of such a situation should be *blamed* for doing so, even if in fact it would have been morally better for them to have refrained from scoring. After all, they themselves may have been confused by the unexpected situation and simply reacted as they were trained to. However, coaches might well think in advance of the ethics of such a situation, and ones relevantly similar to it, before it actually arises. Moreover, rule-making bodies certainly ought to consider a change in such a rule so as to distinguish between teams that intentionally stall in a time out (they might be given a technical foul if not on the floor with, say, ten seconds of a referee's warning) and those that simply are distracted, who would be warned by the referee that the time-out ended.

15. There is a temptation here to say cheating is wrong simply because "deliberate betrayal of the rules destroys the vital framework of agreement which makes sport possible." Kathleen Pearson, "Deception, Sportsmanship, and Ethics," *Quest*, Vol. 19 (1973), pp. 115-118, reprinted in Morgan and Meier, *Philosophic Inquiry*, p. 265. Although I am not unsympathetic to this remark, I doubt if it fully explains the wrongness of cheating. (It may be more acceptable, however, as an analysis of the nature of cheating rather than as an analysis of why cheating is wrong.) After all, deliberate betrayal of the rules that make an activity possible is not always wrong, as when the rules themselves make an unjust practice possible. I suggest that a fuller account than that provided in the text of what normally makes cheating in sports wrong would include (a) a moral defense of the public system of rules that is violated (or at least a defense of why it should not be unilaterally violated in the way in question) and (b) an account of how the cheater acts unjustly by arbitrarily assuming a privileged position

through his or her unilaterally violating the public system of rules that competitors are entitled to have apply to the system.

16. Warren Fraleigh, "Why the Good Foul Is not Good Enough," in Morgan and Meier, *Philosophic Inquiry*, p. 269. A similar point is made by Kathleen M. Pearson, who suggests that "if the purpose of the contest is to determine who is more skillful . . . we can say that a player has entered into a contract with his opponent for the mutual purpose of making that determination. . . . " See Pearson, "Deception," p. 264. Thus, Pearson also seems to suggest that players who deliberately commit strategic fouls are unethical because they violate the implicit contract laying down the mutually acceptable rules that should govern the contest.

17. The idea of a *hypothetical* social contract can be useful in helping us decide what is fair; roughly, a fair contest is one that *would be* mutually acceptable to rational competitors under morally acceptable conditions of choice. We can appeal to such a hypothetical contract to show why cheating is unfair, i.e., that a rational person, under morally acceptable conditions of choice, would not sign a contract permitting others to cheat him as well as those for whom he is concerned, but that is not to say that the cheater violates an agreement he or she *actually* has signed. Thus, the idea of a hypothetical social contract functions in ethical theory more like a method of moral justification than an actual promise.

18. Pearson, "Deception," pp. 264-265.

19. In many cases, it will be controversial what counts as fair or appropriate compensation. One test of fairness in this contest, which might be worth considering, is the following. A penalty is a fair price for the violation of a rule if skilled competitors would be indifferent between two situations: first, in which the rule was violated and the penalty imposed, and second, in which the rule was not violated. Thus, the award of two foul shots would be a fair penalty for being intentionally fouled to stop the clock if skilled players would be indifferent between having the opportunity to shoot the fouls or having an opportunity to try to hold on to the ball against a skilled defense. Of course, actual teams, especially those weak in shooting fouls, may not be indifferent even when skilled players would be. But that is exactly where strategy comes in. As long as the penalty is fair, a team may intentionally foul to take advantage of an opponent's weakness in shooting fouls. The penalty still is fair because if the team with the lead did not have a weakness, which it is the business of athletes to correct, the strategy would not be attractive to their opponents.

20. For discussion, see Fred D'Agostino, "The Ethos of Games," *Journal of the Philosophy of Sport*, Vol. 8 (1981), pp. 7-18, reprinted in Morgan and Meier, *Philosophic Inquiry*, pp. 63-72.

21. Oliver Leaman, "Cheating and Fair Play in Sport," from William J. Morgan, ed., *Sport and the Humanities: A Collection of Original Essays* (Knoxville: Bureau of Educational Research and Service, University of Tennessee, 1981), reprinted in Morgan and Meier, *Philosophic Inquiry*, p. 280.

22. Morgan and Meier, *Philosophic Inquiry*, p. 280.

23. Frank DeFord, "An Encounter to Last an Eternity," *Sports Illustrated*,

April 11, 1983, p. 71. My account of the fight is based upon this article.

24. *Ibid.*, p. 61.

25. Useful philosophical discussions of the nature and justification of violence are included in Jerome A. Shaffer, ed., *Violence* (New York: David McKay Company, 1971). The importance of keeping descriptive and normative analyses separate has been defended by Felix Oppenheim in his *Political Concepts: A Reconstruction* (Chicago: University of Chicago Press, 1981). Although I am not endorsing such a general strategy, I suggest it is useful to define "violence" as neutrally as possible. For a particularly perspicuous analysis of "coercion" that is not neutral but incorporates evaluation in the characterization, see Alan Wertheimer, *Coercion* (Princeton: Princeton University Press, 1988).

26. Many philosophers would deny that an analysis in terms of necessary and sufficient conditions can be given, even in principle, for many concepts employed in ordinary thought and language.

27. *New York Times*, December 14, 1982, p. 30. ©*New York Times*. Reprinted by permission.

28. John Stuart Mill, *On Liberty* (1859), edited by Elizabeth Rappaport (Indianapolis: Hackett Publishing Company, 1978), p. 9. Many other editions of *On Liberty* are also in print.

29. *Ibid.*, p. 56.

30. A committed utilitarian might reply, however, that on the contrary, autonomy itself is valuable only because a society of autonomous individuals is likely to generate more utility than one in which the autonomy of individuals is suppressed, perhaps through tyrannical means.

31. The account of individual rights as political trumps has been advanced by Dworkin in *Taking Rights Seriously*.

32. Mill, *On Liberty*, p. 9.

33. For a defense of such a position, see Gerald Dworkin, "Paternalism," in Richard A. Wasserstrom, ed., *Morality and the Law* (Belmont, Calif.: Wadsworth, 1971), pp. 107-126.

34. An accessible discussion of the medical evidence on the effects of boxing, and of the implications of the evidence for policy, can be found in Robert H. Boyle and Wilmer Ames, "Too Many Punches, Too Little Concern," *Sports Illustrated*, April 11, 1983, pp. 42-67.

35. The example of Mayhem is based upon a similar illustration employed by Irving Kristol in his essay, "Pornography, Obscenity, and the Case for Censorship," *New York Times Magazine*, March 28, 1971, reprinted in Joel Feinberg and Hyman Gross, eds., *Philosophy of Law* (Encino, Calif.: Dickenson Publishing Company, Inc., 1975) pp. 165-171.

36. *New York Times*, December 14, 1982, p. 30.

37. An influential account of the role of models in learning is found in Albert Bandura's *Social Learning Theory* (Englewood Cliffs, N. J.: Prentice Hall, 1977).

38. The views presented here represent only a rough sketch of communitarian approaches, but recent communitarian criticisms of liberal individualist approaches to political theory include Alasdair MacIntyre, *After Virtue* (Notre Dame, Ind.: University of Notre Dame Press, 1984) and Michael Sandel, *Liberalism and the Limits of Justice* (New York: Cambridge University Press, 1982).

39. For extended critical discussions of communitarianism, see Amy Gutmann, "Communitarian Critics of Liberalism," *Philosophy and Public Affairs,* Vol. 14 (1983), pp. 308-322; George Sher, "Three Grades of Social Involvement," *Philosophy and Public Affairs,* Vol. 18 (1989), pp. 133-157; Alan E. Buchanan, "Assessing the Communitarian Critique of Liberalism," *Ethics,* Vol. 99 (1989), pp. 852-882; and Patrick Neal and David Paris, "Liberalism and the Communitarian Critique, A Guide for the Perplexed," *Canadian Journal of Political Science,* Vol. 23, No. 3 (1990), pp. 419-439.

40. Jack Tatum with Bill Kushner, *They Call Me Assassin* (New York: Everest House, 1979), p. 12.

41. *Ibid.,* p. 176.

42. Paul Hoch, *Rip Off the Big Game* (Garden City, N. Y.: Doubleday and Co., Inc., 1972), p. 22.

43. A brushback pitch, designed to move the hitter back from the plate, must be distinguished from a beanball, usually thrown behind the batter (so he will dodge right into it) with the intent to hit him.

44. For discussion, see Eldon E. Snyder and Elmer A. Spreitzer, *Social Aspects of Sport* (Englewood Cliffs, N. J.: Prentice-Hall, 1983), pp. 93-96.

Chapter 4

1. See Terry Todd, "The Steroid Predicament," *Sports Illustrated,* August 1, 1983, pp. 71-72, for a sensitive interview with an athlete and his wife on what they believe the effects of his steroid use to have been on their marriage.

2. John Stuart Mill, *On Liberty* (1849), quoted from the Dolphin Edition (Garden City, N. Y.: Doubleday, 1961), p. 484. Mill's Harm Principle, articulated in the quoted passage, also rules out interference with liberty to prevent offensive acts or to prevent acts simply on grounds of their alleged immorality, independent of any harm to others they may produce.

3. *Ibid.*

4. *Ibid.,* p. 576.

5. Carolyn E. Thomas, *Sport in a Philosophic Context* (Philadelphia: Lea & Febiger, 1983), p. 198.

6. For an excellent discussion of different senses of coercion and an argument that we should think of coercion normatively, as *illegitimate* interference with the freedom of others, see Alan Wertheimer, *Coercion* (Princeton: Princeton University Press, 1989).

7. One can develop along similar lines an argument for legislation limiting the number of hours employees can be required to work. Against the libertarian argument that workers ought to be left free to contract into any working arrangements they wish, it may be objected that workers can then be forced into working ever longer hours for fear of losing their jobs. Hence, it may be in every worker's interest to agree to legislation limiting such contracts even though, without the legislation, rational workers would find it in their interest to work longer hours than the legislation would allow.

8. Norman Fost, "Let 'Em Take Steroids," *New York Times*, Sept. 9, 1983, p. A19.

9. For an extended critical discussion of the claim that users of steroids gain an unfair advantage over other competitors, see Roger Gardner, "On Performance-Enhancing Substances and the Unfair Advantage Argument," in *Journal of the Philosophy of Sport*, Vol. 16 (1989), pp. 59-73.

10. *Ibid.*, pp. 69-70.

11. The idea of the veil of ignorance is presented by John Rawls as part of a complex argument for a conception of social justice in his *A Theory of Justice.*. Rawls's theory is more fully discussed in Chapter 5 of this book.

12. It is a hypothetical contract in that it specifies what persons would agree to under specified (but not necessarily actual) conditions of choice. The contract is held to be morally binding on us, as writers such as Rawls develop the idea, insofar as the hypothetical conditions of choice reflect considerations we think morally *ought* to apply. Thus, to the extent we think choices about what practices are fair ought to be impartial, then to that extent will we be attracted to the veil of ignorance.

13. One line of objection to this argument that needs to be considered is the following. Wouldn't similar considerations show that perfectly acceptable practices in sports, such as rigorous training, would not be agreed to by rational athletes under fair conditions of choice? Thus, if athletes did not know how training would affect them personally, but did know that it takes up time that could be used to secure other goals, wouldn't they vote to prohibit rigorous training? I suggest that there are a number of replies to such a criticism. One difference between training and steroid use is that the latter generally is harmful in an uncontroversial sense of "harm." Training, while it may have opportunity costs for some, is pleasurable for others, and surely is not harmful in any non-controversial sense of the term. A more difficult line of objection to answer would criticize the methodology of appeal to a hypothetical contract. However, the argument in the text can be re-expressed with only minimal reliance on that methodology. Its main point is that if each athlete disregards the impact of steroid use on himself or herself personally, the use of steroids makes no sense as a general practice, because it poses the threat of significant harmful effects to virtually everyone, and at best provides minimal gains in relative performance compared to others who also use steroids.

14. This point is made by Gardner in "On Performance-Enhancing Substances," pp. 69-70.

15. A critic may question whether this requires us to forbid athletes with poor vision from using glasses or contact lenses. This is a good criticism that needs to be fully discussed. One difference between the use of eyeglasses and the use of steroids, however, is that the former does not alter the challenge of the sport but simply allows the athlete with poor vision to "catch up" to those with better vision. Arguably, however, the use of steroids does make achievement easier for all. (Does this mean that steroid use should be permitted, but *only* by weaker athletes?)

16. This point has been developed recently by Michael Lavin in his paper "Drugs and Sports: Are the Current Bans Justified," *Journal of the Philosophy of*

Sport, Vol. 14 (1987), pp. 34-43. In the same issue (pp. 74-88), David Fairchild, in his article "Sport Abjection: Steroids and the Uglification of the Athlete," develops an alternate defense for prohibiting the use of steroids based on abjection.

17. For some sceptical doubts about whether official governing bodies of sports always are reasonable or nonarbitrary, see Fairchild, "Sport Abjection."

18. The Stanford athletes were successful in a lower court decision in *Hill v. NCAA*, but the case is being appealed and no decision has been reached by a higher court as of the time of publication of this book.

19. For a good general discussion of the effect of drugs in the workplace, see "Taking Drugs on the Job," *Newsweek*, August 22, 1983, pp. 52-60.

20. It might be objected that some athletes from disadvantaged backgrounds view sports as their only alternative to a life of poverty and deprivation and thus are, in effect, not voluntary participants. Although I believe it is stretching things to say they are forced to play, this point, even if accepted, does not totally undermine the argument in the text. There is still a moral case for insuring that the rules are applied fairly to all and that athletes not be confronted with undue pressure to use steroids. So even if such athletes are "forced" to play, they themselves, given that they "must" participate, would want, from a position of impartial choice, that the rules applied fairly to all and that they not be required to use such drugs as steroids in order to be competitive.

Chapter 5

1. Thus, for different people to have equal opportunities is for them to have the same (or equivalent) opportunities, while for them to be treated with equal respect is for them to be treated with the same degree of respect.

2. James Michener, *Sports in America* (New York: Random House, 1976), p. 17.

3. *Ibid.*, pp. 171-172.

4. For example, see Jerry Kirschenbaum and Robert Sullivan, "Hold on There, America," *Sports Illustrated*, Feb. 7, 1983, p. 63.

5. Eldon E. Snyder and Elmer A. Spreitzer, *Social Aspects of Sport* (Englewood Cliffs, N. J.: Prentice-Hall, 1983), p. 162.

6. Dworkin, *Taking Rights Seriously*, p. xi. Not all philosophers would regard justice as an overriding value. For example, utilitarians would argue that justice has no value independent of utility, although some would allow that society produces the most utility in the long run by following apparentl nonutilitarian rules of justice. For a discussion of the different positions utilitarians have taken toward individual rights and social justice, see any standard text in ethics or social philosophy, such as Norman E. Bowie and Robert L. Simon, *The Individual and the Political Order* (Englewood Cliffs, N. J.: Prentice-Hall, 1986), pp. 35-45. Michael Sandel puts forth the view that in some contexts, friendship, love, and other personal relationships are more important than justice in his *Liberalism and the Limits of Justice* (Cambridge: Harvard University Press, 1982). However, it is doubtful if injustice actually can be shown to be warranted merely because

it produces gains in utility, or that personal or communal relations, which may well be independent sources of moral value in many contexts, ought to be valued when based on exploitation or other unjust violations of individual rights.

7. Jane English, "Sex Equality in Sports," *Philosophy & Public Affairs*, Vol. 7, No. 3 (1978), p. 270.

8. Of course, it is logically possible that everyone be known to everyone else or that everyone earn one million dollars each year. But in one important sense, being famous entails being better known than most people, and being wealthy (or possessing a fortune) entails being far richer than most people.

9. English suggests such a view in "Sex Equality in Sports," p. 270.

10. Nozick, *Anarchy, State, and Utopia* , p. 238.

11. *Ibid.*, p. 163.

12. This point is made by Henry Shue in his book *Basic Rights* (Princeton: Princeton University Press, 1982), pp. 35-40. I am heavily indebted to Shue's critique of libertarianism in my own discussion.

13. Kirschenbaum and Sullivan, "Hold on There, America," p. 73.

14. For discussion, see Bill Gilbert and Lisa Tyman, "Violence: Out of Hand in the Stands," *Sports Illustrated*, Jan. 31, 1983, pp. 62-74, and Michener, *Sports in America*, Chapter 13.

15. The notion of goods internal to a practice is developed by Alasdair MacIntyre in his book *After Virtue* (Notre Dame, Indiana: University of Notre Dame Press, 1981), especially pp. 175-178. My discussion in the text relies on MacIntyre's, although mine is not committed to his full account of the internal/external distinction.

16. Rawls, *A Theory of Justice*, p. 104.

17. *Ibid.*

18. John Wilson, *Equality*, (New York: Harcourt, Brace and World, 1966), pp. 73-74.

19. Rawls, *A Theory of Justice*, p. 101.

20. A similar objection has been made by Nozick in *Anarchy, State, and Utopia*, pp. 206ff.

21. I did not give adequate weight to this defense of the Rawlsian approach to desert in the first edition of this book.

22. A similar point is one of the main themes of Sandel's *Liberalism and the Limits of Justice*. For Rawls's reply, see his "Justice as Fairness: Political not Metaphysical," *Philosophy & Public Affairs*, Vol. 14, No. 3 (1985), pp. 223-251. In this paper, Rawls draws back from regarding his conception of justice as consisting of universally acceptable principles justified by their derivation from an impartial original position behind the veil of ignorance. In particular, he denies that his conception rests on controversial metaphysical claims, such as claims that the self is separate from its talents and abilities. Instead, he now seems to regard such claims as political assumptions, justified because they do not beg controversial metaphysical questions within liberal pluralistic societies.

23. I have used this example in my essay "The Liberal Ideal of Equal Opportunity and Its Egalitarian Critics," in Masako N. Darrough and Robert H. Blank, eds., *Biological Differences and Social Equality* (Westport, CT.: Greenwood Press, 1983), pp. 93-94.

24. I have more fully developed a version of the argument of this section in my paper, "A Limited Defense of the Merit Principle," *Philosophical Forum*, Vol. 10, No. 2-4 (Winter-Summer Special Issue, 1978-1979).

25. George Sher, "Effort, Ability, and Personal Desert," *Philosophy & Public Affairs*, Vol. 8, No. 41 (1979), pp. 361-376. Although I rely heavily on Sher's argument here, his article is more subtle than my discussion indicates. For example, Sher does not maintain that all judgments of desert arise in competitive contexts. Instead, he suggests that certain judgments of desert may be noncomparative. Presumably, public praise for a heroic life-saving act may be deserved because it is *fitting* or *appropriate*, not because the recipient won in a "heroism contest."

26. Thus, it might be objected that judgments of merit are unfair if some but not all people's combination of talents, bequeathed to them by the lottery of natural endowments and favorable environments, is such that they are unlikely to be successful across a wide variety of highly regarded activities.

Chapter 6

1. Betty Spears, "Prologue: The Myth," in Carol A. Oglesby, ed., *Women and Sport: From Myth to Reality* (Philadelphia: Lea and Febiger, 1978), p. 12.

2. *More Hurdles to Clear: Women and Girls in Competitive Athletics*, Clearinghouse Publication No. 63, United States Commission on Civil Rights, 1980, p. 3. For a full account of the development of women's athletics in the United States, see Ellen Gerber, et al., *The American Woman in Sport* (Reading, Mass.: Addison-Wesley Publishing Company, Inc., 1974).

3. Althea Gibson, Ed Fitzgerald ed., *I Always Wanted to Be Somebody* (New York: Harper & Row, Perennial Library Edition, 1965), pp. 42-43.

4. *More Hurdles to Clear*, pp. 13, 22.

5. "Sport Is Unfair to Women," *Sports Illustrated*, May 28, 1973.

6. For a useful discussion of the background, content, and implications for sports of *Title IX*, see *More Hurdles to Clear*.

7. Richard Wasserstrom, "On Racism and Sexism," from Richard Wasserstrom, ed., *Today's Moral Problems* (New York: Macmillan, 1979), pp. 96-97.

8. *Ibid.*, p. 104.

9. Eldon E. Snyder and Elmer A. Spreitzer, *Social Aspects of Sport* (Englewood Cliffs, N. J.: Prentice-Hall, 1978), p. 158.

10. Wasserstrom, "On Racism and Sexism," p. 104.

11. Pregnancy leaves seem a relevant exception, however, and may show that the assimilationist model should not extend to all areas of economic life or even that it requires severe modification.

12. Perhaps assimilationism can avoid this consequence by distinguishing between the *fact* of fixed sexual preferences of many people and the *social* significance or *importance* attached to such preferences. In this view, the perhaps biological fact of fixed sexual attraction is neither just nor unjust but only given.

What is just or unjust is the special significance and preferential status society attaches to such relationships, particularly heterosexual ones. On the other hand, given the facts that the assimilationist, on this interpretation, acknowledges literal blindness to the sex of other persons seems neither attainable nor desirable. That is, sexual assimilationism implies more than just nondiscrimination against people with different sexual preferences, it requires virtual blindness to the sex of persons which seems to be quite another matter entirely.

13. Wasserstrom, "On Racism and Sexism," p. 97

14. The issue is only "largely" empirical, however, because other evaluative factors come into play. The alleged *fact* of sex differences is one thing and how we *ought* to respond to them is another. Moreover, even if there aren't sex-related physiological advantages, participants may prefer to play on single-sex teams. How we *ought* to respond to such preferences is an evaluative rather than an empirical issue

15. See the discussion in Snyder and Spreitzer, *Social Aspects of Sport*, pp. 155-161, on the association of certain sports with gender-based stereotypes.

16. I am indebted here to Randy Carter's much fuller discussion in his as yet unpublished paper, "Are 'Cosmic Justice' Worlds Morally Possible?"

17. For a critique of the identification of sex equality with sex blindness in areas other than sports and athletics, see Bernard Boxill, "Sexual Blindness," *Social Theory and Practice*, Vol. 6, No. 3 (1980).

18. English, "Sex Equality in Sports," p. 275.

19. *Ibid.* p. 273.

20. This point is made and discussed by Raymond A. Belliotti in "Women, Sex, and Sports," *Journal of the Philosophy of Sport*, Vol. 6 (1981), pp. 67-72.

21. Perhaps a similar argument could justify the policies of single-sex colleges. Particularly in the case of women, such colleges may provide opportunities for leadership not available at colleges and universities open to both men and women.

22. Betsy Postow, "Women and Masculine Sports," *Journal of the Philosophy of Sport*, Vol. 7 (1980), p. 54.

23. *Ibid.*

24. English, "Sex Equality in Sports," p. 275.

25. Even here, there may be exceptions, such as the special right of women to pregnancy leaves. Again, some proponents of the idea that comparable pay for work of comparable worth may defend their proposal on the grounds that women tend to make different but equally valuable career choices than men and should not be penalized for the difference.

26. This point holds whether the attraction is for members of the opposite or the same sex, as long as it is relatively fixed.

27. See Boxill, "Sexual Blindness," for discussion.

28. Carol Gilligan, *In a Different Voice* (Cambridge: Harvard University Press, 1982).

29. Michener, *Sports in America*, p. 120.

30. We should require good-faith effort to achieve equity rather than actual success in achieving it because several factors necessary for athletic prominence,

such as competitive abilities and fan reaction or support, are not necessarily within the control of the institution.

31. Such a requirement is similar to John Rawls's difference principle, which requires that economic inequalities work for the benefit of the least advantaged. See Rawls, *A Theory of Justice* .

32. *More Hurdles to Clear*, p. 29.

33. For discussion of the Oklahoma decision, see the "Scorecard" section in *Sports Illustrated*, April 9, 1990, p. 19, and April 16, 1990, p. 16.

34. In other words, the criteria can be defended along lines similar to John Rawls's defense of his difference principle, which requires that economic inequalities work out for the benefit of the disadvantaged. See Rawls, *A Theory of Justice*, pp. 11-22, 60-83.

Chapter 7

1. Rev. John Lo Shiavo, "Trying to Save a University's Priceless Assets," *New York Times*, Aug. 1, 1982, p. S2.

2. Tates Locke and Bob Ibach, *Caught in the Net* (West Point: Leisure Press, 1982).

3. Shiavo, "Trying to Save a University's Priceless Assets."

4. John Stuart Mill is famous for defending freedom of expression in his *On Liberty* by arguing that freedom of expression gives us the opportunity of correcting our ideas when they are false and strengthening them in the face of criticism, and hence appreciating them more fully when they are true. Without freedom of inquiry, Mill maintains, false and misleading ideas would not be subject to critical scrutiny, and truths would be held merely as slogans because their strength in opposition to conflicting ideas would never be tested.

5. A. Bartlett Giamatti, *Address to the Association of Yale Alumni*, Vol. 16, April 10, 1990, p. 4.

6. The two views may not be in total opposition because, as the passage from Giamatti's address suggests, the Greeks may have regarded the educational lessons absorbed in athletics as tempering the soul, which in turn can be regarded as an extrinsic consequence. Nevertheless, it is useful to distinguish the kind of education that can go on within the sports contest from the effects participation will later have on the participants, such as character building.

7. Paul Weiss, *Sport: A Philosophic Inquiry* (Carbondale Southern Illinois University Press, 1969), pp. 10-13.

8. For a discussion of the acute discomfort engendered in the Swarthmore community by the success of its football team, see Frank Brady, "Swarthmore's Shakespearean Cast and Other Tales," *New York Times*, Nov. 1, 1982, p. C6.

9. Michael Oriad, "At Oregon State, Basketball Is Pleasing, not Alarming," *New York Times*, March 8, 1981, p. S2. ©*New York Times*. Reprinted by permission.

10. Quoted in Ira Berkow, "College Factories and Their Output," *New York Times*, Jan. 18, 1983, p. D25.

11. For an account of the Ross case, see Kevin Menaker, "Casualty of a

Failed System," *New York Times*, Oct. 3, 1982, p. S11.

12. Harry Edwards, *Sociology of Sport* (Homeward, Ill.: The Dorsey Press, 1973), p. 198. See Edwards for thoughtful criticisms of genetic explanations of disproportionate representation of blacks in many major sports.

13. Quoted in Eldon E. Snyder and Elmer A. Spreitzer, *Social Aspects of Sport* (Englewood Cliffs, N. J.: Prentice Hall, 1983), p. 189.

14. Jay Coakley, *Sport in Society* (St. Louis: C. V. Mosby Co., 1978), p. 295, quoted in Snyder and Spreitzer, *Social Aspects of Sport*, p. 190.

15. Reported in the *NCAA News*, Vol. 27, No. 41 (Nov. 19, 1990), p. 16. On the positive side, the survey reported that participation in sports may help reduce racial barriers, as 70 percent of the responding athletes said they had become friends with team members from another racial or ethnic group. Moreover, 74 percent of black athletes, a larger percentage than for whites, claimed that sports helped to keep them away from drugs.

16. Clifford Adelman, *Light and Shadows on College Athletics* (Washington; U. S. Department of Education Office of Educational Research and Improvement, 1990), p. v, p. 16ff.

17. *Ibid.*, p. vi.

18. *Ibid.*

19. Senator Bradley has expressed his views in various forums, including columns and interviews on radio and television. See, for example, *The Lexington Leader*, Lexington, Kentucky, March 31, 1982, Section C, p. 1. Senator Bradley's views have evolved over the years, and he may not now hold the views discussed in the text.

20. See "Black Colleges Threaten to Leave the NCAA over Testing," *New York Times*, January 13, 1983, p. 1.

21. See Edward B. Fiske, "Athletes' Test Scores," *New York Times*, Jan. 14, 1983, p. A11, for discussion.

22. For a relatively moderate statement of such a view, see Frederick S. Humphries, "New Academic Standard: Is It Fair? Will It Work?" *New York Times*, January 16, 1983, p. 2.

23. This point is made by Humphries, "New Academic Standard.

24. Harry Edwards, "Educating Black Athletes," *Atlantic Monthly*, August 1983, pp. 36-37.

25. See Stephen Jay Gould, *The Mismeasure of Man* (New York: W. W. Norton & Company, 1981).

26. In fact, presidents of predominantly black institutions often argue that their schools do an excellent job of taking students with low test scores and developing their academic skills. If the chance to participate in athletics is what motivates such students to enroll in the first place, perhaps they should be allowed to play in spite of low scores if (1) their scores are not extraordinarily lower than those of their classmates, and (2) the institution has a strong record of educating similar students in the past.

27. Perhaps some flexibility should be built into a prohibition on freshman competition. For example, it might apply only to fall sports, or apply for spring sports only to those first-year students who did not do well in the fall semester.

Alternately, students with unusually strong academic high school records could be exempted. Probably, however, a prohibition of all freshman competition at the varsity level, or at least a prohibition for fall sports, is fairest and raises the fewest problems about deciding what exceptions are justified.

28. Dave Meggysey, *Out of Their League* (Palo Alto: Rampart Press, 1971), pp. 43-44.

29. John Thompson, "Students Must Bear the Weight of Education," *New York Times*, Nov. 18, 1990, p.S7.

Chapter 8

1. Not all philosophers find such appeal to versions of the so-called Paradox of Relativism convincing or conclusive. According to the paradox, relativists who assert that there are no truths, only claims that hold within localized cultural, religious, or socioeconomic perspectives are themselves thereby making a claim, which is either true (thereby contradicting relativism) or is itself relative to some particular perspective and therefore need not be accepted by others. Marxists, for example, might seek to avoid the paradox by claiming that the socioeconomic perspective from which they make their own claims is more developed and comprehensive than earlier more parochial perspectives and that they have reached the point in history that comes closer to objectivity than ever before. But doesn't this strategy itself involve claims about which views are more comprehensive and developed than others that presuppose the possibility of comparing perspectives and making a judgment about them which purports to be objective? If so, unless Marxists are to exhibit blatant favoritism for their own views, the position of opponents who also claim to have reached such a point cannot simply be dismissed as false consciousness. Both the views of Marxists and their critics normally should be considered on their own merits.

2. Drew A. Hyland, *Philosophy of Sport* (New York: Paragon House: 1990), p. 12.

3. Albert Camus, "The Wager of Our Generation," in *Resistance, Rebellion, and Death,* translated by Justin O'Brien (New York: Vintage Books, 1960), p. 242, discussed by Hyland, *Philosophy of Sport*, p. 3.

4. There may be unusual occasions when one reasonably might advocate universal cheating, for example as a form of political protest against a regime that sponsors an athletic contest. Normally, however, respect for the rules is a value each athlete, when considering the situation from an impartial point of view, would want all athletes to adopt. For discussion, see Gert, *Morality,* particularly Chapter 7.

5. On the other hand, even if there are defensible standards of excellence in sports, it does not *follow* (although it may be true) that they themselves are justified independent of a cultural context, let alone that ethical, aesthetic, or even scientific standards are justified in some ahistorical or neutral sense. All that is being claimed in the text is that the emphasis on defensible standards of excellence in sports can conflict with more general scepticism or relativism about

standards in the wider culture. Which view is correct is a separate issue.

6. Thus, Carol Gilligan, in her book *A Different Voice* has argued that emphasis on impartiality and universality in ethics expresses a moral perspective more associated with males than females in our society. The implications of a female-oriented approach to ethics is usefully explored by Virginia Held in her "Non-Contractual Society: A Feminist View," *Canadian Journal of Philosophy*, Supplementary Volume 13 (1987), pp. 111-137.

7. For a defense of a "core values" approach to moral education along these lines, see William J. Bennett and George Sher, "Moral Education and Indoctrination," *Journal of Philosophy*, (1982), pp. 665-677.

8. Such a view was argued by Weiss throughout his *Sport: A Philosophic Inquiry*, and was also suggested by our discussion of the ethics of competition in Chapter 2 of this book.

9. Even if the argument sketched in the text that athletes have special moral responsibilities to the rest of us is rejected, we still may be entitled to make unusually severe judgments about the moral *character* of athletes who behave unethically. Thus, there seems to be something especially reprehensible about a professor who upholds strict standards of argument in the classroom but who uses rhetorical tricks to make political points in a faculty meeting, or about a political leader who in public life defends equal rights for all but is blatantly sexist in his personal relations. Similarly, athletes who benefit from universal acceptance of the rules on the field but who cheat off the field sometimes can be justifiably viewed as especially hypocritical because they have violated the very standards that helped generate their greatness in the first place.

10. This already is the case, for example, among some of the nation's academically outstanding liberal arts colleges.

11. Plato, *The Republic*, Book 3, Section 412.

About the Book and Author

We have become used to the world of sports being rocked by scandals. Stars are deprived of their Olympic gold medals because of their use of performance-enhancing drugs; heroes are suspended or banned from their sport for gambling or for connections to gambling; major universities are involved in recruiting scandals and are accused of exploiting their own students.

But ethical concerns about sports run deeper than the current scandals in today's headlines. Athletic competition itself has been criticized as reflecting a selfish concern with winning at the expense of others. Some question the emphasis on an athletically skilled elite at the expense of broader participation by the masses, and many worry about what constitutes sex equality in sports. Others believe the role of sports ought to be greatly diminished in our educational institutions. Do organized competitive sports have a legitimate place in our schools, and, if so, how is that place to be defined?

Professor Simon develops a model of athletic competition as a *mutually acceptable quest for excellence* and applies it to these and other ethical issues in sports. The discussion of each topic deals with examples from the world of sport, illuminated by philosophical work on such values as fairness, justice, integrity, and respect for rights.

Fair Play offers a rigorous exploration of the ethical presuppositions of competitive athletics and their connections to moral and ethical theory that will challenge the views of scholars, students, and the general reader. Our understanding of sports as a part of society will be reshaped by this accessible and entertaining book.

Robert L. Simon is professor of philosophy at Hamilton College and is coauthor of *The Individual and the Political Order* as well as numerous articles on ethical, social, and political philosophy. He has held fellowships at the Center for Advanced Study in the Behavioral Sciences and the National Humanities Center. He also serves as men's varsity golf coach at Hamilton, and his team was ranked fifteenth nationally in Division III for the fall 1989 season.

Index